REFLECTIVE HISTORY SERIES

Barbara Finkelstein and William J. Reese, Series Editors

D1431993

"EVERYBODY'S PAID BUT THE TEACHER"

The Teaching Profession and the Women's Movement

PATRICIA A. CARTER

TEACHERS COLLEGE PRESS

Teachers College, Columbia University
New York and London

Published by Teachers College Press, 1234 Amsterdam Avenue, New York, NY
10027

Library of Congress Cataloging-in-Publication Data

Carter, Patricia Anne.
  "Everybody's paid but the teacher" : the teaching profession and the women's
movement / Patricia A. Carter.
     p. cm. — (Reflective history series)
  Includes bibliographical references (p.) and index.
  ISBN 0-8077-4206-6 (pbk. : alk. paper) — ISBN 0-8077-4207-4 (cloth : alk.
paper)
     1. Women teachers—United States—Social conditions—20th century.   2. Sex
discrimination in education—United States—History—20th century.   I. Title.
II. Series.
LB2837 .C365 2002
371.1'0082—dc21   2001060386

ISBN 0-8077-4206-6 (paper)
ISBN 0-8077-4207-4 (cloth)

Printed on acid-free paper

Manufactured in the United States of America

09   08   07   06   05   04   03   02   8   7   6   5   4   3   2   1

Everybody's paid but teacher
Carpenter, mason, and clerk;
Everybody's paid but teacher,
She gets nothing but work.

Everybody's paid but teacher,
Toiling day and night;
Everybody's paid but teacher,
Drawing her slender mite.

Everybody's paid but teacher,
Butcher, baker, and cook;
Everybody's paid but teacher,
Grafter, fakir, and crook.

Everybody's paid but teacher,
Paid with a scowl or a smile;
Everybody's paid but teacher,
Whose work is not worthwhile.

Everybody's paid but teacher,
Seeking her pay above;
Everybody's paid but teacher,
Living on ethereal love.

—J. H. Harris, "Everybody's Paid But Teacher," 1906.

CONTENTS

ACKNOWLEDGMENTS

Many people have contributed to the completion of this book. First I am grateful to the University of Connecticut and my union, UCPEA, for granting me a 1-year paid sabbatical leave during which I was able to do the bulk of the book's research.

I have derived incalculable benefits from access to several superior research libraries including those at the University of Connecticut, Emory University, the University of Georgia, the University of Minnesota, the University of Cincinnati, and Georgia State University. Special recognition goes to the University of Connecticut Interlibrary Loan staff who were unfailingly pleasant and kind regardless of the burden of their tasks.

Thanks to Bill Reece and Barbara Finkelstein who agreed to include this volume in their noteworthy series. This book was immeasurably improved by the insightful comments of those who read it in manuscript, including the anonymous reviewers. Special thanks to my editor, Brian Ellerbeck, for his confidence in the project and quick responses to my inquiries, and to my development editor, Cheryl deJong-Lambert, and my production editor, Lori Tate, for their careful edits and specific suggestions. Thanks also to my friend Joan Joffe Hall who read the book while still in rough draft and made many helpful and supportive comments. Credit goes to my students for their astute questions and encouragement in my research.

"Everybody's Paid But the Teacher"

The Teaching Profession
and the
Women's Movement

FEMINIST POLITICS AND
THE FEMALE PROFESSION

Throughout the 20th century, female public school teachers (K–12) have undertaken a variety of efforts to expand their rights as workers and citizens. With the guidance of feminist ideologies and the support of local and national women's organizations, teachers worked on numerous workplace issues such as pay equity, the right to marry and take maternity leave, access to principalships and other administrative positions, the right to lobby and collectively bargain, acquisition of a voice within national and regional educational associations and other educational reform activities, and the right to participate in political and social reform movements outside the workplace. In doing so they became active participants in women's and other civil rights movements. The purpose of this book is to provide examples of 20th-century collaborations between female teachers and the women's movement, and to explore the feminist ideologies, strategies, and rationales women utilized in pursuing their goals. It makes a contribution to the growing body of women's history through the connections made between women's career identities and their political and social activities, specifically those guided by a feminist perspective, throughout the 20th century.

Many scholars consider an examination of feminist organizations key to understanding the spread of feminism as an instrument of personal and collective change for women (Buechler, 1990; Ferree & Hess, 1985; Martin, 1990). Although a few feminist–teacher coalitions also existed in the 19th century, the increased percentage of women in teaching and the growing acceptance of feminist political, economic, and social theory and practice in the 20th century expedited the more visible and viable alliances between teachers and the women's movement. The diversity of 20th-century feminist organizations also begins to reflect women's differing responses to political, economic, social, and cultural concerns as affected by their ethnic, racial, class, geographic, age, and other differences. Some of these variations are illustrated in the strategies, influences, rhetoric, and goals of female teachers' organizations and by the women's organizations with which they chose to collaborate.

The history of female teachers is complicated by differences not only among themselves but also among themselves and their male counterparts. Although the work lives of female and male teachers may seem identical, they are in fact very different due to women's unwaged experiences. The female reproductive cycle, traditionally considered in conflict with the ever-pressing demands of the workplace, forced women to either assimilate to a male work model or drop out of the paid labor force altogether. Assimilation demanded that the woman, not the man, take on the burden of the "double shift" that required her to carry out the job of housewife and mother in addition to her duties as teacher. She had to frame her work life around her family responsibilities and vice versa. Schools tended to see a woman's home responsibilities as counterproductive, drawing her attention and energy away from important tasks of the workplace. Yet a husband/father was assumed to be a dependable worker, for whom the role of breadwinner resulted in no parallel criticism.

It is no wonder that female and male teachers were often situated as adversaries on issues related to pay equity, job mobility, and professional representation. Throughout most of the 20th century, both males and females continued to view women's wage earning as temporary and incompatible with women's true roles as wives and mothers. Feminist ideology provided the only antidote to such pernicious conclusions.

PLACING TEACHERS WITHIN A HISTORICAL FRAMEWORK

The difficulties in assessing women teachers' feminist collaboration are confounded by their relative invisibility in the histories of working women, clubwomen, and movement women (Harris, 1978; Hummer, 1979; Minkoff, 1995; Rupp & Taylor, 1987; Scharf & Jensen, 1983; Scott, 1990). Though recent work has moved beyond the too often simplistic, androcentric estimations of female teachers written in earlier decades, we still have difficulty assessing them from a broader political, social, and economic 20th-century perspective. Were they young, barely educated, husband-hunters or old, humorless, spinsters? Is their socioeconomic position working-class unionist or middle-class professional? Were they gatekeepers in a culture that keeps the poor impoverished and the rich in control? Or were they transmitters of true democracy? Were they government drones or community intellectuals? They were, of course, all of these things and more. Their positions as liberators and conservators of the status quo, as political and apolitical, as altruists and opportunists, deserve further investigation. This book is intended as a first step toward that goal.

Much of what has been written about the social history and workplace-reform efforts of 20th-century women teachers has tended to focus on particular periods, in limited locales, or on one issue (e.g., Cordier, 1992; Kleinfeld, 1992; Rankin, 1990; Weiler, 1994). This book provides an investigation of the continuity of feminist–teacher coalitions through the 20th century, through an exploration of the ideologies and strategies that guided them in their efforts to expand professional and personal opportunities inside and outside the education institution. It addresses a variety of teacher perspectives, including racial and multigeographic viewpoints, by utilizing case studies of how a particular issue was treated in a specific locale. It contributes to the history of working women by presenting examples of the value of employment as a means of personal and collective independence for women. It also explores the tensions women felt between their home and work roles and their efforts to make them more compatible. It also illustrates the dichotomy that women teachers experienced between their social and economic status because of their marginalization in the work force, the effect that occupational segregation had on reinforcing the secondary status of women within the economy, and the manner in which institutions, such as schools, benefited by keeping women as marginalized workers.

This book focuses largely on the lives of teachers outside the classroom and on their efforts to improve their day-to-day lives as workers and women. Teachers participated in organizations such as the National Women's Party (NWP), the Women's Trade Union League (WTUL), the General Federation of Women's Clubs (GFWC), the National Federation of Business and Professional Women's Clubs (BPWC), the National Association of Colored Women (NACW), and the National Organization for Women (NOW), as well as many state and local organizations. Such memberships expanded their individual and collective spheres of power and influence while garnering support for their own workplace issues as teachers. Denied opportunities to make significant changes from within the institution—through appeals to principals, the board of education, or professional organizations—they sought outside avenues, most often in coalition with other female teachers or other women's organizations.

Feminism, in its many guises, guided teachers in their reform efforts. Its ideologies sustained them even though few ever utilized the term *feminist* as a self-referent. Whether teachers and their organizations identified as feminist or not, their attempts to make meaning of their lives within the gendered institution of schooling were liberatory. Intellectually motivated and keenly interested in higher wages, improved working conditions, and expanded personal options, they were anything but the altruistic, self-abnegating servants delineated by early school planners. Yet teachers often turned such misguided beliefs to their own benefit. They were well aware that expressions of love for children and a desire to serve the community (although often truly felt) were marketable qualities when hunting jobs or improving their pecuniary conditions. In this and a multitude of other ways they expressed the value of a strategic approach to improving their public and private lives.

Despite (or because of) their exclusion from electoral politics, women in the early 20th century devised strategies that included lobbying, the courts, and the passage of new laws. These clearly demonstrated valid avenues through which women could assert their agendas. They also learned to utilize the press, developing relationships with city editors, pushing newspapers to hire women reporters, and creating their own newspapers and journals and interchanges with other women's periodicals.

CHAPTER OVERVIEWS

Chapter 1 provides an overview of the emergence of women's organizations and female teacher associations, focusing on the strategies and ideologies they exercised in the first decades of the 20th century. By the time women won the vote in 1920, nearly 5 million participated in some sort of women's organization. Over 50% of urban women teachers or former teachers claimed membership in a club aligned with some aspect of the women's movement. Women teachers also formed their own groups in local and state organizations—and, for a period, even a national organization. In addition, Chapter 1 offers a profile of female teachers along with an exploration of the changing socioeconomic conditions that encouraged teacher participation in workplace reform. One of the most critical of these reforms, equal pay for equal work, is discussed in Chapter 2.

Though male and female teachers essentially carried out the same tasks, early in the century women earned only half to two thirds of men's wages. This understandably became an early cause for agitation. Former teacher and women's rights activist Susan B. Anthony pointed out in 1853 that the problem extended beyond the boundaries of the education profession to widespread occupational segregation, which subscribed to sexist notions about which areas of labor were more rationally the venue of male than of female laborers. She explained that by excluding women from all but a few occupations, society forced women to compete for the infrequent opportunities within the few. This drove down women's salaries and the prestige of the occupations where they predominated. Further, school administrators used the theory of supply and demand to rationalize women's low wages, because far more women desired to teach than there were available teaching positions. Moreover, schools rationalized men's wages as an incentive for remaining in a female-identified career and as way of holding them as a contingent force for future administrative work as principals or superintendents. Thus occupational segregation ensured both the ghettoization of women's work lives and the suppression of their wages even within occupations, such as teaching, where they were numerically dominant.

In an effort to explore this dilemma, Chapter 2 investigates the strategies utilized by New York City teachers in their fight for equal pay in the first decades of the 20th century. This case study offers an excellent opportunity to explore women teachers' feminist-coalition-building owing to the extensive press coverage and also because the women were so articulate about their tactics. Teachers utilized press conferences, public debates, political lobbying, rallies, coalitions, and pressure groups to increase community awareness about the issue. In carrying out these efforts, they built a community of diverse constituents—people who otherwise would not have met, spoken to each other, or even agreed on any other subject. The success of such coalitions spotlighted teachers as an obvious and potentially important faction within the burgeoning women's movement.

Community building proved the goal as well as the by-product of the teacherage movement, as examined in Chapter 3. The teacherage, a home for teachers built on public land and at public expense, generated a diversity of opinion as well as varying levels of support or opposition. The teacherage movement illustrates the variegated motivations, intentions, and outcomes that sprang from shifting societal attitudes about the role of women in the family; the legitimacy of women's wage-earning activities; and society's acceptance or resistance to scientific efficiency as a means to solving rural education problems.

What at first glance seems to merit only a footnote in the history of U.S. education provides a fruitful opportunity for assessing the contested terrain of rural school reform in the early 20th century through the lens of feminist ideology. The teacherage concept stood at the interstices of varying factions who competed for authority over the future direction of public school policy in that period. Thus the teacherage can be seen largely as a symbolic, though also practical, response to the shifting and complex objectives of these contending forces. Each bloc—the local communities, state regulators, school consolidators, women's clubs, and progressive reformers—saw the values and problems of the teacherage in terms of its own group's rural school reform agenda.

The history of the teacherage also stands as a paradigm of both urban–

rural cooperation and the dangers of cultural imposition. Women's clubs of the early 20th century were known for their urban institution building. Clubhouses, playgrounds, kindergartens, orphanages, settlement houses, and homes for working girls all constituted a part of their city-improvement plan. In the clubwomen's transition into rural reform, the teacherage became the stimulus for building bridges with farm sisters as well as a response to the problem of escalating teacher shortages and increasingly deficient rural schools.

Chapter 4 explores female teachers' participation in the suffrage movement. Many of suffrage's most well-known leaders had once been teachers and understood the trepidation with which female teachers approached their involvement in this movement. Most teachers worked because they needed their wages to support themselves as well as their elderly parents or younger siblings. As public employees, few teachers could afford to counter local opposition to the vote for women. Thus it was often in the large school districts, especially in the Northeast and West, where public opinion proved more liberal or more heterogeneous, that teachers participated in large numbers in the suffrage movement. Many school boards and administrators eventually came to endorse suffrage, at least rhetorically, in the belief that female voters would be more likely to support increased funding for the schools.

Teachers were attractive participants in the suffrage movement. As trained speakers comfortable in delivering messages to indifferent audiences, they held skills not ordinarily possessed by other community women. Moreover, their visibility and generally esteemed roles provided them access to the local population. Teachers also had the time (during school breaks and vacations) and the skills to produce speeches, pamphlets, and periodicals for the suffrage campaign. In cities like New York, Washington, D.C., Cincinnati, and Chicago, suffrage parades always included a significant coterie of teachers. Many teachers also took stands on the issue in their professional organizations and institutes, addressed it in their classrooms, and assisted students in forming their own suffrage groups. They became lecturers in special suffrage schools, training campaign workers, collecting signatures in support of franchise, and lobbying local and state politicians. Teachers provided a pivotal source of strength in the suffrage movement from its inception to its fruition in 1920.

But teachers gained as much as they gave. From their involvement, they learned the benefits of collective action, public relations strategies, and a greater sense of self-esteem, all of which became integrated into their own campaigns for increased rights in the teaching profession. Over and over again we see women teachers speaking publicly about the relationship of franchise to their own desire to improve the status of women educators. Many teachers firmly believed that the vote would not only remedy their workplace issues but, in essence, become a cure-all of most women's social, political, and legal problems. This was not to be the case, however, and teachers had to attack workplace issues such as equal pay, the right to marry, and maternity leaves on a district-by-district basis in a slow and formidable process of legal change and public protest for often impermanent gains.

Chapter 5 illustrates the many strategies used by teachers to achieve the right to continue working after marriage. This desire, rooted in the radical demand for total equality between male and female workers, was perhaps the first real step in reconceptualizing public work as legitimately the prerogative of women as well as men. Though some women simply wanted employers to stay out of their private lives, others understood that women's lack of economic self-determination and men's control of financial resources lay at the root of female subordination. Men's opposition to lifting the marriage ban provided women teachers with a tangible manifestation of the ways in which male domination limited women's economic enterprise. At the heart of these debates were tensions about the appropriateness of women holding full-time and lifetime careers. These issues also underlie women's marginalization in unions, which steadfastly considered the ideal man's wage as a family wage. This patriarchal assumption permeated all classes, as detailed in the work of Charlotte Perkins Gilman and other theorists whose ideas directly or indirectly influenced the work of women teachers in this effort.

Chapter 6 investigates teachers' protracted effort to develop consistent maternity-leave policies. Though teachers and their organizations began testing this issue in the first decade of the century, no systematic and effective method for dealing with pregnancy leave in the educational workplace was instituted nationwide until the 1980s. The courts, federal intervention, and public opinion equipped women teachers with incremental footholds at each stage along the path to achieving a consistent policy regarding teacher-mothers.

SUMMARY

In summary, this book illustrates some of the key workplace issues faced by female teachers in the 20th century and their strategies for dealing with them. Additionally, it provides examples of women teachers' involvement in women's groups whose goals and influences extended beyond the school. The women's movement, its ideologies, vision, and participants, became essential factors in the successes and achievements of female teachers during the 20th century. And just as critical was women teachers' participation in various facets of the women's movement, which included their roles as coalition builders, activists, visionaries, and educators of the next generation.

Chapter 1

COALITIONS AND STRATEGIES FOR CHANGE

Though women always participated in mixed-sex teachers' associations, their positions in them were ancillary, at best, until well into the 20th century. For instance, in the United States in the mid-19th century, the constitution of the country's largest education organization, the National Education Association (NEA), read: "Ladies engaged in teaching may on recommendation of the board of directors become honorary members, and shall thereby possess the right of presenting in the form of written essay (to be read by the secretary, or an other member whom they select) their views upon the subject assigned for discussion" (Alexander, 1910, pp. 71–72). Similar conditions existed at the state-level organizations.

WOMEN AND EARLY 20TH-CENTURY
TEACHER ASSOCIATIONS

It took the efforts of former teacher Susan B. Anthony to open the New York State Association to women as members in 1853. A year later, they elected a woman as their first vice president. Few organizations were fortunate enough to have a woman of Anthony's political acumen lead them along this path. State organizations resisted full-gender integration and only did so incrementally, allowing women as associate members or occasionally letting men read their essays, but in these early years few women held roles sufficient and prominent enough to create a mandate for real and lasting change.

One attempt to change business as usual occurred in July 1902 when a group of disgruntled female NEA members held a meeting at the Unitarian Church in Minneapolis to discuss the formation of a feminist alternative. Ella A. Rowe presided and Carrie Chapman Catt, president of the National American Woman Suffrage Association (NAWSA), gave an impromptu and inspirational talk on how important it was for female teachers to organize. Margaret Haley, cofounder of the notorious Chicago Federation of Teachers (CFT), claimed a new organization was necessary to secure better conditions for teachers. The *Chicago Teachers' Federation*

Bulletin (National Federation of Teachers, 1902) for September 5, 1902, reports that a committee drew up a constitution overnight and presented it the next morning, at which time 60 members paid dues. They elected Margaret Haley as president; K. Maud Clum, president of St. Paul Teachers Association, as first vice president; Mary McGowan, president of the Cincinnati Women Teachers' Association, as second vice president; Annette Rosenthal, of the Milwaukee Grade Teachers' Federation, as secretary; and Emma McCabe of New York City as treasurer. Afterward, the group met annually at the NEA conference and worked assiduously to rouse the larger organization into some sensitivity about teacher wages and to secure positions for women on the NEA's governing board.

Ella Flagg Young's election in 1911 to the NEA presidency gave evidence of female members' frustration with their denied voice and mobility within the association. Although women made up 75% of the membership, no woman had ever before held executive office in the NEA. The year before was typical: Only 1 woman out of 12 vice presidents, 2 of 51 state directors, and only 17 on the 120-member Council of Education. The main program listed only 1 woman out of 14 speakers, and in the general session, only 2 out of 60. The same condition existed in state associations where women made up between 39% and 89% of the members but rarely held positions on executive committees or served as key speakers at conferences (Alexander, 1910, pp. 39–71; National Federation of Teachers, 1902).

Local Teacher Groups

Women were more influential in city organizations, such as those in Chicago, New York, Buffalo, Cincinnati, Boston, San Francisco, and Denver, where separate female organizations were also popular. In these, women generally held far more influence than they did in NEA and the state organizations. Feminist grade school teachers Margaret Haley and Catherine Goggin, who founded the CFT in 1902, provided an illustration of women's local power. They received nationwide attention for their effectiveness in exposing municipal corruption and tax evasion, thereby gaining newly discovered tax dollars to improve teacher salaries ("On the Resolution," 1902). As a result, the CFT became a model to many of its contemporaries in other cities. The concept of teachers as city watchdogs appealed to middle-class reformers, as it represented the ethical high ground (Murphy, 1990, p. 66). Yet the idea of women, and teachers at that, taking such public positions fighting corporate giants surprised and concerned many in the community. Throughout its efforts, the CFT relied on several Chicago women's groups for help in gaining publicity, meeting space, and money, providing a good example of teacher–clubwomen coalitions that sprang up during this period ("Chicago Women's Club," 1900; Suratt, 1974).

Chicago women's groups were also significant in Ella Flagg Young's successful bid to become that city's first woman superintendent of schools in 1909. Just 2 years later, a coalition of women teachers' groups from Boston to San Jose also assured her installation as the first female president of the NEA. Upon her election to superintendent, Young predicted great things for women:

> Women are destined to rule the schools of every city. I look for a large majority of the big cities to follow the lead of Chicago in choosing a woman for superintendent. In the near future we shall have more women than men in executive charge of the vast educational system. It's woman's natural field, and she is no longer satisfied to do the greatest part of the work and yet be denied the leadership. ("Mrs. Ella Flagg Young," 1901, p. 515)

Though Flagg's vision was not realized, one could understand why she might predict such an outcome in the heady days of this era. Women appeared to be making unprecedented progress. Given Flagg's personal victories, the Chicago Teacher's Federation discovery of tax evasion, and the New York City teachers' success in their equal-pay campaign, there was no reason to believe that similar successes would not be achieved in cities across the country. In addition, the formation, in 1908, of NEA's Department of Women's Organizations, representing some 900,000 clubwomen sympathetic to female teacher issues, would surely have a far-reaching effect on the NEA and beyond (General Federation of Women's Clubs, 1911; Gill, 1901).

One educator surveying the growth of teacher associations in the first decade noted the changing mood:

> With the increasing feminization of the teaching profession, especially during the last few years, there has been considerable discussion of the proper place and relative importance of women in these associations. Women teachers themselves, the country over are showing signs of uneasiness and disinclination to remain nonentities in the associations much longer. . . . Probably the most important thing in the whole matter of separate organizations of women teachers is their affiliation with general women's clubs. (Alexander, 1910, pp. 69, 82, 91)

Teachers Define the Clubwoman's Agenda

Across the country, teachers' reading and social groups metamorphosed into organizations that actively campaigned for issues such as equal pay and female principalships. Some of these groups aggressively brought issues of workplace discrimination before their school boards and the public while working in cooperation with city women's organizations. In turn, clubwomen and female social reformers actively sought teacher membership in their organizations. Teachers helped to define clubwomen's educational agenda, which resulted in such progressive school platforms as student health programs, playground beautification, open-air classrooms, and art and music programs (Englehardt, 1987; Reid, 1991).

In their activities within these organizations, female teachers became prominent members of the controversial population, the *new women*. This concept, reflecting the changing morals and manners of urban middle-class women, emerged between the end of the 19th century and World War I. The history of the teachers' reform efforts helps to document changing attitudes and shifting discourses as to the effect of reforms, such as women's economic freedom and family planning, on American family life (Chafe, 1972; O'Neill, 1969; Tax, 1980). The ideological shift in societal thinking about the feminine sphere contributed to such positive attainments for women as suffrage, better educational and career opportunities, and marriage and divorce rights; but it also contributed to media distortions as illustrated by the hedonistic "flapper" image that began to appear in the late 1910s (Freedman, 1974; Smith-Rosenberg, 1975). One of the most controversial issues surrounding the new woman was that of female economic independence. Much of the economic discussions taking place in feminist circles could be traced to the theories of Charlotte Perkins Gilman (1898) and her widely read book *Women and Economics*. In this text she argued for the elimination of women's economic and psychological dependence on men, their nonvoluntary domestic servitude, and sexual oppression (Hill, 1980). The question of economics took on increasing importance for teachers and became a central tenet of many of their battles, as is shown in the following chapters.

A PROFILE OF THE "FEMALE PROFESSION"

Many factors determined the acceptance of women into the teaching profession, including an exploding student population triggered first by the establishment of the common school and later by an ever-increasing immigrant population, child labor laws, western growth, and the emergence of urban centers. The rapid increase in the nation's student population required a commensurate increase in teachers. Whereas the student population almost doubled in the years between 1870 and 1900, the number of teachers increased about 300% (*Census Statistics of Teachers*, 1905,

p. 8). In the same period, female teachers increased from two thirds to almost three quarters of the profession (Woody, 1929/1980, p. 499). Though men continued to enter teaching, their percentage decreased steadily until the 1930s when it stalled at 16.1%, then slowly edged back to prewar levels.

As clarified in Chapter 5, this increase was due to Depression-era marriage bans as well as men's desire to find a stable income, even in a female-identified occupation, during this period of economic hardship. Alice Kessler-Harris (1990) notes that during the Depression public disapproval attempted to restrict those who earned a "luxury" wage in favor of those who depended on a "necessity" wage. This meant that married, white-collar women were especially targeted for layoffs. Teachers' visibility as civil servants only increased their vulnerability to public opinion. Later, as men returned from World War II, they moved into teaching jobs at an unprecedented rate during the 1950s. Over the next two decades (1960 to 1980), the percentage of males slowed to a steady 1.5% to 3.2% per decade. The 1980s reversed this trend, dropping the male–female ratio back to a mid-1950s level.

Part of the explanation for the shift between 1960 and 1990 can be attributed to expanding occupational opportunities for women. Encouraged by feminist ideology, legal reforms such as Title VII of the Civil Rights Act, and changing marriage and divorce demographics, women considered an array of job and educational possibilities broader than ever before. Another explanation is that once men entered teaching in large numbers in the 1950s, the occupation lost some of its identification as women's work. Furthermore, a precipitous expansion of the school's central administration and business office after 1950 provided male teachers with a widening range of positions to which to aspire. During the Vietnam War, men also pursued education degrees as a refuge from the draft. Later, affirmative action policies meant to open positions to women and minorities had the effect, in this female-predominated occupation, of concretizing the continuing preference for male teachers in high schools and administration.

Gender and Wage Discrepancy

Although men have traditionally had many options within the professional class, few women have worked in any segment other than teaching. Though they received much media attention throughout much of the early 20th century, women physicians, clergy, attorneys, architects, and political office holders have been a very small proportion of their fields and the professions as a whole. In 1920, over one third of all professionals were teachers. Yet only 10.8% of the male professionals were teachers compared with 62.8% of the female professionals. This is a clear indication of the limited professional opportunities for women outside of teaching. These statistics altered gradually throughout the rest of the century as women began to make wider inroads into the professions.

Additionally, the gender hierarchy that existed within the professions at large was paralleled within the teaching occupation, where men received higher wages and moved more readily into institutional positions of power and authority. This resulted in higher starting salaries for men teachers in an effort to pave their road to upper administration. School boards believed that unless men were attracted to and kept in the profession with higher salaries, they would not be available to take leadership positions. In 1905, female elementary school teachers received an annual average salary of $650, whereas their male colleagues earned $1,161. In high schools, men received an average salary of $1,303 a year but women made $903 (*Survey on Salaries*, 1891). Salaries also differed dramatically from one area of the country to the next. Cities such as New York, Chicago, Philadelphia, and Boston, which employed 27% of all teachers in 1900, inflated the national median wage for teachers, because wages paid in those cities were comparatively high. Excluding those four cities from the survey, the annual median salary for male high school teachers was $1,106 and for women $817, and $653 and $556, respectively, for elementary school teachers. Of the 1,500 men teaching in the elementary schools, 900 were employed by the four cities named above (Coffman, 1911).

According to the U.S. Census Bureau data in 1940, only 13% of U.S. male teachers earned less than $600, compared with 26.6% of women. At the opposite end of the salary scale, 30% of men earned more than $2,000, whereas only 14.4% of women did. In 1981, men received $18,473 to women's $16,558, and in 1991, men earned $34,491 to women's $30,781 (*Status of American Teachers*, 1992, p. 18). The differences in the salaries, especially in the years after 1960, are attributable to the greater percentage of men in the high schools, which paid more than the elementary grades, as well as to overt sex discrimination in salaries. A comparison of elementary and secondary salaries, respectively, for the years 1961 ($5,090, $5,489), 1971 ($9,092, $9,449), 1981 ($16,873, $17,360), and 1991 ($31,231, $32,265) indicates a consistent gap between the two salary ranges.

Geography of Teachers

Gender differences also exist by region. In 1900, women accounted for 82.1% of all city teachers and 70.6% of all those working in smaller and rural districts. The states with the lowest percentage of women teachers were generally in the South and the highest in the North. However, census data reveal that by 1971 the Southeast had the greatest percentage of women (77.9%), whereas men were most populous (35.5%) in the West.

Race of Teachers

In 1900, the majority of women teachers, 63.5%, were American born and White with parents who were also native born. Another 27% were American-born White women who had one or more foreign-born parent. Less than 10% of the female public-school-teaching force was foreign born, only 4% was of African American descent, and less than 0.1% was Asian American or Native American. For Whites and African Americans, the proportion of teachers to their respective racial populations (age 15 and over) increased from 1890 to 1900. About one quarter of White teachers were male and one third to two fifths of African American teachers. On average African American teachers were older than White, American Indian, and Asian teachers. Young male teachers were most numerous among the Whites and least among the African Americans. Young female teachers were most numerous among American Indians and Asians and least among Whites. By 1991, 86.6% of all American schoolteachers were White, 8% African American, 3% Hispanic, 1.4% Asian/Pacific Islander, and 0.9% American Indian/Alaska Native. Minority teachers constituted a larger percentage (28.8%) of the teaching population in large school districts than in medium districts (9%) or small systems (4.3%) (*Status of American Teachers*, 1992, p. 78).

Age of Teachers

Throughout the 20th century, the trend has been to a more mature teaching force. At the beginning of the century the youngest teachers were more numerous in the North Central states and least in the Western states. Elderly teachers were more common in the North Atlantic states and least in the North Central states. The proportion of youthful teachers was greater in the country than in the city. Census data indicate the median age of female teachers increased from a low of 23 years in 1900 to a peak of 44 years in 1960, dipping the following decade to 37 and then slowly increasing back to 42 in 1990. Explanations for the trend toward maturity include the initiation of pensions, which became available to those who remained in the profession until retirement age, a lack of other professional opportunities available to women, and greater public acceptance of married women teachers.

Marital Status of Female Teachers

Shifting attitudes about married women teachers, and married women workers in general, are mirrored in their steady increase throughout the 20th century. In 1900, married women constituted only 4.5% of all female teachers, but in 1990, over 73% of all female teachers were married. This trend parallels one taking place in the larger female working population in the same period. In 1900, only 1 in 20 married women held a job outside the home; the majority of these were employed in low-paying and physically demanding jobs in domestic service, in agricultural labor, or in textile, box, paper, or cigar factories. A very small percentage of married women were employed in the professions in 1900. In the following decades, middle-aged, married women with grown children came to be viewed as a newly available labor supply (Van Horn, 1988; Weiner, 1985). Before the 1970s, this supply, like that of single women in generations before them, tended to be treated as a temporary work force to be drawn on in periods of labor shortage only. Furthermore, as is illustrated in Chapter 5, public opinion restricted the workplace to those married women who labored out of emergency or dire necessity. Teachers whose husbands drew a respectable income did not fit this category and had to fight to remain employed. Prohibitions against married women teachers slowly abated in the latter quarter of the 20th century, resulting in an occupation where female workers tend to start out single, soon marry, take child-rearing leaves, and return to teach until retirement age.

The Cost of Preparation and In-Service Training

A 1910 survey (Coffman, 1911; see also Coffman, 1913) found that 50% of the male teachers had from 2 to 5 years of education beyond elementary school, whereas 50% of the women had between 3 and 5 years. This can be attributed, at least in part, to a feeling among males that greater education would not provide any greater salary reward. As a result, men recovered their investment more quickly than did women teachers. For instance, in 1900 the median salary for male teachers with 5 years of experience was $534; with 6 years of experience, $658; with 7 years of experience, $800; with 8 years, $983; and with 9 years or more, $1,083. The average female public school teacher with 5 years experience received $504; with 6 years, $543; with 7 years, $594; with 8 years, $671; and with 9 years or more, $688 (Coffman, 1911, pp. 32, 37–38).

TEACHERS RESENT INEQUITIES

Teachers expressed resentment over the inequity of this situation in an NEA survey (*Teachers' Salaries and the Cost of Living*, 1913). One Atlanta high school teacher clarified:

> My work has been given the unqualified indorsement [*sic*] of the Board of Education and the public and yet in our school system inexperienced men are given less advanced work than mine on a salary which exceeds mine by $263. (p. 243)

Compared to other occupations in which women could participate in the early 20th century, teaching demanded more training and gave less immediate financial reward. This was especially true of the nascent clerical force to which female teachers often compared their situation. One question in the 1913 survey inquired about the cost of professional preparation. A New Haven, Connecticut, grade school teacher with 4 years of high school and 2 years of normal school (teacher) training responded: "Have two sisters who went two years to high school. One receives $200 more a year than I do, the other about $500 a year more. One is a bookkeeper, the other a stenographer" (p. 217). An Atlanta woman principal agreed:

> Much better salaries are paid here in other lines of work. I have a sister employed as a stenographer who received several hundred dollars a year more than I do, and then too, without the years of preparation I have given for my work. (p. 217)

A Cincinnati grade school teacher expressed remorse for her lack of forethought in choosing her profession: "Had I given the thought, time, labor, and earnestness to any line of mercantile employment, I should today be earning a better salary, have more opportunity for investments, and not have had a nervous breakdown" (p. 219). A Denver teacher compared her wages to those in other public service jobs: "In this city post-office clerks, policemen, firemen, and clerks in the Capitol and City Hall, and others serving the public are better paid than teachers, and organized workers in almost all lines receive a greater compensation" (p. 219).

Time and money spent on teacher education was only one factor in the discontent women felt about their salaries. The continuing need for upgrading one's education and skills was another. A Cincinnati grade school teacher expressed this concern:

> The demands on a teacher are very great in these progressive times. A teacher cannot confine herself to schoolwork alone. She should hear the best of music, see the best works of art, be acquainted with all current events of interest, and all this on a salary of the average stenographer. (*Teachers' Salaries*, 1913, p. 218)

Inflation worsened matters. The U.S. Bureau of Labor found that between 1897 and 1911 inflation increased by 44.1%. Food prices had increased by 61.7% from June 1896 to June 1912 (*Teachers' Salaries*, 1913, p. xi). This meant that a teacher, whose salary had remained fixed since 1897, would in 1911 have the purchasing power of only $693.76 per $1,000 salary. Unfortunately for teachers, their communities did not affirm the realities of inflation through salary increases. Although most other occupations received cost-of-living raises, these proved too infrequent. And as a New Haven, Connecticut, teacher complained, salary increases incurred higher charges for services:

> Since the last increase in salary, I have not been able to save any . . . as soon as the tailor knew I was a teacher, he charged $2 more to make a suit. The dressmaker charges as much per day as I earn. The dentist charged me $3.50 to do the identical work for which I formerly paid him $2. (*Teachers' Salaries*, 1913, p. 223)

A Denver teacher concurred: "Teachers are required to pay a higher rate for board and lodging than are other workers because the public considers us better paid" (pp. 222–223).

To compound matters, some women teachers believed that communities and school boards expected them to appear to be members of the middle class on their working-class salaries. One woman noted: "More is expected of a woman teacher [than of a man] in the way of social life, accomplishments, culture, and style of living. These things entail a large expenditure of money" (*Teachers' Salaries*, 1913, p. 221). A Denver teacher reported the increased stress on such requirements over time:

> In returning to school work after an absence of twenty-two years I noticed a marked increase in the demands made upon the teacher's time, skill and money. Teachers have to dress much better and more is expected of them in every way. . . . Salaries have not increased in proportion to these demands. (p. 221)

Another teacher complained: "I am required to dress well in a rather aristocratic school in which I teach, and altogether, with the present high cost of living, [I] find the salary inadequate" (p. 221).

One of the reasons for the community's misconceptions about the adequacy of teachers' pay was that it represented only 9 (or less) months of work. Although some teachers supplemented salaries during nonschool periods, acquiring such a job was difficult because most employers preferred permanently available workers. The absence of such employment forced some women to become dependent on relatives. Others, the sole support of siblings or elderly parents, made heroic efforts to bring in extra money. The NEA survey noted one woman who supported her mother variously through private tutoring, proofreading, cashiering in a dry goods store, operating an excursion tour, waitering, and clerical work in addition to her full-time teaching position.

These female teachers did not support the commonly held assumption that women worked for "pin money." In 1913, over 28% of all single women teachers lived apart from their parents. Furthermore, the parents of 1 in 4 female teachers were deceased, twice as many as for male teachers. Few of those with surviving parents could depend on them for their sole financial support. The median income of the parents was only $767 in 1910. The majority of teachers came from farming or industrial families with an average of seven people, considerably more than the average U.S. family of 4.7 members. In fact, many female teachers supported elderly parents, younger siblings, or invalid relatives. One example was provided in a Cincinnati survey where 264 out of 434 unmarried teachers provided at least partial support to one relative (Coffman, 1911, pp. 60, 69, 73). Other cities reported similar findings.

Although the evidence challenged the assumptions about unmarried, working women's economic motives, it also proved an incentive for teachers' support for equal pay for equal work. A Cincinnati teacher argued: "To sum it all up: the women have the same amount of school duties as men, they have the same amount of family responsibilities, very much less time for intellectual pursuits, and less pay. Raising salaries of the women to equal the salaries of men would do the men no injustice, and would only be doing justice to the women" (*Teachers' Salaries*, 1913, p. 239).

Even though many women teachers agreed, few school boards did. The fact that women comprised such a large percentage of the profession made it a fiscally problematic proposition. Taxpayers, they felt, would not support higher taxes to equalize salaries. On the other hand, the idea of downgrading men's salaries to the level of women's proved an equally distasteful option. Some argued that men simply would not work for the same salaries as women. They rationalized that men had families to support, greater salary expectations, and more job opportunities outside the teaching profession. The following chapters explore the continuing problems of salary inequities and gender discrimination in public schools and women's attempts to ameliorate them. Women's organizations would prove pivotal in these efforts and, in turn, female teachers helped bring a broader feminist agenda to fruition.

TEACHERS AND WOMEN'S ORGANIZATIONS

Teachers proved a most salient force in the development, leadership, and vision of women's organizations. Women teachers played an important role in the expansion of the American women's movement through their membership in general women's organizations as well as in groups specifically dedicated to improving the status of women teachers. In crossing the boundaries between their professional identities and their community identities, teachers forged links between the schools and reform organizations, shaped policies and set precedents for the new woman's agenda, and provided role models for wage-earning women in all areas of the economy.

The origin of the American women's club movement is most often traced to Sorosis, established in 1868 by former teacher Jane Cunningham Croly. Sorosis, informed by a domestic feminist ideology, nevertheless claimed many career women among its charter members, including 9 teachers, 22 authors, 6 artists, 6 editors, 1 historian, 2 physicians, and 4 science writers (Blair, 1980). The percentage of teacher-members in Sorosis set a standard in many clubs to come. Teachers, or former teachers, often constituted a very visible and substantial proportion of women's club members across the country from the late 19th to the mid-20th century. A 1922 survey (Force, 1922) reported that more than half (53%) of all female teachers living in cities with populations greater than 100,000 participated in women's clubs (see also Threlkeld, 1923).

Given that women were often expected to resign from their teaching positions upon marriage, it is understandable they would search out other intellectual and social opportunities with which to occupy themselves. A case in point is Martha E. White (1903), a member of the New England Women's Club, who organized the Woman's Club of Arlington, Massachusetts, and chaired the Department of Literary and Library Extension in both the General Federation of Women's Clubs and the Massachusetts Federation of Women's Clubs. She explained, "When I gave up teaching after my marriage [in 1889] I missed the job so much that I sought another way to teach. Women's clubs offered me the opportunity for platform work [where] I could become a lecturer" (p. 614).

A similar pattern existed across race, such as in the National Association of Colored Women (NACW), where teachers constituted about 67%

of its mostly middle-class club affiliates. Kathleen Berkeley (1985) notes that NACW members were likely to reside in large urban centers, to be college graduates, and to have taught school before retiring upon marriage. As clubwomen, they continued to serve their community as "influentials and activists." The NACW assured all "Negro women's groups" who joined the national organization, including church clubs, sewing circles, trade unions, self-improvement/literary associations, and college organizations, of an integral but autonomous identity (Giddings, 1984; Jones, 1985; Salem, 1990).

Although the women's club movement included both Black and White women, it was for the most part a middle-class activity. Both races tended to limit their memberships, either overtly or covertly, to those with similar social and educational backgrounds. Middle-class African American clubwomen, Sharon Harley (1982) notes, disassociated themselves from women of lower status in an attempt to distance themselves from the stigma of racism. Standards of dress, fine homes, social manners, and community status enlarged that chasm further still (Dickson, 1987; Foster, 1991). For instance, John Reid (1991) notes that Black women teachers comprised "a disproportionate number of both members and leaders" of Detroit's Black women's clubs (1865–1915). He also notes these women came from relatively prosperous families and of "mixed heritage or at least a light complexion, suggesting that a light complexion aided one's entrance into the black elite and into the public school system" (pp. 3, 5).

In many cities, however, African American and White teachers crossed class lines frequently as they helped working-class mothers organize groups directed to the improvement of child-rearing practices as well as to the creation of a political voice for mothers within the schools (Neverdon-Morton, 1989).

When teachers had large enough numbers to form their own groups, they often did so. For instance, in 1894, when the Sarah E. Doyle Club for Teachers of Providence, Rhode Island, formed, most of that city's women's clubs experienced a drop in membership of single women. The club's namesake, Sarah E. Doyle, a public school teacher and suffragist, merged these two concerns in her organization (Blair, 1980, pp. 64–66). Other cities formed similar organizations and by 1910, 50% of all U.S. cities with populations over 30,000 had at least one organization representing women teachers. These included the Boston Teachers Club; the Canton, Ohio, Teachers' Club; the Interborough Association of Women Teachers in New York City; and the Chicago Federation of Teachers. Specialty groups such as the Ella Flagg Young Club in Chicago, the Jersey Primary Principals Association (New Jersey), and the Pittsburgh Teachers' Art Club also formed in addition to statewide associations such as the Califor-

nia Federation of Schoolwomen's Clubs and the Vermont Schoolmis-
tresses' Club.

In joining these latter groups, which organized to increase wages and
opportunities for women in the profession, teachers risked being fired,
denied promotion, or ostracized by colleagues (Berkeley, 1984; Clifford,
1978; Collins, 1976; Koehler, 1984). Thus coalitions between teacher organizations and outside women's groups (in which teachers often held dual
memberships) became an effective 20th-century strategy for protecting
teachers while pressuring school boards and directing public attention to
the sexist hiring practices and workplace policies of American schools. If
individual teachers or groups of teachers were threatened with dismissal
or treated unfairly, women's groups could aid them by organizing letter-
writing campaigns, individually confronting school board members, or
holding public debates to sway community sentiments in favor of the
teacher's cause.

WOMEN'S CLUBS AS FOUNDRIES FOR FEMINIST THOUGHT

Early 20th-century women teachers quickly discovered that their professional skills were a valuable asset in assuming leadership positions in
organizations like the Women's National Loyal League, the National
American Woman Suffrage Association, and the Women's Christian Temperance Union (Clifford, 1987). Such organizations reflected the heart and
spirit of the progressive movement, which was an amalgamation of reform
efforts spanning the late 19th through the early 20th centuries. The progressive movement allowed women unprecedented opportunities to in-
vest in both political and personal change. Mary Martha Thomas (1992)
reports:

> While male Progressive leaders talked about efficiency, regulation, and scien-
> tific management in factories, female Progressives directed their attention
> toward humanitarian and social reforms, such as the abolition of child labor,
> wage and hour reforms, and the improvement of health conditions in the
> workplace. (p. 2)

Kathryn Kish Sklar (1988) describes female progressive era reformers as
involved in "devoted friendships, overlapping networks, [and] multiple
organizations." She explains that a "fundamental feature of women's reform activism" was the "emergence of middle-class leaders who experienced a congruence between their search for power over their own lives
and their search for influence in society as a whole" (p. 176).

Yet some historians have had problems aligning progressive reform organizations, particularly those whose focus was on educational reforms, with the goals of feminism. Many of these groups initially rejected or continued to show little interest in the more colorful and radical positions of feminism that involved suffrage and economic independence. Sari Knopp Biklen (1978) found that progressive education leaders "failed to make women's equality a goal" and that "though education was still a concern of feminists, feminism was not a concern of the progressive education movement" (p. 316). However, by claiming progressive education reform largely as the domain of male ideologues, Biklen fails to explore the pivotal role played by women's clubs in setting and pushing forward the progressive educational agenda items. Beyond this she tends, as did many historians writing in the 1970s, to define feminism narrowly—as related to suffrage, birth control, and economic emancipation.

This perspective hints at a persistent division among historians in describing female reform efforts, particularly in the progressive era but extending before and after the period: that is, the determination of what constitutes feminist praxis and what does not. Another example is James L. Leloudis's 1983 study of the Women's Association for the Betterment of Public School Houses (WABPSH) work in North Carolina between 1902 and 1919. In this study, he asserts that although these women saw themselves as competent and resourceful individuals, they did not possess a feminist consciousness. In defining the term *feminist consciousness* Leloudis uses the standard definition of "an awareness of and determination to transform the social and economic systems that have structured women's lives and defined their subordination to men" (p. 893). The issue here is one of perspective: Leloudis views only the WABPSH's stated agenda—that of school reform—not the activity itself, in which women moved out of their formerly restrained domestic spheres to work in public ones where they not only ventured opinions but demanded respect for them.

This book assumes that the participation of women in woman-identified, woman-led groups was in itself a feminist act, because it illustrated a confidence in women's intellectual, political, and social abilities to create change. Historians exploring progressive era women often refer to this distinction in female social reform movements as stemming from *domestic* or *social feminism* (Cott, 1989; D. S. Smith, 1979). Although domestic feminist groups took up various agendas for social, cultural, and community change, they tended to share a belief, at least in their public rhetoric, in their moral obligation to bring the special insights of women into the public sphere. What particularized this insight was their roles or potential roles as mothers. Other feminists, whom O'Neill (1968) and Lemons (1973;

see also Steinschneider, 1994) call *hard-core* or *extreme* feminists, tended to deny that women had any special insights related to their reproductive roles. Rather, their insights related to their male-dominated position in society. Whereas hard-core feminists placed women's rights at the top of the agenda, domestic feminists subordinated individual women's rights to other social reforms.

Distinctions between feminist organizations continued to be made in later decades of the century. For instance, the *liberal feminists* of the 1970s believed in changing the governance system to make it more accountable to women, whereas *separatist feminists* (Bunch, 1987; Johnston, 1973; Kerber, 1988) expressed no confidence in the possibility of such a transformation, preferring instead to create alternative, autonomous institutions of their own. It is interesting to note that in many ways liberal feminists had more in common with their more radical sisters of the 1920s, whereas separatists shared the institution-building proclivities of their social-reform domestic-feminist foremothers (Freedman, 1979). Other terms used to describe differences in contemporary (after 1970) feminist activities or ideologies include *radical* versus *reformist feminism* (Ferguson, 1984), *socialist feminism* (Hansen, 1986; McIntosh, 1978), and *cultural feminism* (Alcoff, 1988; Echols, 1989). Some African American scholars have adopted the alternative *womanist* to underscore the idea that for African American women the concepts of race and gender are not separable (Gilkes, 1980). Still other distinctions include *protofeminism* (Epstein, 1981) and *material feminism* (Hayden, 1981). That all these terms appear to describe feminism in different times, places, and political and cultural contexts underscores the dynamic nature of the women's movement.

In the early 20th century, domestic feminist ideology dominated the rhetoric of the woman's club movement. Clubwomen justified their new activities with frequent references to woman's "natural talents" and "God-given feminine abilities." Instead of denigrating the home as intellectually limiting and physically confining, these women argued that their work in school and community reform simply extended the skills and concerns so well developed by women in the home. Thus participation in voluntary activities could meet women's intellectual and social needs while being applauded by the community as benevolent, virtuous, and well within the accepted role of women (Forderhouse, 1985; Hine, 1990; Moses, 1987; Perkins, 1983; White, 1993).

The rise of domestic feminism is tied to the ascent of the modern ideal of childhood that cast the mother as "moral anchor of family." In this ideology, the home was seen as the "foundation of social order" in an era beset by the economic and ethical upheaval accompanying modern industrial growth (Pickens, 1989, pp. 17–18). Although domestic feminism rationalized specific gender roles for men and women, it nevertheless served as a cleaver with which women cut wider and wider paths into public life.

An example of this rhetoric can be seen in Grace H. Dodge's (1895) statement favoring women serving on school boards and in educational administrative positions. Dodge, a wealthy philanthropist, founded the Association of Working Girl's Societies and served as national president of the YWCA in 1906, among her many interests (Graham, 1926; Peiss, 1986). She argued: "[A] true mother should be a citizen mother, interested in the city and country because children live and grow in them . . . women have been trained as housekeepers; there is much housekeeping in connection with schoolwork" (Dodge, 1895, pp. 439–440). Ellen E. Price (1898) agreed, claiming:

> The ignoring of women in school offices is depriving the state of many of her most loyal citizens, qualified and ready to serve her. . . . Yet in many of our states women have been almost entirely ignored in the management of our Public School. A school board composed entirely of men—even properly qualified men—cannot fill the requirements of the ideal board, for it lacks a very essential element—the qualities of the mother heart and soul. (pp. 299–300)

Helen L. Grenfell (1909), ex-superintendent of public instruction for Denver, Colorado, echoed this sentiment when she proclaimed, "A woman on the school board ought to be regarded as a matter of course and of necessity" (pp. 998–999). Women's clubs actively lobbied for the placement of women on local school boards and in leadership positions within educational institutions (such as in "Want Five Women," 1913, p. 6).

There were complications in using a domestic feminist rhetoric, however. An editorial in the *Denver Times* used the same logic to urge women to resign from the most powerful positions on school boards. They argued:

> Probably no woman member of the board would be expected to devote her energies on committees to intricate questions of finance or troublesome problems of the selection of school sites or the letting of contracts. But in the matters of sanitary interests or school discipline, in subjects, which touch child life and child development her presence would be most valuable. There she stands supreme because of her blessed womanhood. ("Women in the School Board," 1901, p. 24)

Though African American women's clubs also participated in domestic feminist rhetoric, they were, perhaps, the first to defend women in the teaching profession strictly on the grounds of common sense and economic justice. Utilizing a more radical feminist (or womanist) stance, teacher Josephine Turpin Washington claimed the right of African American women to be admitted to all fields of employment. Educator and clubwoman Anna Julia Cooper supported married women because it "renders woman less dependent on the marriage relation for physical support (which, by the way, does not always accompany it)" (Giddings, 1984, p. 108; see also Hutchinson, 1994). Both concepts—of a fully integrated job market and the economic independence of women in marriage—certainly qualified as radical and feminist in the early decades of the 20th century.

TEACHERS AS FEMINISTS

The varying standpoints taken by clubwomen paralleled those of women teachers' organizations and are aptly defined by Kathleen Weiler's (1989) reference to the "woman schoolteacher" as a "contested and contradictory identity within shifting historical contexts" (p. 11). From the beginning of women's involvement in American public schooling, prescriptive literature constructed sundry and competing identities for the female teacher. Historians generally note that the integration of teaching was facilitated by a gender ideology that deemed women morally superior but intellectually inferior to their male cohorts. This presumed moral-aptitude/cerebral-deficit polarity presented women teachers with a dilemma as they became regarded as parallel, but not equal, to male teachers. In fact, elementary school teaching was more often emphasized as a patriotic or religious duty for women than as waged work. The argument that teaching duties were analogous to maternal ones only complicated the dilemma of admitting women to a profession while not accepting that women could be professionals (Clifford, 1982; Grumet, 1981). Thus, although teaching allowed women to expand their life choices beyond the confines of familial tasks into the realm of waged work, this shift proved only incrementally emancipating.

Jo Anne Preston (1993) claims that few women ever conformed lock-step to ideals prescribed for "teaching ladies." She argues that Catharine Beecher, the first prominent advocate of female teachers, "sought to limit men's power by increasing women's" and that "schoolteaching was a vehicle by which women as a group could establish cultural hegemony . . . expand[ing] their sphere of influence and . . . effect[ing] . . . events both local and national" (p. 533). Preston further contends: "Beecher's primary concern was to maximize the potential of women within the confines of domestic ideology." In fact, she argues that architects of public schools, such as Horace Mann and Henry Bernard, essentially co-opted the rhetoric and intentions of domestic feminism as a means of "establish-[ing] . . . a centralized, universal, public education system" (p. 537). In their zealous promotion of women as teachers, these early school reformers constructed an identity for female instructors: They embodied self-sacrifice, sentimentality, patience, and docility, and, though lacking "natural brilliance," they "willingly" worked for low wages. Such rationalizations allowed reformers the opportunity to build schools on the backs of women while simultaneously appearing to assist women's progress toward economic opportunity (Conway, 1987).

Teaching came to be viewed as an appropriate occupation for African American women for many of the same reasons it did for White women. As Mary Church Terrell (1940), the first African American woman to serve on the board of a public school in Washington, D.C., stated: "Among colored people, school teaching offers one of the most desirable vocations which an well-educated representative of the race can enter" (p. 141). Terrell was the founder and first president in 1896 of the National Association of Colored Women, which established many progressive education-related institutions including kindergartens, day nurseries, and mothers clubs (B. Jones, 1994). Racism, classism, and sexism limited higher educational opportunities for African American women. Early women had to fight for admission to the profession. In 1895, Susan Elisabeth Frazier became the first African American teacher in an integrated public school in New York City, but only after initiating legal proceedings against school authorities (Brown, 1926; Collier-Thomas, 1982).

Both African American and White teacher-leaders were known to use the domestic feminist discourse of women's "moral superiority," especially when challenged as being self-indulgent. But teachers soon realized the importance of a liberal or hard-core feminist response to the workplace issues. For instance, in their equal pay for equal work campaigns, teachers argued that they deserved pay equity on the grounds that they performed tasks equal to those of their male colleagues. And when defending married women's right to work, they argued that their home lives should be as sacrosanct as men's. Throughout the 20th century, female teachers actively resisted and challenged social prescriptions that circumscribed them ideologically and materially. After all, most women joined the labor force for the same reasons that men did; they needed and wanted to work (Hoffman, 1981). Although their lives in the classroom differed very little from men's, their efforts nevertheless came to be seen as "women's work"—inferior and disdained by men, even their male colleagues (Apple, 1985; J. A. Preston, 1993).

Several historians have attempted to assess whether female teachers' reaction to sex bias in the profession constituted a feminist response and, if so, what kind. Courtney Ann Vaughn-Roberson (1984) claims that teachers in Oklahoma, although struggling for independence and economic equality with men, nevertheless viewed teaching as an extension of a woman's domestic role; the classroom was her family. And in a 1985 study, Vaughn-Roberson positions traditional domestic ideology against feminism to find that antifeminist attitudes were still common among the female teachers of Oklahoma, Texas, and Colorado in the 1970s. In describing teachers' work in the Americanization movement, John F. McClymer (1991) claims that women teachers lacked a feminist perspective even as they opened opportunities to immigrant women through the curriculum they taught. Richard A. Quantz (1985) finds that the professional organizations to which female teachers of Hamilton, Ohio, belonged were the Classroom Teachers Association, the Federated Women's Clubs, and the American Association of University Women. Homosocial activities held at these events leads him to incorrectly assume that: "Luncheons and other such activities are hardly the kinds of activities that one would expect to find if the teachers were organizing for the protection of salaries and seniority" (p. 454). In fact, women did use these "feminine" settings to strategize some of the most crucial changes occurring in the profession in the first decades of the 20th century, as shown in later chapters.

On the other hand, in her study of hierarchical power in the Chicago school system between 1890 and 1920, Cherry Wedgewood Collins (1976) finds that increasing power of the superintendents "was opposed by feminist grade teachers, led by the Chicago Teachers Federation and its officers, Margaret Haley and Catherine Goggin." Collins also recognized the "existence of women grade teachers as a major pressure . . . [which] can be explained in terms of the rise and fall of feminism" (p. 2). Thomas and Moran (1991) imply the existence of a similar feminist agenda among Buffalo, New York, teachers, as does Laurence Block's (1972) study of Baltimore teachers. Robert E. Doherty (1979) notes a "lively suffrage movement in New York [City]" that "might" have provided encouragement for women teachers to assert themselves (p. 417).

Marjorie Murphy (1990) asserts that teachers' unions founded in the first two decades of the 20th century "were not just women led, they were feminist" (p. 61). Yet she sees feminism as both strength and weakness in these groups, explaining that although feminist ideology indubitably helped create strong leaders, too much of the energy was focused on the attainment of suffrage and, once it was won, the associations lacked focus to carry on. Sarah King (1987) believes that in comparable British organizations, members of the National Union of Women Teachers (NUWT) "perceived themselves as feminist educationalists" who "campaigned with immense vigor and dedication as part of an extensive feminist movement to challenge the oppression imposed upon women and the educational practices which perpetuated that subordination" (pp. 31–32). In another study of the NUWT, Hilda Keen (1990) reaches a similar conclusion.

The connection between feminism and economic independence is undertaken by Geraldine Clifford (1978), who disagrees with Mary Ryan's (1975) assessment that "preferences aside young unmarried women were not capacitated by the meager wages of schoolteachers to challenge the hegemony of fathers, brothers, and grooms" (p. 94). Clifford (1978) argues that even their small wages made teachers "economically important" to their families "especially in cash-poor and small town America where most of the population still lived" (pp. 10–11). Furthermore, "Married or single, women who gained some sense of self through employment as teachers were carriers of potentially dangerous feminist tendencies or sympathies" (p. 13).

TEACHERS AND SOCIAL CHANGE MOVEMENTS

The failure to recognize multiple identities held by women teachers within women's organizations, their communities, and educational institutions has led many historians to discount them as a potent force in social and political reform movements. Instead the focus has been more on their repression within the system and the culture at large than on how teachers utilized their meager resources to transcend the economic, social, and political barriers imposed by the patriarchy. Such a critique is understandable given the overwhelming evidence of gender discrimination experienced by women teachers since their entrance into the occupation in the 19th century.

The Hegemony of Patriarchy

Moreover, contemporary studies of teachers suggest that bias still exists. Meg Maguire (1993) notes: "The values of neutrality, impartiality and professionalism have served to disguise power relations" and shaped "perceptions, attitudes, and opportunities for teacher educators" (p. 269). Sandra Acker's (1992) study of how women view their careers found that though most women teachers believe that men have career advantages, they demonstrated little sense of outrage about this state of affairs; some even blamed themselves. Their inability to regard the problem as systemic rather than individual is characteristic of the dynamic of hegemony. As feminist philosopher Alison Jaggar (1983) notes, a dominant group maintains its dominance by controlling the *social reality* or *hegemony* to such a degree that it is accepted as common sense and a part of the natural order by even those subordinated by it. The hegemony of western thought is determined by *patriarchy*, classically defined as "rule by the fathers." Contemporary feminist thought sees patriarchy as supported by and supportive of the dominant cultural, social, and economic structures—including capitalism itself. This means that patriarchy is so all encompassing that it imposes values, rules, and assumptions that we rarely even think to question. This is possible because patriarchy functions at two elemental levels: private and public (Brown, 1987). The private patriarchy has traditionally controlled women through the family by making the husband the sole owner of the wife's labor, both productive and reproductive. The public patriarchy operates through and requires the cooperation of male-dominated public institutions that are religious, governmental, cultural, social, and educational. In turn these institutions help create public policy that influences and reinforces family norms and roles. The interconnectiveness and the apparent seamlessness of the patriarchal hegemony contribute to our acceptance of it as "common sense" or even gender neutral.

Schools as Patriarchal Structures

The meaning that this has for teachers and educational institutions is complex. Following one scenario, we can see that the traditional belief that gender differentiation is natural in our culture is reinforced by educational policies in which female and male students are expected to behave differently and have different destinies. Teachers, career counselors, and administrators cooperate in preparing girls and boys for their different futures. Employers further reinforce these assumptions by dividing the workplace into jobs segregated by sex. Male coworkers may harass female coworkers who step out of traditionally ascribed positions in the workplace.

As illustrated by Maguire (1993) and Acker (1992), one's inability to see the problem as structural and systemic often leads to worker self-doubt and self-blame. It is to the institution's benefit to orchestrate such an individuation of workplace difficulties. If workers see the problem as their own fault, they are less likely to ask the institution to respond by making structural changes. Patriarchy by its very nature is resistant to change, because it might undermine the stakes held by the power holders. Others simply choose to conform their lives to the prevailing norms of the system. When the educational realm embodies only male norms, it is inevitable that women participating in it will be forced into a masculine mold if they hope to be successful (Martin, 1982). Others might avoid career and home conflicts by prioritizing their home lives over their professional development (Biklen, 1995). Even in educational institutions where counterhegemonic work appears to be the goal, covert or hidden agendas get played out consciously or unconsciously (Ellsworth, 1989; Sadker & Sadker, 1994). Furthermore, commitment to change can be encoded but not enforced. An example of this can be seen in Title IX of the Equal Educational Act, which outlawed sex bias in the treatment of students in federally funded schools. Though it became law in 1972, it was subsequently narrowly reinterpreted by the courts and, with some exceptions, largely ignored by public school systems across the country for over two decades. Schools routinely spent 10 times more on boys' sports than on girls'. Vocational schools segregated boys into mechanics and girls into cosmetology. Schools expelled pregnant females but not the males who impregnated them. Suits were lodged, but not one school lost a single dollar of federal funds because of sex discrimination between 1972 and 1991 (Sadker & Sadker, 1994, p. 36).

Radical critics of schooling in the 1970s emphasized three primary functions of schooling: channeling, socializing, and legitimizing. In part, they argued that schools legitimize existing class divisions constructed on the basis of differences in financial inheritance. The needs for self-development or self-expression are inevitably sacrificed when they come in conflict with the cultural-assimilation function of the school; schools then shape personalities that are necessary to the functioning of a hierarchical and authoritarian structure. All these functions not only authorize class divisions but are gender-encoded, validating certain types of characteristics as the property of males and females and certain *knowledge*, and thus occupations, more legitimately as the prerogative of men (Nicholson, 1980).

The powerful position that an educational institution holds within the patriarchal hegemony is due in large part to its high level of interchange with people throughout the life cycle. The lessons learned by children as students are often reinforced later in adulthood through their interactions with the schools as parents. Furthermore, educational institutions are endowed with the authority to confer degrees, certifications, and other methods of acknowledging special status in our society through the acquisition of knowledge.

Yet too often this conceptualization of the patriarchal hegemony fails to recognize the more complex probability that at least some teachers reproduce and accommodate the hegemony while also questioning, resisting, and trying to change it. Kathleen Weiler (1988) rejects the notion that reproduction and resistance are dichotomous practices in her study of contemporary female teachers, arguing instead that they are "mutually informing relationships of contradiction" (p. 188). Other research has indicated that the teacher's consciousness of her own gender oppression may in turn contribute to her consciousness about the oppressions of others (Culley & Portuges, 1985; Lather, 1991). It is at this point that the teacher starts to operate from a counterhegemonic position, meaning that she no longer sees the problems from an individualized point of view but from a position within a larger context such as her gender, race, class, ethnicity, or geographic location.

Throughout the 20th century, female teachers moved to this consciousness as a part of their membership in teacher associations and/or other women's groups. Coalition building is a key mechanism in developing counterhegemonic thinking. Exposure to different perspectives and experiences enlightened teachers to needs within the larger female community and vice versa. The many forms of community that women developed in this process sustained them through denigrating experiences, contemptuous colleagues, and concerns about whether their political activities might lead to joblessness.

The teacher's contradictory positions—as a white-collar worker at a blue-collar wage, as a gatekeeper who was often barred from reaching her own goals, and as a female role model who could not possibly hope to measure up to all stereotypes of acceptable female behavior—helped to define her influence on society and it on her. As workers, teachers were positioned to understand the need for workplace changes for all women wage earners. Yet, as public employees, teachers found that their efforts at workplace reform constituted a double-edged sword when the teacher's prestige within the community became tainted by such activities. The demand for higher wages and better conditions was viewed not only as unladylike but also as lacking the altruism that taxpayers had come to expect of female teachers (P. A. Carter, 1992b). Thus women's marginalized position within the teaching profession necessitated a gendered response because female and male workers were treated differently by the system. When marriage, motherhood, and dual careers conflicted with the schoolwork culture, women were forced either to assimilate by remaining single or to create institutional changes that would accommodate them as married women and mothers. With school administration, school board membership, and leadership positions virtually closed to women, teachers had no choice but to create coalitions with other women inside and outside their workplaces to take on these challenges.

SUMMARY

At first glance, teaching might be seen as a gender-free occupation with rewards based on one's qualifications, intellectual abilities, and demonstrated teaching expertise. But from its inception, the profession has been defined from every aspect by gender assumptions. Early administrators' ability to pay women far less than men proved instrumental in the establishment of the nation's common school system. Throughout its history, public schooling depended on women's willingness to subordinate their own economic interests to the community's. In return the community tacitly condescended to grant women the opportunity (albeit a temporary opportunity) to enter an occupation that could provide them with at least a marginalized middle-class status. Thus the class identification of female teachers proved tenuous and frustratingly amorphous. Although ubiquitously regarded as "ladies," they often had less disposable income than did their sisters employed in the factories. Though teaching provided an avenue through which working-class girls could become middle-class ladies, this transition was anything but smooth. In the title of "lady" resided expectations regarding deportment, dress, and other aspects of physical appearance not easily achieved on a woman teacher's salary. Moreover, as schools ratcheted up credentialing procedures, women teachers were forced to deplete precious personal funds to pursue higher education.

Issues of race, geography, and cultural context also intersected with class and gender to place additional boundaries on teachers. African Americans and other women of color had to fight to obtain places in normal schools, then to win teaching positions. Overt and covert hierarchies and biases kept minorities in their place.

That women teachers formed coalitions among themselves and with other women is evidence of their marginalization within the profession and the degree to which teachers' goals corresponded to the objectives of the American women's movement at large. Victories achieved by teachers were victories for all women and vice versa.

Chapter 2

EQUAL PAY FOR EQUAL WORK:
FROM LOCAL DISPUTES
TO FEDERAL INTERVENTION

Campaigns for equal pay for women teachers took place in towns and cities nationwide, and in courts and legislatures over several decades of the 20th century. Though dealing with a common problem and doubtlessly influenced by the successes or failures of teachers in other cities, each campaign had to be site specific, taking into consideration the peculiarities of its own location. Earlier attempts had been made to draw attention to the problem, but little coalition building occurred until after the turn of the century when expansion of the nation's common school population and massive waves of immigration clarified the profession's increasing dependence on women.

Higher education (largely limited to normal schools) and public skepticism about overeducated females worked in tandem to funnel thousands of young women into often short-term and poorly paid school careers. Though these same women might have earned more as factory workers, their desire to maintain or adopt a middle-class status left them with little occupational choice other than teaching.

Throughout the period in which teaching emerged as a profession for women, men retained control and direction of the schools as administrators, policymakers, politicians, and school board members—though the popular term "the feminization of the schools" would have led us to believe otherwise. Although in the majority, women teachers had little control beyond their own classrooms and, because of the increasing application of theories of scientific efficiency, not even there. A great deal of what happened in the classroom was guided by the theories of male pedagogues, usually college professors, who spent little or no time in public school classrooms themselves. The charge of "feminization" became an all too easy device to deflect attention from the large and seemingly intractable problems of shifting societal mores, demographics, and complex tax structures that stymied progressives' efforts at school reform.

The principles of scientific efficiency may have seemed genderless but were in fact based on patriarchal suppositions that viewed work done primarily by women as inherently inferior. This habit of denigrating women's work existed for several reasons, including the following three. First, there was a belief that women did not deserve the same pay as men because they did not, or least should not, work to support families. A second prevailing notion was that women workers were naturally inferior due to perceived biological, mental, and physical deficiencies (P. A. Carter, 1992a). A third, involving a conscious division of labor, held that even in occupations like teaching where the labor was reasonably similar for men and women, women should be paid less because they predominated in the lower grades, whereas men worked in the higher.

The division of labor for teachers was determined by several factors. At the turn of century, as today, females constituted the majority of elementary school teachers. Skills required of teachers in the lower grades were oriented to nurturing, patience, and affiliative activities, whereas the higher grades called for the more disciplined and directive capacities of men. There appears to have been little discussion as to why men and women could not possess both sets of these characteristics. And domestic feminists fell into this conundrum by insisting that women possessed different, feminine, if often superior, teaching skills to men (Brown, 1990).

Even if it were true that female and male teachers possessed only the attributes ascribed to them, why did they not receive comparable pay if they both fulfilled a necessary labor? Indeed, if it weren't for the fundamentals taught by women to younger children, what knowledge building would have been possible for students in the upper grades? Although these arguments were offered, boards of education did not engage in such debates. For them, everything hinged on their inability to rationalize the additional expenditure that equal pay necessitated. Proponents of pay differentials claimed that males should be provided better salaries on the expectation that they would later ascend to administrative positions. Women could not anticipate similar mobility within the system. They moved into elementary principal positions with relative ease, because few men competed for these positions, but rarely into high school principalships or further up the ranks.

The belief that women, in economic terms, were worth less than men pushed women into a ghetto within their own profession. Kessler-Harris (1982, p. 21) notes several factors that hindered working women in fighting inequitable treatment: the necessity of income, the lack of union protection, the lack of personal negotiation skills, and the fear and social stigma of bargaining for an improved position. However, as shown in this chapter, women teachers, by virtue of their higher education, breadth of occupational experience, and acquired negotiation skills, positioned themselves to overcome some of the disadvantages experienced by workers in other fields. The marginalization of women teachers within their profession provided them the incentive for coalition building. The issues were far too structural and complex to fight on an individual basis, and teachers faced dismissal if viewed as too combative. The women's movement offered both the ideology of equal rights and a collaborative model through which women teachers could pursue economic justice.

EQUAL PAY FOR NEW YORK CITY TEACHERS, 1900–1911

Of the political efforts undertaken by New York City women teachers between 1900 and 1920, the campaign for equal pay proved most divisive. It played on long-simmering antagonisms between male and female teachers, suffragists and anti-suffragists, Democrats and Republicans, and state politicians and local New York City office holders. What logic could women teachers utilize to convince the city to spend a million dollars more a year on their salaries? Would the adoption of a feminist agenda hurt or help them in their efforts? Who would support their cause and what did they require in return? How could they limit opposition? Would it be more efficient to work through the New York City Board of Education or would the New York State Legislature be more responsive to the needs of the teachers? Despite such apprehensions, the New York City equal pay campaign provided teachers across the country with hope and a model for changing their own inequitable circumstances.

Background on Equal Pay

From women teachers' entrance into the profession, some voiced concerns about the inevitability of a lower wage scale for women. However, the idea that women would, and even should, accept less reward remained a qualifying factor in determining their proliferation in the profession. By 1850, women had been declared the answer to escalating school enrollments and reluctant taxpayers. School leaders counted on women's social consciousness, passivity, and sense of duty to God and country to subdue their desire for equitable salaries. In some cases, the female/male pay differential proved so great that rural districts hired as many as four women for the equivalent of one male teacher's salary. In Eastern cities, low pay forced female teachers into poor boarding places where they scrimped on food and leisure activities. As early as April 21, 1855, a

Philadelphia periodical, the *Woman's Advocate*, exposed the problems faced by its poorly paid teachers:

> We are struck by the great discrepancy between the amount paid to male and female teachers. . . . We do not understand why the principals of the schools, so precisely alike in their nature and requirements, should receive such unequal pay, nor do we believe any of the board could render a substantial reason if required to do so. We can imagine no valid reason why a woman, who has spent time and money in acquiring an education, and who is engaged to teach as many hours, as many pupils, and as correctly and thoroughly, should not receive as large a salary.
>
> This keeping down the salaries of women obliges them to practice the most rigid economy, and the consequence is, that in a city like this it is almost impossible for them to get respectable places to board, because they can not pay the price that men do. No, no, it is not because it costs men more to live, that women's salaries are being kept down. It is from a long practice of injustice, and it is their meager pay that obliges them to be more economical and forego many of the comforts and all the luxuries, which are obtained by the fortunate recipients of large salaries, for the same work which brings them but half pay. ("Compensation," 1855, pp. 94–95)

Feminist sentiment certainly precipitated such arguments for equal pay. In fact, Susan B. Anthony was the first to broach the subject at the 1853 meeting of the New York State Teachers' convention. Anthony, a former teacher herself, broke a long-held sanction against women speaking at teacher conventions when she stood and demanded to be heard on the subject. After a half-hour debate, she was allowed to speak. In her short lecture, Anthony pointed out that a sex-segregated job market suppressed both the wages and social status of teachers, and rationalized pay inequities for women. She scolded the men present, arguing they had to advance women's lot in order to improve their own:

> None of you can quite comprehend the cause of the disrespect of which you complain. Do you not see that as long as society says woman is incompetent to be a lawyer, minister, or doctor but has ample ability to be a teacher, every man of you who chooses the profession tacitly acknowledges that he has no more brains than a woman? And this, too, is the reason that teaching is a less lucrative profession, as men must compete with the cheap labor of women. . . . Would you exalt your profession, exalt those who labor with you? (Lerner, 1977, pp. 234–236)

Despite such early enlightenment, the concept of equal pay for equal work remained just that, a concept. It was a theory rarely applied, primarily because sexist prescriptions continued to exist, schools couldn't find the funding, and male teachers fought to keep the wage discrepancies in place. Even as the percentage of male teachers dwindled, women found no stronger voice with which to demand equal pay.

Although numerous, women teachers lacked solidarity, owing in part to their high turnover. At the end of the 19th century, it was still common for women to consider teaching a short-term experience. Most taught only 2 or 3 years before marriage. This began to change slowly in the early 20th century as women waited longer to marry or chose "single-blessedness." Harsher economic realities forced many young, middle-class women to seek jobs to help support parents and siblings. The death of the family breadwinner also pushed some women into the work world.

Feminist awareness increased women's desire for and access to higher education, making it a more natural event in the lives of middle-class women. Given the fact that few other options existed, the majority of those who entered higher education left as teachers. All these factors influenced a stronger commitment on the part of the woman teacher to maintain her teaching career and expand its pecuniary rewards.

New York City Women Teachers

New York City provided one example of a school system in which women teachers began to actively promote an increased respect for their gender in the profession. One of the first avenues they chose to pursue in achieving this goal came through the campaign for equal pay for equal work. Although New York City women teachers were already the highest paid in the country, they chafed under the obvious evidence of their second-class status. In 1900, the New York State Davis Law upgraded salaries for all teachers. Women teachers who lobbied for the law were surprised to learn that the new legislation set their salary schedules at a rate substantially lower than those of their male colleagues. The New York City charter set a minimum annual salary for men teachers at $900, but $600 for women. After 16 years of employment, female primary school teachers reached a wage maximum of $1,240, whereas men reached their maximum of $2,160 after only 10 years. Women principals who supervised elementary schools began at $1,750, reaching a maximum of $2,500 after 4 years of service, whereas their male cohorts began at $2,750 and obtained the maximum of $3,500 in the same time period. In the high schools, women earned between $1,100 and $2,500 to men's $1,300 to $3,000 (Maxwell, 1903).

Under the Davis Law, a woman had to be 19 years old and a normal school graduate (or equivalent) before she could teach. She then entered a year of apprenticeship at a salary of $408 prior to being assigned a regular teaching appointment. This created a great deal of consternation, because even the city's elevator boys received salaries between $600 and $900 a year. After several meritorious years of service, women teachers still earned less than city street sweepers, the health department's stable hands, and janitors in the local jails.

With the help of local women's groups, the concept of equal pay for teachers began to attract notice and become a cause célèbre. In November 1904, the New York City Federation of Women's Clubs held a program titled "The Equalization of Salaries of Public School Teachers." The program scheduled Alida S. Williams, principal of P.S. 33, to speak in favor of it and Dr. B. Crowson, Principal of P.S. 125, to speak in opposition. However, Williams did not appear and Crowson faced the group alone. The *Woman's Journal* ("Should Women Have Equal Pay?" 1904) reported that Crowson "made his audience so indignant, that almost all women there seemed to wish to get up and speak on the other side" (p. 356). The *Journal* summarized his main points: that women are physically and mentally inferior to men, and apt to take up teaching as a temporary thing and resign in order to marry. He also claimed women teachers supported only themselves, whereas men's larger income was necessary to support families.

In response to Crowson's assertions, Alice Stone Blackwell, editor of the *Journal*, argued that a large majority of female teachers supported others and that salaries should not be set according to the number of persons dependent upon the worker. Connecting equal pay to franchise, Blackwell also noted: "While in our Eastern cities male teachers are advocating large pay for themselves and small pay for women, in Wyoming and Utah the law expressly provides that women teachers shall have equal pay for equal work" ("Should Women Have Equal Pay?" 1904, p. 356). Increasingly, the concept of equal pay for equal work became aligned with suffrage and a radical feminist agenda, even though many feared this association would lead to greater enmity from the larger public and politicians.

New York Class Teachers' Association

The point that Blackwell made about male teachers being the foes of equal pay was well taken. In New York City, the issue became a dividing point for the sexes, and it split pro- and anti-suffrage women. The New York Class Teachers' Association (NYCTA), representing some 2,000 members, became painfully aware of the fragmenting effect that the issue could have on organizations. In April 1905, a group with the NYCTA began circulating a flyer, which declared:

The time is ripe to establish the principle of equal pay. Why should a woman's minimum annual salary be $300 less than a man's and why should her maximum [of] $900 be less than a man's? The women teachers do the same work, are exempt from no rules or duties, and most of them have fathers, mothers, sisters, or brothers dependent upon them. Why then should women not receive the same salaries? Let us make a strong united effort to bring about a consummation of what is manifestly just. ("Schoolma'ams Want," 1905, p. 8)

At this point, the circular suggested that the best way to begin this effort was to depose the current president, George Cottrell, and replace him with a "womanly woman, one loyal, faithful, conscientious." Approached by the press for his reaction, Cottrell expressed both surprise and anger. "It implies that I have not done my work properly." "Not at all," responded the equal pay contingent, "we presented our proposition to you last fall and you frowned upon it. You said that it would only result in lowering the male teachers' salaries. Thereupon we have taken the matter into our own hands" ("Schoolma'ams Want," 1905, p. 8).

The *New York Times* monitored the situation, reporting that the "anti-suffragist members" had organized to keep George Cottrell as president. Helen Aiken, a Cottrell supporter, explained why: "I know I am voicing the sentiments of many members when I say because of the nature of the duties of a President a man is better fitted for the position" ("Teachers' Election Fight," 1905, p. 12).

At the NYCTA's May 9th meeting, "the man crowd," so dubbed by the suffragists, "fired the first shot" by reading resolutions eulogizing the work accomplished by Cottrell. They were received by boos and hisses from the "suffrage side." Then Augusta Black, a Cottrell opponent, took the floor to ask: "How many of you ever signed a payroll and seen upon it the name of a man who is doing the same work as you are, but who is receiving double your salary?" This was met with cheers and applause. "Haven't you felt humiliated?" she continued. "Then let us insist that the injustice be remedied" ("Teachers' Election Fight," 1905, p. 12).

On May 17th, a vote was taken and Cottrell was retained. Anna Goessling, his presidential opponent, mused that though the battle had been lost, an important point had been raised. "I did not expect to win," she claimed. "I only started the movement to arouse the teachers. Thus far I have succeeded, and I am confident that sooner or later women will rule this organization. They have a right to, for there are only about a dozen men who belong to it altogether" ("Class Teachers Wage War," 1905, p. 9). In spite of the fact that men made up such a small percentage of the whole, their influence loomed large. In 1905, the concept of women's suffrage was still not highly regarded by the majority of the population, and the idea of equal pay stood in danger of being tied to it.

THE INTERBOROUGH ASSOCIATION OF WOMEN TEACHERS

The issue of equal pay resurrected the next spring in New York City when several hundred women teachers founded the Women Teachers' Organization (WTO). Anna Goessling proved instrumental in its establishment, and was elected vice president on April 8, 1906. The president, Kate Hogan, defined the group's purpose:

> Our proposition is reasonable. It seems that teaching is the only profession in the city, which still adheres to the old idea of paying women less than men. Women physicians and women lawyers receive as much as men. Such should be the case in our profession. ("Class Teachers Wage War," 1905, p. 9)

Fully convinced of the merit of their position, the WTO took their proposal to the board of education who voted it down without a hearing, explaining that it was "not feasible to amend the by-laws." Hogan, indignant at the decision, warned the board: "We will hold a big mass meeting in June. We will get ten thousand interested persons to attend. We will see if we can't accomplish something that way"("Board Rules," 1906, p. 9).

Although some must have scoffed at the idea that the WTO could turn out "ten thousand interested persons," Hogan's estimate wasn't that far off the mark. By their September meeting, the organization, now called the Interborough Teacher's Association (ITA), counted some 4,000 members. Within 2 years, membership expanded to 14,000. At the September meeting, the ITA decided that the most expedient way to achieve the goal of equal pay was to lobby the state legislature directly. In this effort, they hoped President Roosevelt would be helpful. Roosevelt had been New York governor when the Davis Law passed and had remarked on the wide discrepancies between male and female salaries. However, when informed that the new schedule represented substantial wage increases for women, he signed the bill despite whatever misgivings he had ("Women Teachers Want," 1906).

In November 1906, the Board of Estimate cut the education budget by $1,879,400 and, in turn, the New York Board of Education appealed to the state legislature for a change in how the General School Fund was raised. The fund had been overestimated for 6 years in a row. The teachers, now organized under the title of the Interborough Association of Women Teachers (IAWT) saw this as an opportunity to again approach the board of education about their equal pay proposal. They reasoned that as long as the board was going to the legislature over budget concerns, they might as well ask for the money necessary to cover the costs of equal pay. Once again the board rejected the proposal. IAWT member Grace Strachan, a Brooklyn school district superintendent, advised her organization not to overestimate their power and to be patient with the situation ("Women Teachers Begin," 1906, p. 3). Members were clearly impressed by Strachan's strategic insights as well as her unusually high position (for a woman) in the school system, and this event apparently paved the way for her eventual ascent in the association.

A New Leadership for the IAWT

Later in November, the IAWT suffered a blow with the sudden death of president and founder Kate Hogan, creating much dissension within the ranks. The group broke into two factions, each supporting a different successor to Hogan's post. Anna Goessling was pitted against Sarah J. J. McCafferty, the principal of P.S. 116 in Manhattan. Although the December 8, 1906, meeting was called to hear memorials to the late president, the group quickly broke into argument when Goessling took the president's chair. When questioned by what right she did so, Goessling replied that as vice president, it was expected of her. Debate ensued, with some members claiming that the Brooklyn contingent was trying to take over the organization because they already held three of four officer positions. Another faction claimed that a class teacher (Goessling) and not a principal (McCafferty) should be president, as this more closely represented the majority of the members. Parliamentary procedure flew fast and furious. By the end of the meeting, a compromise candidate, Nora Curtis Lenihen, the former IAWT treasurer, had been elected president. Her reign was a short one; at the beginning of the 1907 school year, when nominated again for president, she declined for health reasons.

At this point, Grace Strachan became president of the IAWT ("Alliance," 1906). No details are available as to what led to Strachan's sudden rise to power. The local newspapers do not report on it, and in her autobiographical book, *Equal Pay for Equal Work* (1910), she leads the reader to believe there was never any question that she would eventually inherit the position. It is hard to say whether someone else could have led the IAWT to victory in the equal pay struggle. There is no doubt that Strachan had a certain political savvy, a clue to which is seen in her own climb up the administrative ladder. In 1907, her position as district superintendent and her aspirations for a still higher niche made her stand out. Although the women of the IAWT may have had misgivings about her, because she was not then a teacher like the majority of members, they nevertheless decided to give her the reins.

One of her first actions as president must have helped to reassure the IAWT, as well as many outsiders, of her leadership ability. In March 1907, in a totally unladylike style, Strachan led over 600 women into the halls of the legislature in Albany to attend the hearing of Senator Horace White's equal pay bill. The *Woman's Journal* described the convergence on the capitol: "We are told that the teachers pervaded the capitol building and overflowed the rooms and corridors, that all the Senators were besieged by rings of teachers three deep, plying them with arguments" ("Teachers Ask Equal Pay," 1907, p. 1).

Although the bill passed quickly through both houses, New York City Mayor George B. McClellan vetoed the bill, citing financial hardship to the city. The IAWT's lobbying efforts contributed to their public exposure, if not notoriety. Newspapers and popular and educational journals editorialized, often in a negative vein, about the efforts of the women teachers. The popular magazine *Outlook* was particularly scandalized, editorializing on the untoward effect that equal pay would have on male students:

> It is the general opinion of educational experts that in the higher schools more men teachers are needed. This is not because the pupils of men teachers pass better examinations than women teachers; it is because the masculine is needed in the educational community; because for example, the average boy, if he is taught only by a woman, comes to regard scholarship as a purely feminine accomplishment and looks upon it with something like contempt. He needs to understand that manliness and scholarship, may and often do go together, and he can only learn this by seeing them together in the teacher whom he respects both for his manliness and for his scholarship. ("Equalization of Salaries," 1907, p. 595)

The *Journal of Education* prophesied that if the equal pay concept was put into effect, it would mean a loss of jobs for women teachers:

> Men, as men, will probably favor this, since it would offer a salary for which men would at once compete, and the proportion of men in the profession would be quadrupled within four years. The chances are that the great majority of grammar and high school positions would soon be filled by men. ("New York Women Teachers," 1906, p. 479)

The *New York Herald* agreed, as did Edgar Levy, former deputy comp-troller for the City of New York, who wrote in the *Educational Review*: "The most extreme demands of trade unionism have scarcely equaled those of the women teachers. When has a greater danger to democratic government arisen than this new theory of compensation which is to ignore wholly the operation of natural laws?" ("New York Women Teach-ers," 1906, p. 479).

None too subtly implied in these articles were several points of inter-est. The first, ironically, was the agreement that the women teachers were underpaid. In fact, Levy considered underpayment a rational means of forcing an imbalance of women out of the system. The second implication was that male students were more important than female students or female teachers. The anxiety for boys, as future family breadwinners, seemed to take precedence over the concern for justice or the reality that many female teachers were the sole support of family members, whereas not all men were. The author in the *Journal of Education* article implied that equal pay was not in the best interest of women and that women could not be the competitive equals of men. And Levy implied inexplicably that the campaign for equal pay was an antidemocratic movement and that some greater force worked through the "operation of natural laws" to shift wages in favor of men.

Another source of opposition to the activities of the IAWT was the Association of Men Teachers and Principals (AMTP) of the City of New York (1907). This organization formed on the heels of the IAWT's trip to the New York State Assembly. The group of 600 to 700 men, with representatives from the Brooklyn Teachers' Association, the Bronx Princi-pals' Association, the Principals' Association of New York, the Assistant and Junior High Teachers' Association, the Schoolmen of New York, the Schoolmen of Queens, and the Male Teachers Association, was obviously threatened by the power they perceived the IAWT to possess.

Taking a clue from the IAWT's lobbying tactics, the AMTP quickly released a lengthy circular that attacked the latest equal pay bill proposed by Senator White. Among the 24 arguments they made in opposition to equal pay were that the White bill (1) was mandatory legislation, (2) was based on a false economic principle contrary to accepted practice in the business world, (3) would "work injury to the public schools and to the children," (4) would create extensive litigation, and (5) "would bring about a reorganization of the administration of the State and of other municipalities." The emergence of the AMTP motivated former bystand-ers to choose up sides. Though it often appeared as though the split was down gender lines, some men supported equal pay because they believed to do otherwise would be unchivalrous.

Carrie Chapman Catt, president of the NAWSA, speaking at an equal pay rally, claimed that the men teachers' circular contained "24 excuses not 24 reasons against equal pay." The *New York Evening Sun* called the male teachers "self-seeking male persons opposed [to] a simple act of justice." The AMTP lacked the more subtle and persuasive qualities of the IAWT lobbyists, using strong-arm tactics that offended some, including Assemblyman Hoey, a New York Democrat. He complained: "Few people realize the campaign of misrepresentation and deceit that has been waged by the men teachers against this bill. It is unworthy of them. I have been actually insulted and threatened by one male teacher because I dared to vote for this bill" (cited in "Teachers' Equal Pay Bill," 1907, p. 82).

On May 15, 1907, the New York House and Senate again voted on the bill, this time passing it over the veto of Mayor McClellan by a margin of 82 to 55. Although there was reason for jubilation, few could ignore that the bill passed by a smaller margin on the second vote. Nevertheless, the IAWT members were again present in great numbers at the assembly vote. The *New York Tribune* commented on the frenzied atmosphere:

> The women teachers who have won such a reputation as lobbyists of unexcelled ardor and persistence, as usual stood around the rail of the assembly floor. . . . Assemblyman after assemblyman flocked to the railing for a word or a smile from the lobbyists. "Did you ever see anything so disgusting in your life?" asked an assemblyman of many years service pointing to an active group around the rail. (cited in "Teacher's Equal Pay Bill," 1907, p. 82)

The Long Effort

Governor Charles Evans Hughes vetoed the bill. He explained that the question of equal pay was a local one and should not fall under the jurisdiction of the state legislature. However, before the legislature had an opportunity to override the veto, the session adjourned. The next year (1908), despite an enormous lobbying effort by the IAWT, the equal pay bill was killed in the Committee on Rules of the Assembly. Strachan felt that the demise of the bill could be attributed to the work of one person, the chair of the Republican Rules Committee. This led her to publicly urge teachers to work only for political candidates who were sympathetic to the equal pay cause. When this action came to their attention, the board of education sharply criticized Strachan and threatened to charge her with "gross misconduct and insubordination." Several board members decided that it was wiser to make future occurrences of such political activity by teachers illegal. The following amendment emerged from the October 28, 1908, board meeting (Meeting of Board of Education, 1908):

> No member of the supervising or teaching staff shall be permitted to join or become a member of any club or take part in any movement intended or undertaking to affect legislation for or on behalf of the Department of Education or any official thereof, or to contribute any funds for such a purpose. Any combination or concerted effort among members of the supervising staff or other employees of the Board of Education to elect or defeat any candidate for public office by reason of his having favored or opposed or having agreed or refused to agree to favor or oppose any legislation affecting the salaries of any members of said supervising staff or other employees shall be deemed to constitute gross misconduct and insubordination. (pp. 2126–2127)

However, after it was pointed out at a later meeting that such charges might be considered in violation of a teacher's civil liberties, the board decided to retract the amendment. Instead, they voted to refuse any future requests by teachers for time off to attend the assembly session ("Board Retracts Threat," 1908, p. 6).

In 1909, another equal pay bill passed through the legislature and, unexpectedly, Mayor McClellan again vetoed it. The women of the IAWT felt sure that their previous year's work had convinced the mayor of the merit of equal pay. They had secured thousands of signatures on petitions sent to the mayor. Public debates had been held, and letters written to the mayor by prominent people in favor of equal pay. On March 7, 1908, they had filled Association Hall with over 3,000 women teachers, businessmen, and political figures, all raising their voices in favor of the bill.

A few months later, 1,500 people had turned out to an "Equal Pay Dinner" at the Hotel Waldorf Astoria. In attendance at the formal affair were presidents of most of the local and state women's clubs, expressing their solidarity with the "woman's cause." Arthur Brisbane, editor of the *New York Evening Journal*, told the gathering that the only way for women to achieve equal pay was first to get the vote. Widespread applause answered his suggestion, but Rabbi Wise of the Free Synagogue of New York and member of the editorial board of the *Woman's Journal* countered that the women must not wait to vote because the cause of equal pay was every bit as important as the vote. Charles Edward Russell, editor-writer for the *New York American*, reminded the women, "You teachers are fighting the fight of every woman who toils." Senator Grady spoke of Governor Hughes's veto of the bill and suggested, "If it is presented to a Democratic governor I am sure it will pass" ("Equal Pay Dinner," 1908, p. 8).

Unexpectedly and much to the dismay of IAWT members, the male teachers' organization came out in favor of raises for women teachers in

1909. The AMTP passed a resolution along to the board of education recommending an initial salary increase to women teachers from $600 to $720. Strachan was livid. She saw the recommendation as a shallow attempt by the male teachers to improve their tarnished image. She knew that the board of education had already scheduled a minimum increase to $700. She pointed out to the board of education that the action of the men was unnecessary and insincere: "This association was not only organized for the purpose of defeating women teachers in their efforts to obtain a just salary schedule, but . . . it has continuously been active and bitter in its opposition to the women teachers" ("Tell Men," 1909, p. 16).

In 1910, a new board of estimate came into power and one of its earliest acts was to authorize the appointment of a commission of four men and one woman to study the question of equal pay. The 170-page report, in essence, recommended "an aggregate increase of $1,700,377 be made in salaries and the salaries be graduated according to position and not according to sex," creating new hope for the women of the IAWT ("Recommends," 1910, p. 184). IAWT had actively pursued pledges from candidates for the Equal Pay Bill throughout election year 1910. With both the offices of mayor and governor up for reelection, the IAWT saw their efforts as crucial in overcoming the two major stumbling blocks to the bill's passage. Following the earlier advice of Senator Grady, the IAWT helped elect two Democrats to the offices. In autumn of 1911, with no hesitation, the legislature, with its two newly elected officials—Governor John Alden Dix and Mayor George B. Gaynor—signed into law the Grady Equal Pay Bill.

Although the Grady Bill was a pared-down version of the IAWT's original plan, members were justifiably proud of the victory. The bill, which became Chapter 902 of the 1911 Laws of New York, carried the basic principles long fought for by the equal pay supporters. It specified that teacher salaries were to be regulated only by merit, length and degree of experience, and grade level. But more important, the 19 words that had taken some 5 years to obtain were now present in the Greater New York City Charter: "In the schedule of salaries hereafter adopted there shall be no discrimination based on the sex of the member" (see "Recommends," 1910, p. 184).

SUMMARY OF NEW YORK TEACHER ACTIVITIES

Teachers in New York City made two major attempts to secure equal pay for women teachers. The NYCTA proposed the first, but it was quickly defeated, perhaps because of its association with suffrage. A second organization, the IAWT, represented many members of the earlier association. Throughout its 5-year campaign, as several bills were developed, reviewed, and rejected, the IAWT grew. By the time of the White Bill's passage, the IAWT represented over 15,000 members. A major factor in the strength and growth of this group was its leader Grace Strachan, who demonstrated political savvy, perseverance, and an ability to motivate.

Aside from achieving the goal of equal pay for equal work for teachers, the IAWT secured a number of other accomplishments. First, the women of the IAWT made an enormous impression on the people of New York City and educators nationwide. They helped to break stereotypes about the docility of female teachers. They challenged the public and politicians to face facts about sex discrimination in the job market. They demonstrated the power of even voteless women, with sobering results for a few elected officials who lost their offices. They solidified a network of 15,000 members under oppressive circumstances for a lengthy 5-year campaign. Furthermore, they situated themselves as an active facet of a larger network of women's clubs and feminist organizations. They provided role models for women in other occupations and for women teachers in other cities. They helped set an example that gave encouragement to others to examine their work lives and their goals and to move together toward a more secure future.

Though suffragists firmly believed that acquisition of the vote would circumvent the necessity of undertaking struggles such as that carried out in the New York City equal pay campaign, this was not to be the case. After 1920, the wage situation for female teachers continued to be fought, on a district-by-district basis, nationwide, incrementally, and in a frustratingly repetitious pattern ("Equal Compensation," 1929; "Teachers' Pay Is Below," 1916). The song sung by Cincinnati Women's Teachers Association, though humorous, accurately points out the continuing struggle of many female teachers living on a less than adequate wage:

A LONG WAY TO REACH THE MAXIMUM

Mary started teaching
at the age of twenty-three;
She got six hundred dollars for her yearly salary;
She bought the teachers' papers,
Took a course at 'Varsity,
And hopefully looked forward
To the age of thirty-three.

Mary tried to live within
Her yearly salary;
She made her clothes and trimmed her hats,

And did her laundry
She patronized cheap restaurants,
And often went hungry;
But hopefully looked forward
To the age of thirty-three.

Mary woke one day to find
That she was thirty-three;
The increased cost of living now eats up her salary;
The big folks all have autos,
Not a skatemobile has she;
But she's looking to her pension
At the age of thirty-three.

Chorus
For it's a long way to reach the maximum,
It's a long way to go;
It's a long way to reach the maximum,
But we'll get there, we know,
Good-bye, books and travel, music concerts and dress!
It's a long, long way to reach the maximum;
But we'll get there, we guess. ("A Long Way," 1915, p. 5)

THE GROWTH OF THE SINGLE SALARY
SCHEDULE, 1920–1950

Toward the end of World War I and beyond, colleges and other institutions of higher education saw a phenomenal growth in women's admissions. Between 1917 and 1921, women's enrollments increased by 76% at some 127 coeducational colleges and universities (compared with a 48% increase in male enrollments). In 22 women's colleges, their percentage increased by 50% and in 9 universities by 110% (*Who's Who and Why*, 1921). Because social expectations continued to limit women's career options and aspirations, the majority of these female graduates left with a teaching certificate in hand.

In the period between 1925 and 1940, numerous changes occurred in the country's educational infrastructure, including the proliferation of junior high schools, the doubling of high school enrollments, and increased teacher certification requirements. Between 1925 and 1931, teachers received modest wage increases followed by Depression-induced reductions in the period between 1931 and 1935. In most large cities, teachers saw their 1935 salaries decline to 1925 levels. Salaries were eventually restored, increasing by some 62% from 1939 to 1949.

During World War II, higher salaries attracted many teachers, particularly men, to war-related industries, resulting in a serious teacher shortage. Other factors in the shortage related to the teacher layoffs during the 1930s, rapidly expanding school districts, and increased teacher dissatisfaction with their careers. While the schools pleaded for teachers, the army had no difficulty securing all the instructors it needed, because it paid 50% to 100% more than local school districts. In 1945, Amanda M. Ellis (1945) of the National Federation of Business and Professional Women's Clubs (BPWC) asked the question on many minds: "Will the teachers who left poorly paid [school] positions . . . to take up more lucrative employment growing out of the war return to their classrooms now that the war is over?" (p. 247). Ellis concluded the answer was no. Her research had found teachers had several criticisms of the profession. They experienced too much public scrutiny, had too little personal time, and did too much work for too little pay.

Boston University investigated the question of whether teacher dissatisfaction was key in women's reluctance to engage or stay engaged in the profession. The study explored the social obligations and restrictions placed on small-town (populations of 12,000 or less) teachers. Teachers responded that they resented small-town scrutiny and the expectation that they be involved in an endless stream of community events. Many mentioned that the war had added greatly to such obligations, including bond drives, war-stamp collections, Red Cross work, scrap collections, and registration for rationing. Furthermore, local social prescriptions precluded women teachers from smoking, drinking, dancing, card-playing, dating, marriage, divorce, certain types of dress, and taking weekend trips. Still others noted the lack of equal pay for equal work. As teacher dissatisfaction reduced the ranks, boards began to reevaluate the effect of community meddling and poor compensation on employment patterns (Lichter, 1946). Women's groups such as the National Federation of Business and Professional Women's Clubs stood ready to drive the point home at every opportunity.

The National Federation's periodical *Independent Woman* and more mainstream magazines such as the *Ladies Home Journal* regularly published articles decrying the shortage and linking it to the lack of salary and respect accorded teachers. They exploited predictions that as many as 6,000 schools would close for lack of teachers and cited research that showed that teacher morale had dropped to an all-time low ("$37 a week," 1947). The National Federation pushed local clubs to prioritize the issue and bring it before their own communities on a regular basis (Bayard, 1947; Brokaw, 1946). The Office of War Information got into the act by distributing circulars and posters urging women to consider teaching a patriotic activity (Davis, 1943).

Partly as the result of such efforts, by 1949, 90% of city school systems with populations over 50,000 had adopted single salary schedules (Mueller & Bunn, 1951). Female teacher organizations, most prominent in the cities, worked tirelessly to obtain this goal. An early form of "equal pay for comparable worth," the single salary schedule proposed that elementary and secondary teachers of comparable training and years receive the same salary regardless of sex. Male teacher groups were less than enthusiastic about the concept and organized against it. Typical was the protest of the Schoolmen's Club of Kansas City, who argued that the plan ignored the law of supply and demand and that its implementation would eliminate "men fit to train and inspire our youth for good citizenship." The superintendent of the Little Falls, New York, schools went even further by implying that a state equal pay law would fundamentally alter the course of "relation[s] of the sexes in all spheres of human activity: industrial, economic, civic, domestic, and social." He demanded to know among other questions: "What are the inevitable economic consequences as regards the home, childhood, and the whole social fabric, of the universal application of the theory of equal pay?" It was a question on many minds (Cowan & Bird, 1925, pp. 596–597; see also Hervey, 1925).

Gender and the Salary Schedule

Men, nevertheless, continued to receive better salaries than women due, in part, to the growing trend of districts to pay more to teachers with dependents. In 1940, 5.7% of all districts paid dependency bonuses (increasing to 6.8% by 1956). Superintendent Harold T. Rand of the Melrose, Massachusetts, schools explained the rationale behind dependency bonuses:

> We have on our staff a number of excellent men teachers who would long since have been obliged to accept, in fairness to their families, positions in higher paying communities were it not for the fact that they receive up to $600 above their salary schedule on account of their dependents. ("Extra Pay," 1960, p. 53)

Superintendent C. E. Jones of the Beloit, Wisconsin, public schools clarified that though women were eligible, the "origin of the dependency stipend was not to care for the needy widow but based on the recognition of salary competition with business and industry in an attempt to provide additional compensation for men in the field of education" (p. 54).

Another method for increasing the salaries of male teachers was through compensation for extracurricular activities. Typical activities providing extra revenue included coaching football or cheerleading and directing school dramatics or conducting the marching band. The Roslyn Public School in New York established a point system to determine each activity's remuneration. As a result, the football coach received $810, the marching band director $600, the school dramatic coach $440, and the cheerleading supervisor $250. Sex-bias, conscious or unconscious, obviously guided the point spread.

The appointment of men to administrative and supervisory positions continued as another well-utilized method of increasing male salaries. One teacher referred to this as a "modified spoils system" in which any male teacher reaching the upper limit of his salary range would be pushed up the administrative ranks whether adequately prepared or not (Lafferty, 1948).

Race and the Salary Schedule

African American women teachers faced a separate and additional struggle for pay equity in these years: getting paid on the same scale as Whites (Littlefield, 1994; Shaw, 1996). This proved particularly difficult to achieve in the South and even more so in Southern rural schools where the vast majority of African American children were educated in dilapidated, one- or two-teacher schoolhouses. In the academic year 1934–35, two thirds of all African American rural schools were either one-teacher (39.3%) or two-teacher (28.4%) structures. Teachers in these segregated facilities generally obtained less training than their White counterparts. Though African American educators waged a vigorous battle against dual standards for White and Black teachers, problems like the lack of scholarships and access to normal schools produced hurdles often too difficult to overcome (Fultz, 1995). Some women's groups and female teacher leaders (including some White women) played a significant part in trying to bring local schools through this minefield. But in doing so, they jeopardized their jobs and exposed themselves to community animus (Calloway-Thomas & Garner, 1996; Clark, 1962; Giddings, 1984; Kaufman, 1991; Weider, 1992).

In 1931–32, the average salary of African American public school teachers in 15 Southern states was $433 for elementary teachers and $758 for high school teachers. This placed Blacks' salaries at about half those of Whites ("Salaries," 1936; "Educating," 1938). In a series of court cases, the National Association for the Advancement of Colored People (NAACP) addressed racially discriminatory wages. Lemann (1991) notes the NAACP, a middle-class organization, would barely have existed without teacher-members, who were forced to join secretly to protect their jobs.

Judge W. Calvin Chestnut, in one of the first federal cases, issued an order in late 1939 restraining the Arundel County, Maryland, school board from paying less to African American than to White teachers in comparable positions ("First Federal Injunction," 1939). Then, the U.S. Supreme Court upheld the case of a Norfolk, Virginia, African American teacher, finding in *School Board of the City of Norfolk v. Alston* (1939) that separate salary schedules violated the due process and equal-protection clauses of the 14th Amendment of the U.S. Constitution.

During the 1939–40 school year, the salaries of Norfolk African American teachers with normal school certificates ranged from $597.50 to $960.10 compared with those of similarly qualified Whites who earned $850 to $1,425. African American elementary school teachers who were college graduates earned from $611 to $960, whereas Whites with the same qualification earned $937 to $1,425. African Americans teaching high school earned from $784.50 to $1,235, whereas White high school teachers received from $1,200 to $2,185 ("Equal Pay," 1941). Despite the Supreme Court's decision, the fight ahead would be a lengthy, attenuated, and daunting experience for the teachers involved. African Americans came down on both sides of the issue, with some fearing the loss of their jobs if school boards were forced to pay them salaries comparable to those of White teachers. Though their fears proved to be well founded, most teacher organizations pressed on in favor of a single salary schedule.

AFRICAN AMERICAN COALITION BUILDING

In 1944, Mary L. Williams, president of the American Teachers Association (ATA), charged the nation's schools with perpetuating racial discrimination in several ways. She noted that school boards routinely evaded court mandates by (1) placing African American teachers on the lowest scale regardless of qualifications, (2) dismissing African American teachers from jobs, (3) replacing African Americans with Whites when salaries were increased, (4) failing to provide transportation to schools for African American children, (5) failing to provide vocational training to schools for African American children, and (6) offering only substandard and discarded buildings and equipment to schools in African American communities ("A Plea," 1944).

The ATA faced a difficult path, but the 40-year-old organization had already battled near overwhelming odds. The association organized in

1904 as the National Association of Teachers in Colored Schools (NATCS) when African American teachers were excluded from attending the National Education Association (NEA) conventions, even though many were dues-paying members. The NATCS grew slowly, changing its name at the 1937 Philadelphia conference to the American Teachers Association. Pushing forward its motto and agenda, "Equality of Educational Opportunity for Every Child and Equality of Professional Status for Every Teacher," the ATA increased its membership from 3,100 to 11,000 in only 3 years (from 1944 to 1947) (Neverdon-Morton, 1989), largely as the result of outreach strategies that encouraged membership beyond the Southern states.

The ATA's problems with the NEA were long-standing, beginning when the NEA appointed an informal committee in 1926 to "study the problem in Negro schools." Two years later the committee urged the NEA to cooperate with the NATCS. The negotiations to that end, however, were slow in developing—taking some 17 years, at which point the NEA offered only to provide a separate "Negro Department" within the organization. In 1943, the NEA adopted a resolution to hold conventions in only those cities where equal accommodations were afforded to every NEA delegate. Yet complaints of segregated treatment emerged at the conference held in St. Louis in 1950. In 1953, a convention scheduled for Miami was moved to Miami Beach when the city of Miami failed to provide assurance of equal treatment and accommodations (Ridley, 1966). One contemporary assessed the NEA's civil rights policies as good on paper but "in the realm of practical action . . . a different picture emerges showing . . . a disinclination to become entangled in controversies involving segregation, regardless of what happens to tenure and academic freedom" (Lieberman, 1957).

When the NEA began to push for integrated schools in the 1960s, the ATA voiced concern about this goal. Integration meant unemployment for African American teachers in the South. A prime example could be seen in Giles County, Virginia, where the closure of an African American elementary and high school led to the dismissal of seven African American teachers who were "not needed" in the now racially integrated schools.

With the help of the Negro Virginia Teachers Association and the NEA, the Giles County teachers went to court in 1965 to protest their dismissal and won. But the court only went so far as forbidding the wholesale firing of African American teachers. Though the U.S. Department of Education threatened to withhold federal aid from school districts that did not integrate teachers, this strategy did not have much immediate impact because little effort was put into its implementation. That year it was estimated that 55,000 African American teachers could lose jobs in the South if the process of "integrating out" continued at its current rate.

Those teachers, both African American and White, who spoke out against the process found their names placed on a "black list" ("Discriminatory," 1965; "Integration," 1965). Sometimes the black list had the force of law. In 1956, the South Carolina legislature passed a bill that no city employee could affiliate with any civil rights organization. Septima Clark was dismissed from her teaching position in the Charleston public schools for refusal to resign from the NAACP. At the time she was 58 years old and had taught for 44 years. She spent the next 20 years working to get her retirement benefits restored (McFadden, 1993).

Only a decade after *Brown v. Board of Education of Topeka, Kansas* (1954), some 38,000 African American teachers and administrators had lost positions in 17 Southern and border states. The repercussions are still being felt today. In 1996, nearly 90% of the U.S. public school teaching force was White. As the number of minority teachers continued to dwindle, the number of minority students increased, resulting in a deficit of adult role models in the schools as well as a lack of advice from minority educators. Research has cited lack of educational opportunity, racial discrimination, and low prestige among the reasons that African Americans fail to pursue degrees in education (see, e.g., Ehrenberg, Goldhaber, & Brewer, 1995; Ethridge, 1979; Gordon, 1995; Hudson, 1994; "Teachers Lack," 1996).

Despite such largely unintended outcomes, most believed that desegregation would be a positive step in the history of American schooling, moving from poorly funded, dilapidated school buildings, with a lack of textbooks and other materials, and undereducated teachers toward some kind of parity with the schools in which Whites predominated. But the paradox of desegregation was that where material improvements were obtained, teacher–pupil relationships suffered as Black teachers were replaced with White (Foster, 1991).

EQUAL PAY ACT OF 1963

As was the case with race prejudice, gender bias ran so deep that by the 1960s women's groups realized that district-by-district efforts, and even state-by-state efforts, were futile and began to work for legislation at the federal level. In 1963, the right to equal pay for equal work, which teachers had fought for since the early years of the 20th century, was finally set into law. Key in the passage was the BPWC that, from its inception in 1919, placed equal pay as its primary objective. The federation represented some 60,000 women whose membership in hundreds of business and professional women's clubs across the country made them eligible for national membership. Throughout its history, teachers or former teachers represented a significant proportion of the BPWC's membership. In 1931, for instance, a low point for many clubs because of the Depression, teachers constituted approximately three fifths of the professionals in the Federation. As will be seen in Chapter 4, the influence of the teachers on the organization's priorities was clear-cut (Manson, 1931).

The BPWC's nationwide campaign began to meet real success during the 1950s when several states enacted equal pay laws (Women's Bureau, 1965). By 1963, 23 states had such laws in force. During the Kennedy administration, the U.S. Women's Bureau's director, Esther Peterson, transformed the concept into federal law. Unfortunately, a conservative Congress placed so many exemptions within the bill that it became inapplicable to the majority of the nation's female workers. The Equal Pay Act, an amendment to the Fair Standards and Labor Act, covered only wage and hour employees, exempting employers with fewer than 25 employees, those working in most domestic service and agriculture jobs, and those holding executive and professional positions, including teachers in educational institutions at the K–12 and university levels. Over the next decade, teachers and their coalitions, including the BPWC, lobbied Congress for their inclusion in the law. In 1972 their efforts finally met with success when the provisions of the act were extended to management and professional employees as well as to state and local government employees (Linden-Ward & Green, 1993; Lindgren & Taub, 1988; Rupp & Taylor, 1987; Stetson, 1991).

However, as in previous decades, school districts managed to develop mechanisms to evade the law. In 1977, Women's Educational Action League (WEAL) published research that found that the old point systems were still in place for teachers' extracurricular work, and as a result female teacher salaries lacked parity with salaries of their male colleagues. This practice, as WEAL pointed out, constituted a violation of the amended Equal Pay Act. Those not voluntarily complying with the law, they warned, would be in jeopardy of litigation. Two years later, the NEA reached the same conclusion. In a study of the existing literature, teacher opinion polls, and teaching salary schedules, the NEA discovered serious discrepancies in the salaries paid to coaches of female and male athletics teams in the public schools. Furthermore, they learned that teachers felt that efforts to comply with the provisions of Title IX of the Education Amendments Act of 1972 were dismal if existent at all (Boring, 1977; "Title IX: Parity," 1979). A more recent survey (*National Center for Education Statistics*, 1992) found that in 1987–88, 43% of all teachers received supplemental income from schools. Today such pay discrepancies remain an issue of contention within many school districts.

SUMMARY

The decision to form separate women teachers' groups often took place on the discovery that they did not always share with men the same goals or status. Having struggled through the same teacher training courses, taught in the same classrooms and under the same obstreperous administrators as their male colleagues, women naturally expected that they would be treated as "fellow" professionals. Yet this was rarely the case, as evidenced in this chapter. The question of whether women were considered "equal to" or "different from" men guided the arguments revolving around many of the issues facing female teachers, including equal pay for equal work. In an occupation increasingly defined as a "woman's profession," men often did all they could to rationalize distinctive positions for themselves, including separate career ladders, pay scales, and other privileges. Men argued that they had sacrificed better salaries in other lines of employment to become teachers, and as family breadwinners they needed and deserved the best rewards that the profession could offer.

The "difference" argument was also used by some feminists who claimed women were "natural" teachers, and thus superior to men as teachers. But the stronger feminist argument centered on proving that regardless of biological differences, as professionals they were equals. In doing so, women were able to use the gains won by men to their own advantage. If men received wage increases, then why shouldn't women? Men won their rewards not only because of their gender but also because they constituted a powerful minority. Commensurate rewards for women often meant economic hardships for school districts. Thus the dilemma became whether to eliminate the inducements paid to men to stay in the profession or to convince the public to expand the tax base to adequately compensate all teachers equally.

The case for adequate compensation was more compelling during times of teacher shortage. During both world wars, labor shifted from the public sector to the war industry where greater incentives were provided. Schools, with budgets that remained stationary or in decline, futilely competed to attract workers. Boards hoped to motivate applications with sentimental discourses about women's innate sense of patriotism or community spirit. And although many women responded to such lures, they were quick to form coalitions through which they could utilize this temporary leverage to reap greater restitution or better job security.

Even as White women made some inroads to equal pay by leveraging teacher shortages to their benefit, Black women, particularly those in the

South, faced a separate struggle. As schools were forced to integrate through federal intervention, Black teachers lost the little security that they had achieved in the segregated schools. Not only did Blacks have to fight to obtain parity with Whites with regard to teachers' salaries; they also had to battle for the right to teach in integrated schools. It was through federal intervention and the Equal Pay Act of 1963 that teachers finally possessed a weapon with which to acquire this long-sought goal of pay equity.

Chapter 3

BUILDING HOUSES FOR TEACHERS:
HOME, HEARTH, AND THE
GENERAL FEDERATION OF WOMEN'S CLUBS

In 1905, unable to find lodging with a local family in a well-to-do district of Walla Walla County, Washington, a young female teacher commandeered a cook-house wagon and hauled it into the school yard where she lived for the rest of the year. The situation was far from ideal. Covered only in canvas, the 20-foot structure let in rain and snow. Passersby at the train station inquired about the wagon, and, when told the story, they chastised the townspeople through neighboring newspapers. When the embarrassed citizenry pressed the school board director to come up with a better solution, he went to the county superintendent with a plan to build a permanent home for the teacher on the school grounds. By the next fall, the district teacher was housed in a neat two-room cottage adjacent to the schoolhouse ("Where Shall the Country Teacher Live?" 1916). Josephine Corliss Preston, the assistant county school superintendent, and later state superintendent of public instruction, immediately saw the replicability of the solution (Cattell, 1932). She began, with the help of the GFWC, a national movement to educate community people about the value of these homes that became known as teacherages.

Over the first two decades of the 20th century, lumber companies, federal education agencies, civic organizations, and philanthropists joined the GFWC in advocating the teacherage as a means of school improvement. Such support led to the rapid adoption of the housing alternative. The U.S. Bureau of Education estimated that between 1915 and 1923, approximately 3,000 teacherages were erected, 567 of these in Texas alone ("Teachers in Rural Districts," 1922). In Hawaii, one third of all schools had cottages for teachers built at public expense (Vincent, 1916). The architectural styles and building costs ranged from a primitive $50 log cabin, to a $50,000 five-apartment structure (Gray, 1916; Muerman, 1922).

The teacherage movement emerged during the progressive era that spanned 1890 to 1920, a period when women held an increased presence as reformers and took the lead in efforts as diverse as suffrage, temperance, consumer protection, child welfare regulations, city housekeeping, and school improvement (see, e.g., Blair, 1989; Davis, 1967; Giddings, 1984; Hewitt & Lebsock, 1993; "Kansas Federation," 1986; Salem, 1993; Scott, 1993; Sklar, 1988). In cities, women's clubs and organizations participated in social architectural reforms such as the development of playgrounds, day nurseries for the children of working mothers, and homes for young working women. This chapter explores the teacherage concept as one example of the transition of such urban "female institution building" to the rural areas of the United States (Freedman, 1979, 1995; Gibbons, 1979).

CLUBWOMEN AND SCHOOL REFORM

As part of the activities in the broader, somewhat inchoate, rural reform agenda of clubwomen in the early decades of the 20th century, the teacherage continued clubwomen's well-established connection to school reform. From its inception in 1890, the General Federation of Women's Clubs (GFWC) embraced the educational mission already central to many of its 500 affiliate clubs and over 100,000 members. Participation in school reform activities aided clubwomen in their shift from self-improvement to civic reform activities so widely observed at the time (Allen, 1988; Blair, 1980; Reese, 1978).

Middle-class White and African American women rationalized their involvement in schools as an extension of their domestic roles as mothers. They struggled to unite home and school out of a belief that "the ideal school was really an extension of the ideal American home" (Reese, 1978, p. 4). Although many club members would later become vigorous participants in the suffrage movement, not all were ready to take such a bold step in the 1890s. The transition from domestic to public politics proceeded incrementally in many women's groups. With small footholds in educational politics, women enlarged their niche in rural school reform activities as they lobbied for improved teacher training, an end to political patronage in the selection of school superintendents, school consolidation, and better facilities and instructional materials for students, among their many other campaigns (e.g., McBride, 1994; Thomas, 1992). Along the way they established foundations, organizations, and periodicals, through which their agendas were formed and operationalized. Though at times resistant to their intrusion into school politics, for the most part state and rural county educational administrators applauded clubwomen's efforts, which not only improved the material conditions of the schools but also established a base of public support not previously apparent (Evans, 1898; Thomas,

1992, p. 59). At its 1905 national convention in Portland, Maine, the GFWC committed to rural education, stating:

> Whereas, education in the U.S. is not a national, but a state affair and there is such diversity in the educational methods of various states that the education of a child depends altogether too much upon where he lives, it shall be our aim to bring about such an equalization of educational advantages that any child in any nook and corner of the nation may receive as good an education that any child in the most favorable locality now receives. (Wood, 1912, p. 205; see also Wood, 1915)

The transition from urban school reform to rural school reform was not an easy one. Despite democratic intentions, too often the agendas of urban clubwomen were pushed onto rural communities without adequate preparation, integrated participation of local community people, and, most important, without serious self-criticism about the repercussions of these activities. Their fears and their will to do good works propelled women into rural reform. The primary fear was that the poor state of rural schools would continue to drive a flood of ill-prepared youth into the city streets in search of jobs. This would weaken both the urban and farm economies. Good schools, it was hoped, would stem this tide and shore up the American tradition of family farms and the agricultural economy.

Women's clubs were not alone in such fears. But an argument can be made that too often rural female reformers simply bought the agendas of state and federal bureaucrats as whole cloth. For instance, in discussing their efforts to eradicate the one-room schoolhouses, in which 60% of all rural children were enrolled, the chair of the GFWC's educational division, Mrs. Ellor C. Ripley (1915), explained: "We are told that these facilities . . . are possible only under exceptional conditions" (p. 89). By whom she was told we can only presume, probably not local community people, not students, and maybe not even teachers. Although all three of these constituencies might have agreed with the sentiment, it is far more likely that the information came from someone outside the rural areas, someone more authoritative in the club movement, a professor at a prestigious university, or an authority from the NEA. Many reforms, whether intended or not, often took control out of the hands of local people and put it into those of a bureaucracy. Too many times this fundamental redistribution of power and authority seemed to go largely unexplored by the women's clubs, even though sustained efforts at cooperation were always listed at the top of their agenda (Forderhouse, 1987; Reese, 1978).

That the more than 200,000 rural school districts had their problems cannot be denied. Illiteracy was twice as great in rural areas as in urban.

In 1911, over two thirds of all pupils were enrolled in rural schools. The per pupil expenditure in these schools was $24.19, compared with $41.85 in the cities ("Rural vs. City," 1911; "Teachers' Cottages," 1916; Tyack & Hansot, 1982). The average school term in 1906, though on the increase in all areas of the country, remained shorter in regions that were primarily rural. The U.S. average stood at 150.6 days per year, but the South Central states averaged 108.2 days, whereas the North Atlantic area with its surfeit of urban districts topped the list at 174.8 days. More important was the number of days that students actually attended school. The United States averaged 106.6 days, the North Atlantic region 133.6 days, but the rural South Central states only 68 days (*Report of the Commissioner*, 1907).

The ambition of each rural community to have its own schools resulted in a proliferation of schools with conditions that depended largely on local prosperity and concern. Though plentiful, school buildings in the rural areas of the United States, especially in the South Atlantic and South Central regions, were valued at only a fraction of those in the more urbanized regions of the North Atlantic and North Central states. According to the *Report of the Commissioner of Education* (1907) for the school year 1906, the estimated value of the average schoolhouse in the North Atlantic stood at $7,602.74, whereas such a building in the South Central region averaged $751. Clubwomen hoped to end such disparities by improving rural school facilities, stabilizing the teaching force, and encouraging greater community support for the schools. The teacherage proved a favorite item on the rural agenda of clubwomen in the period between 1910 and 1930 because it developed and improved relationships between female teachers and the community and embodied familiar associations with their urban institution-building work.

Circumscribed by the lack of franchise, clubwomen utilized what was called "indirect influence" with public policy/decision makers, and others they hoped to win over in their rural school reform efforts. Thus the arguments and strategies they used appealed to the broadest base of support possible. In talking to educational policymakers, clubwomen usually focused on the teacherage's potential to help professionalize a poorly trained and peripatetic teaching force, or on its assistance in consolidating public schools. With farm women they discussed the merits of the teacherage as a community center, a demonstration school for domestic training, or a mechanism to liberate them from the drudgery of caring for teacher-boarders. Businessmen were diverted with arguments of scientific efficiency, expert wisdom, model projects, and cost savings. Yet just as interesting is what was not being said: that many clubwomen were current and past members of the teaching force who saw the teacherage as a means of elevating the living conditions of the "female professional" (Bullock, 1916). One element of the historical importance of the teacherage lies in its ability to provide insight into the lives of early 20th century teachers and the difficulties that they faced in bringing education to the rural and frontier areas of the United States. Michael Apple (1993) states that society often blames teachers for the failures of public policy that they have been excluded from making in the first place. Yet as teachers and former teachers saturated the ranks of women's clubs, they were uniquely positioned to influence social reform from both within and without educational institutions.

RURAL TEACHER HOUSING PROBLEMS

Several factors contributed to the teacher housing shortage and, in turn, made the teacherage a viable concept. First was teachers' frustration with the accommodations afforded them through the traditional "boarding-around" system. In 1900, one out of four female teachers boarded in a home owned by someone other than parents or relatives. Only three female occupations claimed higher boarding rates than teaching: domestic service, waitressing, and nursing. This clearly indicated the extent to which it was necessary for women to leave home in order to obtain a teaching position. The percentage of teachers boarding varied by race, nativity, and marital class from 56.2% among single, foreign-born White women to 13.3% among married, native-born White women (*Statistics of Women at Work*, 1907, p. 121). Though conditions varied widely, many teachers endured hardships that they felt endangered their health and imposed obstacles to the preparation of their lessons. Second, teachers increasingly expressed a desire for greater autonomy and a refuge from the prying eyes and stern criticism of townsfolk. Farm women also idealized privacy and sought a greater amount of free time. But it was only as economics improved in agriculture that farm women and teachers were able to gain a little control over their living conditions.

History of Rural Teacher Housing

In the 19th century, lodging with community families—"boarding 'round" in common parlance—proved the ubiquitous form of housing for rural teachers who didn't live with their own families. It allowed the school district to exercise its responsibility for the moral guidance and protection of the usually young, single, and female teacher (a type of in loco parentis), and she in turn played a role in transmitting appropriate social and cultural values to her pupils (Manning, 1990).

Boarding around was seen as mutually beneficial to both the teacher, who received shelter and protection, and the boarding family, who received financial compensation from the school board or directly from the teacher. Because lodging conditions varied greatly depending on the prosperity and generosity of the families, teachers often spent much their careers moving from community to community in search of better housing and school facilities. Even those who remained in the same community often shifted from one home to the next so that no one family would have greater responsibility or authority over the teacher. These stays could be as difficult as they were short.

Dr. Anna Howard Shaw, later to become president of the National American Woman Suffrage Association, recalled her predicament as a 15-year-old teacher on the Michigan frontier: "In 'boarding round' I often found myself in one-room cabins, with bunks at the end and the sole partition a sheet or a blanket behind which I slept with one or two of the children. It was custom for the man of the house to delicately retire to the barn while we women got to bed and disappear again in the morning when we dressed." On another occasion she paid her host the board in advance, only to find the house "nailed up and deserted" when she arrived, leaving her to walk 8 miles a day from her own family's home (Lerner, 1977, pp. 232–233). Although privacy proved a precious commodity, so did heat, light, and water, as illustrated by the woman who wrote the following in a letter to her former teacher, Catharine Beecher:

> I board where there are eight children and the parents, and only two rooms in the house. I must do as the family do [sic] about washing, as there is but one basin, and no place to go to wash but out the door. I have not enjoyed the luxury of either lamp or candle, their only light being a cup of grease with a rag for a wick. . . . Occupy a room with three of the children, and a niece, who boards there. The other room serves as a kitchen, parlor, and bedroom for the rest of the family. (Woody, 1929/1980, pp. 163–167)

The Beecher Plan

Though Beecher's primary ambition as an educator was to recruit women from the East to act as "missionary" teachers in the West and South, she probably cringed at the conditions faced by her students (Hoffert, 1985; Hoffman, 1981). Housing remained a fundamental concern throughout her life. In 1841, she published one of the first books on housing in the

United States directed to a female readership, *The Treatise on Domestic Economy* (1858). It contained her designs for Gothic-style cottages as well as a variety of mechanical work-saving devices. Later, with her sister, Harriet Beecher Stowe, she published a second text, *The American Woman's Home* (1869), which provided designs for the model American home as well as for settlement houses, tenement houses, churches, schools, and an independent residence for frontier schoolteachers.

However, it was not until the 20th century and under the direction of Josephine Corliss Preston that the Beecher sisters' idea for a teacher residence gained popular approval. Though Preston offers no credit to—or even awareness of—the Beechers' earlier work, the parallel is intriguing, for it posits an enduring concern for the shelter of women teachers and the continuing problems of rural living conditions (Preston, 1916a, 1916b).

Another teacher illustrated how little had changed in the intervening half century between the Beechers' and Preston's advocacy of the teacher-age. She described a situation in the late 1910s, in which she slept in a haymow in a barn for 2 months along with her landlady and her four children. In an improved boarding place, she had been given a bed so small that her 5′9″ frame dangled through the metal bars of the footboard (Schuler, 1922). Another teacher of 26 years' experience, on reading about the General Federation of Women's Club's (GFWC) support for the teach-erage, wrote its president: "My eyes filled and my heart ached, because at last someone had realized and given voice to the needs of rural school teachers." She went on to describe her difficulties in finding appropriate housing:

> Last autumn I was appointed principal of a four-room school. I applied to several patrons for board and finally got permission to stay a week on trial. The room had a bed, a washstand and a dresser, a worn-out couch and two broken rocking chairs ... no stove or grate or means of heating; bare floor, bare walls, no closet. (Pennybacker, 1915, p. 25)

The landlady in her next position, she claimed, was "addicted to drugs" and as a consequence provided an unsanitary home with far less nutritious meals than the teacher had expected. She attributed a long illness to these conditions and prophesied that the acquisition of a teacherage would allow her to become "a real living individual ... for ... when you live in the home of others you must conform to their customs, their requirements" (p. 25).

In advocating the teacherage, J. S. Pardee (1916) claimed that such situations were not all that unusual: "Literally the teacherage may save the teacher's life. In more than one case, girls who went out in the fall to their schools in sound health, have been taken with tubercular trouble" (p. 24). Moreover, mental health was also an issue, as teacher Beatrice Stephens Nathan (1956), affirmed: The "private lives of the single women [teachers] were subject to unofficial but rigid censorship by the local citizenry" (p. 100).

The Privacy Issue

This issue of privacy concerned landladies as well. Community women who supported the teacherage concept seemed compelled to justify their reluctance to board teachers in their home. The general consensus was that the strain of caring for another household member, in addition to the myriad of farm, household, and childrearing duties, required too much work for too little economic return (Pennybacker, 1915, p. 25). One woman complained that teachers "expected first class hotel service in the busy farm home" (Preston, 1916c, p. 110). A farm woman worked hard during the spring, summer, and fall and looked forward to the winter for rest and recreation. The presence of the teacher-boarder denied her that opportunity. Others expressed the middle-class trend toward more familial privacy. One farmer said: "I do not want a teacher sitting around my fireside every evening. I want to be alone with my family once in a while" (p. 110).

Those who could afford large, comfortable homes with contemporary amenities, homes most attractive to teachers, were no longer interested in taking in boarders ("Cottages for Country School Teachers," 1916). They didn't need the money or the problems involved (Cordier, 1992, p. 86; Link, 1986). Though by 1900, over 44% of all rural schoolteachers also came from farm families, class differences between boarding families and teachers increased as the prosperity of families became inversely related to available boarding places (Cordier, 1992; see also Coffman, 1911; Lewis, 1937). With only the more impoverished families willing to take boarders, the disparity between the teacher's family home and her boarding quarters became all the more apparent. So when teachers could find housing, it was usually with the poorer families who needed the money but who could rarely offer the type of accommodations most attractive to teachers. This brought greater embarrassment and pressure to bear on middle-class rural women to defend their unwillingness to board teachers.

Thus mutual dissatisfaction with the boarding-around scheme allied teachers and middle-class farm women in the teacherage strategy. The formation of this alliance can be seen with the first reports of widespread complaints in 1907 from teachers about the near impossibility of finding boarding places in the rural areas of the country, and reached an apex only 15 years later (Muerman, 1922, p. 1; "Rural Teacher Notes," 1907).

The Teachers' Discontent

Teachers' discontent with their boarding places confirmed the notion that housing, in addition to salary, validated their importance to the community. Proponents claimed the teacherage would provide teachers with "dignity and independence" where "respectability of a definite status" could be achieved and professional work carried out (Lowth, 1926; Rapeer, 1920). Dignity and independence were hard to come by on the meager salaries paid to women teachers. In 1905, U.S. women teachers averaged a monthly salary of $43.80, with women in the West earning the most ($57.09) and Southern Atlantic women the least ($33.54). Women spent from a third to half of their monthly salaries on housing and, as one historian noted (Rankin, 1990, pp. 162, 166), merely redistributed tax money back to the community, at rates sometimes bordering on extortion considering what teachers acquired for their expenditure (see also Coney, 1920; Wilson, 1990). Although teacher shortages provided leverage in their bargaining position for higher salaries, housing afforded another currency with which they could improve their professional and community status.

Independent housing also satisfied the teacher's desire for greater autonomy in her private life. Demographics had changed significantly since the mid-1800s, when a teacher's career began around age 15, required little more education than the grade levels she taught, and often ended a few years later upon her marriage. By 1910, the average beginner was at least 19 years of age, with a high school degree and an awareness of the women's rights movement (see Chapter 4). Although rural teachers still lagged behind their urban counterparts in age, education, and economic rewards, the trend represented at least an incremental advancement toward professionalism (Coffman, 1911, pp. 25, 28, 30, 80). Furthermore, teaching offered one of the few employment opportunities to rural females beyond marriage and motherhood.

THE FARM WOMAN'S SUPPORT OF THE TEACHERAGE

Two major factors motivated the farm woman's support for the teacherage: economics and domestic harmony. Agricultural prosperity in the period between 1900 and 1920 relieved many farm women of the need to take in boarders. As the urban population grew exponentially, the demand for agricultural products rose at an unprecedented rate and was elevated further still by the onset of World War I (Fink, 1988; Jensen, 1991; Jones, 1988). Advancements in agricultural technology, encouraged by private industry and government, brought work relief to the farm man but not the farm woman. Whereas farm men invested in heavy machinery to lighten their workloads, rural homes lagged decades behind those in towns and cities in work-saving appliances and indoor plumbing, and rural electrification was not widely available until mid-century. As women began to recognize the inconsistency between their husbands' and their own work lives, their discontent with household labor intensified (Mc-Murry, 1988). The increasing autonomy and vocality of rural women can be gauged by organizations such as the Grange and Farmer's Alliances that, as one historian notes, "provided forums in which women voiced their support of prohibition and equal suffrage and inveighed against the drudgery that they thought ruined the farmwomen's physical and mental health" (Marti, 1991; see also Bush, 1987; Watkins, 1993).

Beyond the concern about drudgery was the growing emphasis on the positive relationship between housing, consumerism, and character formation in the latter 19th century, as possessions became the outward mark of middle-class virtue (Grier, 1988). In the Western territories, a "proper home" identified a woman's connection to the greater comforts and culture of the East (Riley, 1988, p. 88).

As rural economics allowed, the home shifted from mere shelter to a marker of personal prosperity and virtue, and then to a national indicator of the relative health and well-being of agriculture itself. This latter point spoke to the general American fear that agricultural production would not be able to keep pace with the consumption of an increasingly urbanized country (Knowles, 1988). Citizens questioned: "With so many country dwellers moving to the city, especially the children of farmers, could American agriculture continue to feed its people?" (Jeffrey, 1987, p. 287). Thus farm women began to realize that they could justify home improvements as a mechanism for stabilizing the agricultural economy. As historian Julie Roy Jeffrey (1987) notes: "If the home was to be made attractive enough to discourage children from abandoning farm life, if it was to be a place of rest, of comfort, of social refinement, and domestic pleasure, then women would have to make it so" (p. 287).

The preservation of domestic harmony was another critical factor in farm women's support of the teacherage. The ideal of family privacy moved from middle-class urbanized homes into rural areas as part of a broader movement to separate the nuclear family from the work world (Cowan, 1983; Lasch, 1979; Motz & Browne, 1988; Strasser, 1982; Wright, 1985). On the 20th-century farm, this shift was most often signaled by

the adoption of separate quarters for nonfamily farmhands and the eleva-
tion of the kitchen to the woman's sanctum sanctorum (McMurry, 1988,
p. 89). The teacherage became an extension of this same trend by removing
the teacher boarding quarters from the rural home altogether.

THE TEACHERAGE AS SCHOOL REFORM

What motivated clubwomen's efforts on behalf of the teacherage? A number of factors convinced women to expend their energies on its behalf,
including economic, political, and social arguments. One of the most
common justifications offered by rural women centered on their desire
for their children to receive the best education possible. The teacherage,
when placed in the context of progressive reform, can be seen as an effort
to democratize schools by providing rural communities with educational
opportunities equal to those of the cities. The argument continues: If you
want good schools, you must be able to attract good teachers. At their
1914 biennial convention, the GFWC passed a resolution to encourage
teacherages in all the communities in which a woman's club existed ("The
Teacherage," 1914, p. 5; see also Riley, 1988, p. 180; Schneider & Schneider,
1993). GFWC president (1912–1916) and former teacher Anna J. H. Pennybacker implored rural mothers to demand the teacherage as an asset to
their children's education. She explained:

> We believe the teacher's cottage [is] the best way to obtain better teachers;
> better teachers the best way to create community centers; community centers
> the best way to revive rural life with far-reaching economic effects in making
> possible rural organization. ("New Teacherages," 1916, p. 4)

To those who decried the extravagance, Pennybacker suggested that
they think of the teacherage in the same terms as school libraries, art and
manual training, and domestic science. Moreover, mothers in a small
town that could ill afford a library or art museum could still point with
pride to the teacherage as a status symbol (Lesser, 1991, p. 185).

A more critical perspective might see the goal of such reform work
as a type of Machiavellian imposition of middle-class urban values on
rural people through their schools. Certainly this is what some had in
mind when they presented the teacherage as a new scientifically efficient
model home, which might shame rural people into upgrading their own
poor abodes (Carney, 1912, p. 37). Whether such goals provoked class
tensions is unclear, but these concerns did not deter the GFWC from

taking up the teacherage banner as a part of its broader platform for rural school reform.

The GFWC's work dovetailed with that of the larger rural progressive educational agenda of consolidating schools, attracting better teachers, standardizing the curriculum, and upgrading the school's physical plant (Gulliford, 1984; Leloudis, 1983). In her addresses to the NEA, Josephine Corliss Preston focused on the ability of the teacherage to draw the "very best teachers for less salary" and to retain them for longer periods (Thomason, 1915, pp. 554–555). This certainly appealed to those concerned with increasing the efficiency of the rural schools. Aside from attracting better trained teachers and providing them with greater privacy and better living conditions, rural education advocates also stressed the benefits of the teacherage in lengthening the tenure of teachers, terminating what was known as the "suitcase teacher syndrome," and promoting school consolidation (Vincent, 1917).

School consolidation was scientific efficiency's cure-all for the ills of rural schools (Rankin, 1990, pp. 156–157). By unifying several one-room decentralized schoolhouses into centrally administered multigraded schools, reformers sought to gain uniformity, control, and greater professionalism in rural education. A significant force in the rural school consolidation movement was the General Education Board founded in 1902 and financed by the Rockefeller Foundation (Link, 1986, p. 116; see also Jones, 1937). Among the board's goals was to systematize educational philanthropy throughout the nation, with a special emphasis on developing a comprehensive educational policy (Leloudis, 1983, p. 898). Among its various projects the General Education Board helped finance many teacherages. The Julius Rosenwald Foundation, at the behest of Booker T. Washington, also built schools and teacherages for African Americans in some rural areas of the South ("Education," 1915; Fultz, 1995; Keatley 1951; Neverdon-Morton, 1989). The concept of the consolidated school was built on the economies of scale, with the expectation that fewer but larger schools would result in increased enrollment and attendance at a lower price. Moreover, it would standardize and upgrade rural schools, putting them on par with those in more urbanized areas (Link, 1986, pp. 139–141).

Consolidation was seen also as a measure for improving school personnel, as teachers constituted a major factor in the disparity of schooling from region to region (Coffman, 1911, pp. 25, 28). For decades ambitious teachers had used rural schools as stepping-stones to better salaries and conditions in city schools. Others, without the training or initiative, dropped in and out of teaching or shifted from one rural locale to the next.

As U.S. Commissioner of Education Dr. P. P. Claxton ("Cottages for Country School Teachers," 1916, p. 293) noted, the turnover was so great that each year two thirds of all rural schoolteachers had never taught before (for a different view, see Carter & Savoca, 1992). This left communities with an ever-changing cast of newly minted or poorly prepared teachers. Claxton saw the teacherage as a method of stemming this tide of teachers while creating a more stable work force with greater loyalty to their districts. When a few critics voiced the concern that the teacherage would hinder school consolidation by negating the incentive to close small district schools, superintendents began to champion teacherages as part of a new consolidated school package (Rapeer, 1920, pp. 190–207).

The strongest opposition to the teacherage was its cost, and as a result its proponents began to argue its versatility as a community center, domestic science lab, or model home, in order to justify the expenditure. As a model home it was intended to inspire community people to replicate the latest labor-saving devices and safety mechanisms in their own homes (Preston, 1915). The kitchen would become a home economics lab where students could prepare lunches from milk and vegetables donated by local farmers (Preston, 1916b). Others argued that the presence of a teacher would extend the school's usefulness as a community center, because the nearby teacher would provide maintenance and protection of the school property both day and night. Likewise the school grounds could be used as an after-hours playground or a community garden under the watchful eye of the resident teacher. Such extracurricular duties were likely to have met with resistance from teachers.

THE TEACHERAGE IDEAL AND REALITY

By 1922, a U.S. Bureau of Education survey (Muerman, 1922, p. 18) found that out of a total of 2,816 teacherages across the country, fewer than 20% could be considered "modern." Andrew Gulliford (1984, pp. 159–229) notes that early 20th-century rural schoolhouses ran the gamut of vernacular architectural styles, including tents, log cabins, dugouts, and sod houses. Teacher housing followed a similar pattern. Sometimes the same structure served both purposes, as did the dugout in the timber-poor community of Pleasant Hill, Texas. The facility, according to the teacher who lived and taught there, was gloomy, poorly ventilated, and subject to vermin including sand fleas, snakes, frogs, and spiders. The walls and floors were covered in canvas, and children gathered around a table in the center of the room to study in the dim light (Sitton & Rowald, 1987, p. 39).

Discussions of "model" teacher homes seem ludicrous in light of such realities. Yet planners continued efforts to reach a consensus about minimal standards for the teacherage. Often repeated were the following: (1) It should be located on or near school property, on at least an acre of land, which would furnish a kitchen garden, a chicken house, a cow or horse stable, and perhaps an area for agriculture demonstration. (2) It should be warm and substantial in order to economize on fuel. (3) It should be constructed of local materials, again to save money. (4) It should be a model for the neighborhood to stimulate the farmers to build better homes.

Though some districts hired architects to design teacherages, many more simply adapted existing structures or built the cheapest structure possible without attention to developing a community prototype (Kellogg, 1916).

Model Homes

The Radford Architectural Company of Chicago produced three teacherage plans with the assistance of the National Lumber Manufacturers Association. Design 1, a three-room one-story bungalow, with total dimensions of $33' \times 27.5'$, was designed to accommodate two women teachers or a teacher and spouse. An optional basement with a finished cement floor held the furnace and laundry rooms, coal bins, and vegetable and fruit storage areas. The interior contained a combination kitchen and dining room, with a drop-leaf table built into a bay projection with benches on either side. The adjacent cupboard served as a repository for dishes, pots, and pans. The living room, designed of sufficient size to entertain, included a built-in sofa with storage space in its bottom in the bay window. A larger structure, Design 2, housed four single teachers or one teacher's family. The story-and-a-half residence measured $22' \times 28.5'$ and was covered with beveled siding and a shingle roof. The basement replicated that in Design 1, and the kitchen contained similar arrangements for the storage of dishes, pots, and pans. The dining and living rooms opened into one large $12' \times 27'$ room for neighborhood gatherings. Though the Radford designs indicate indoor plumbing and whole-house heating, these are repeatedly delineated as optional. Unfortunately, this allowed communities one more opportunity to economize.

The appeal to economy-minded citizens permeated teacherage advocacy strategies. Most people focused on cost-cutting measures in the building itself. But some encouraged the multiple uses to which the teacherage could be put, such as labs for home economics training, meeting space for local organizations, a social center for student parties, and even a place where local merchants and farmers could bond, encouraging mutual "understanding, confidence, and business" (Kellogg, 1916, p. 21; Preston, 1916b, p. 144).

The State and Teacherage Funding

Between 1915 and 1921, 15 states passed laws allowing districts to raise money to build, own, and control teacher homes. As a result, district funds for the teacherages most often came from tax levies or fund-raisers. Indiana and New Jersey made several failed attempts to pass laws that would allow public support of teacherages. However, California, Oregon, and West Virginia specifically passed legislation denying the use of public school funds for the purpose of building or purchasing homes for teachers (Muerman, 1922).

Public opposition to the teacherage appeared on several fronts. Although boardinghouse owners in Minnesota declared them a "communist invasion," in general, anxieties revolved around the increase in community bonded indebtedness and the continuing expense of the home's maintenance (Vincent, 1917). Thus offers of matching funds to build the homes often proved key in convincing the local citizenry to support the teacherage. The General Education Board extended such an offer to several towns including Alberta, Minnesota, in 1916. Within a few months the building was erected ("City Comforts," 1917).

The three-story structure, considered a model, contained a domestic science lab, a sewing room, a modern laundry, and a model practice dining room in the basement. The first floor accommodated a separate apartment for the superintendent and his or her family. The second-floor apartment included four bedrooms and housed six single women including the domestic science teacher who managed the home, and a school graduate employed as a maid. The third-floor attic provided three more sleeping rooms, which could accommodate additional teachers, a housekeeper, or older students whose parents lived in the outer reaches of the district. The mechanical operations included a hot water furnace, electricity powered by a gasoline generator, and indoor plumbing that received water stored in the school's pressurized water tank. The cost of the house totaled $7,500, $3,500 contributed by the General Education Board, $3,000 from the district, $500 from the state, and $500 in in-kind services contributed by architects and local merchants ("City Comforts," 1917, p. 406).

The return on the local investment came in under 5 years. The first year the superintendent's family paid $240 in rent and the single teachers a total of $555. Living cooperatively, the teachers shared the costs of supplies (food, coal, oil, etc.) at $40.55; the maid's wages, $18.00; electricity, $1.00; laundry, $3.00; and rent, $35.00 per month. This meant that each of the five teachers paid $19.51 a month, a good savings when compared with their former boarding places, which charged an average of $22 to $25 per month. However, few districts invested the money, time, or energy to replicate the Alberta experiment.

TEACHERAGE AS FAILED IDEAL

The failure of the teacherage movement to recreate model programs such as the one carried out in Alberta, Minnesota, can be attributed to a number of factors. These include the unwillingness of districts to support the building or maintenance of teacher housing, the increasing accessibility and affordability of regular housing, and the Depression of the 1930s (Stephens, 1990). Teachers themselves rejected those teacherages that afforded them too little privacy or allowed for too much public scrutiny (Muerman, 1922, p. 6; Schuler, 1922).

Rural parsimony often overwhelmed the more altruistic motivations of the teacherage advocates, resulting in cheaply built structures, with too many teachers sharing too little space, ironically replicating the problems teachers experienced when they boarded around. Although some towns produced the "model cottages" proposed by the movement, many more simply turned deserted schoolhouses or shacks over to teacher housing or constructed the cheapest structures possible. Thelma Esterling described one teacherage near Olney, Texas, in 1929, where she lived with three other teachers in three small rooms with no indoor plumbing and a roof that leaked. She recalled that they had to set a dishpan on the foot of the bed when it rained, and carried water from a pump when it didn't. They shared one double and one single bed among four adult women, and hung their clothes on pegs on the wall. Another Texas teacher, Pauline Underwood, described her four-room teacherage as "unpainted and completely unfurnished . . . no gas, no electricity, no water, no bathroom . . . and the raw wood clapboard had shrunk so that the prairie wind whipped through bringing with it every element, snow, rain, and sand" (Sitton & Rowald, 1987, p. 176).

Additionally, the economic downturn of the 1930s put another nail in the coffin of the teacherage concept. As farmers took a second look at the extra income that boarders could provide, teacherages began to be seen as undesirable competition (Fink, 1988, p. 61). Though the teacherage did not immediately disappear, large-scale organized efforts on its behalf dissipated after the 1920s.

SUMMARY

The moral imperative that rural families provide housing and protection for female teachers weakened in the early 20th century as shifting economic and social factors brought the tradition of "boarding around" into disfavor. The new middle-class farm woman no longer needed or wanted to board teachers. Teachers sought better conditions and greater autonomy than that offered them in the homes of poorer townsfolk. The desire to upgrade and consolidate rural schools in an effort to stabilize the agricultural economy led educational reformers to look for methods to attract and keep good teachers. The teacherage appeared to meet all these needs.

Though the concept received strong support from a powerful coalition of entities—women's clubs, teachers, school consolidation advocates, government agencies, lumber companies, and philanthropic foundations—the alliance could not overcome the public's misgivings about the expenses involved. That more than 3,000 teacherages were erected in only 8 years should be an indicator of some success, but this success was diminished because too many of these structures departed from the ideals expressed by the social architects of the teacherage concept. In part the demise of the teacherage can be attributed to a decentralized national schooling system, which allowed each district to decide whether to support the concept, and to what extent. Thus, although a few prototypical structures were erected, usually in towns that sought additional outside funding from philanthropic foundations, a much greater proportion of teacherages were little more than shacks. Even those built to an ideal standard usually housed too many teachers in far too little room, depriving individuals of the privacy and professional conditions they sought. Had there been a centralized federal authority with specific and coherent regulations and funding appropriations, as was the case in many European countries, it is possible that the outcome of the teacherage movement might have been different (Gray, 1916; Herrick, 1921; Vincent, 1916).

The failure of the women's clubs to establish greater visibility and support for the teacherage was at least in part due to their inability to alter the more urbanized agenda of the women's club movement to suit a rural environment (Wilson, 1979, pp. 95–96). Mrs. Ellor C. Ripley, chair of the GFWC's Education Division, noted the difficulty of women's clubs in achieving a working relationship with rural women, especially around school issues. Speaking of urban organizers who made such attempts, she said:

> They are confronted in many quarters with a firmly established belief that the interests of rural schools and urban schools are entirely different. More

than this, they are too often told that town people should take care of town schools and country people of country schools . . . such a fallacy causes many town clubwomen to hesitate to enter directly their help in the solution of the rural school problems and makes women regard their help as an intrusion. (Ripley, 1915, p. 19)

Thus the strategies clubwomen felt compelled to use to counter rural communities' resistance relied on indirect methods that often involved the imposition of top-down planning. Direct methods, utilized in those villages more amendable to the clubwomen's ministrations, started with a study of the problems and the needs of individual schools. They then tried to organize local women into women's clubs and school-improvement societies to work on the problems discovered. However, Ripley admitted that too many times the studies were done haphazardly or by outsiders, who had little knowledge or compassion for the people within the community. Thus their failure to include local women from the very beginning set a pattern of urban and middle-class imposition to which resistance seemed the only common-sense response.

Chapter 4

THE SCHOOLMARM AND THE VOTE

Teachers were a pivotal source of strength in the suffrage movement from its inception. They worked in coalition with women's groups to promote the female vote first on school matters, then on municipal referendums, and finally on local, state, and federal issues. Some of the earliest advocates of the woman's vote, Susan B. Anthony, Lucretia Mott, and Carrie Chapman Catt, asserted that the inequitable treatment they received as teachers had been a factor in their decision to become women's rights activists (Stanton, 1898, pp. 161–162). These early suffragists eagerly anticipated the potent force of educators once converted to the cause ("Chicago Teachers Join Labor Union," 1902). Teachers represented the largest group of professional women in the country and held one of the most visible and respected positions for women in the community. Furthermore, as members of local, state, and national educational associations, they had contact with even greater numbers who could be encouraged to work on behalf of the vote.

As a result, teachers became the dominant occupational group within the suffrage movement. An example of this was seen at a national suffrage convention held in Buffalo, New York, in 1908 when a presiding officer asked all women present who had ever been teachers to stand, and one third of the audience arose ("Do Teachers Need the Ballot?" 1908). A few years later, a poll discovered that of all women, teachers (94.09%) were most likely to favor women's suffrage (Blackwell, 1905). Historian Genevieve McBride (1994) claims the most significant coalition in Wisconsin's suffrage campaign was that between clubwomen and that state's teachers' association. The two groups, she notes, shared not only a commitment to education but also a mutual membership and leadership. In fact, the first two Wisconsin Teachers Association presidents were Wisconsin Federation of Women's Clubs officers. Similar relationships occurred in other cities and states. Sharon Hartman Strom (1975) notes that teachers' work "gave them new skills and self-confidence" (p. 300) which in turn enhanced suffrage.

As women's suffrage gained greater public acceptance, some teachers saw the vote as a means to improving working conditions for themselves

(McNaught, 1917). U.S. education was paternalistic at best and misogynis-tic at worst. Female teachers received one half to one third the wages of their male peers. Few women held hope for any upward mobility within the profession. In 1905, men held only 8.6% of the nation's 85,042 public school teaching positions but claimed 91.9% of all high school principal-ships in cities with populations greater than 1 million, and 100% in cities with populations between 100,000 and 200,000. Increasingly, bureaucrati-zation removed what little power women teachers had even within their classrooms ("Sex of Teachers," 1905). An abundance of aspiring female teachers stood ready to fill any vacancies left by those teachers daring to question patriarchal authority.

In some towns, teachers became political pawns of corrupt school boards or city officials who lined their pockets with gratuities from teach-ers hoping to obtain or retain positions (Blackwell, 1909; Nolan, 1992; Shelton, 1976). At times cities compensated for city budget deficits by failing to keep raises promised to teachers ("Teachers and Their Pay," 1906; "Women Teachers Envy Fish," 1915). City reformers abhorred such practices and suffragists expressed the belief that women voters would rid the cities of such graft, corruption, and blatant injustice (Allen, 1911, pp. 243–275). Additionally, they argued that these new "child-centered" voters would be a major resource in school improvement.

SCHOOL SUFFRAGE

Women often used these arguments in order to gain school suffrage. Historian Anne Firor Scott (1993) refers to school suffrage as "the most visible practical achievement of the [women's] movement in the twenty-five years after the Civil War" (p. 138). This restricted right permitted women to vote in matters regarding the public education of their children. Kentucky became the first state, in 1838, to grant school suffrage to women, though limited it to widows with school-age children. Kansas extended it to all women in 1861, as did Michigan and Minnesota in 1875, Colorado in 1876, New Hampshire and Oregon in 1878, Massachusetts by 1879, New York and Vermont in 1880, Nebraska in 1883, and North Dakota, South Dakota, Montana, Arizona, and New Jersey in 1887. Illinois granted school suffrage in 1891, Connecticut in 1893, Delaware to tax-paying women in 1898, Wisconsin in 1900. When Oklahoma was admitted as a state in 1907, it continued the school-suffrage law in existence since it had become a territory (Hecker, 1914, p. 167). Women in many cities and states fought simultaneously for school and full suffrage, utilizing the former as a fall-back position (Stanton, Anthony, Gage, & Harper, 1922).

LOCAL SUFFRAGE

Other variations on women's suffrage existed. For instance, in 1887 Kansas gave women what was known as municipal suffrage, meaning they could vote on certain issues related to town management including school matters. Iowa allowed women "bond" suffrage in 1894, as did Kansas in 1903. This meant that tax-paying women could participate in questions related to the bonded-indebtedness of their towns, which included some school issues. In 1898, Minnesota women won the right to vote for library trustees. Two states, New York (1901) and Michigan (1908), gave tax-paying women the vote on all questions of local taxation. In 1912 the Louisiana legislature agreed to allow women to vote for and serve on school boards ("Louisiana Legislature," 1912).

In some cities and states, school and municipal suffrage acted as a precursor to full suffrage, as a mechanism by which women could gain a foothold in the voting process. Suffragists tried to use the example of school suffrage to convince the general public of the absurdity of keeping women from full suffrage. But too often Byzantine voting restrictions caused indignation or confusion over eligibility. For example, Massachusetts passed the School Suffrage Act in 1879 and amended it in 1881, making women eligible to vote for members of the school committees of the towns in which they resided.

The statute provided two methods of qualifying: If a woman owned property she could register *if* she could prove she could read and write, and women with no taxable property could register if they could demonstrate that they had paid a 50-cent poll tax. Some women resented that, unlike men, they were required to go to the city or town hall to be assessed a poll tax, and provide a statement of all their assets under oath. Sometimes unsympathetic registrars would drop a woman's name from the voting lists. As a result, so few women voted in school elections that anti-suffragists gleefully pointed out women were simply not interested in the vote. A case in point occurred in one Massachusetts district where not one woman voted, including resident Lucy Stone, founder of the Massachusetts School Suffrage Association (organized in 1880). Stone explained that her town registrar required her to register under the name Mrs. Blackwell, a name that she never used and refused to use even to vote (Merk, 1956; "Mrs. Chapman's Warning," 1897).

The struggle to gain and maintain school suffrage was just as difficult as that to place one's vote. This is illustrated aptly by the case of Ohio. After years of compromise, suffragists introduced a bill that would allow women to vote for and seek election as members of school boards, but not for the office of state commissioner of education or on any question related to bonds or appropriations (Lerner, 1977, pp. 357–361). Even with these restrictions, legislators were unenthusiastic about the bill and twice rejected it, in 1892 and 1893. The Ohio Women's Suffrage Association worked tirelessly to get similar bills reintroduced four more times before a school suffrage statute became law in April 1894. Yet when women tried to register that December for the April election, the law was challenged as unconstitutional. Over the next 2 years, the issue played out in the courts, where women's right to school franchise was upheld first in a lower court and then again on appeal by the Ohio Supreme Court. In 1897, more than 30,000 women voted in their first election. But during the following year, a bill to repeal the law was reintroduced into the legislature. Suffrage clubs around the state met the challenge, gathering some 40,000 names on a petition in less than one month's time. The house overwhelmingly defeated the repeal, and women again went to the polls in 1900, this time voting in even larger numbers than before (Lerner, 1977, pp. 357–359). Other states including South Dakota fought off similar attempts to eliminate school suffrage (Reed, 1958).

Despite the difficulties involved, school suffrage elevated women's attention to the need and the possibility of getting women on school boards. Suffragists often stressed the idea that women would prove a cleansing force on city school boards. In rhetoric typical of the period, one Ohio woman claimed:

> The Boards of Education, most unfortunately, have for too long been the tool of politics, and men have been elected who neither were the fathers of families nor had any particular interest in the education of children. This is true in Columbus today. There are said to be two men who had been nominated, neither of whom have [sic] a knowledge of the school questions and whom [sic] have secured the nomination purely in the interest of party politics. It is for these reasons that the women of the state ought to awaken to the limited privileges, which have been granted to them and exercise their rights in the selection of members of Boards of Education. ("Women and the School-boards," 1913, p. 4)

WOMEN AND THE SCHOOL BOARDS

The election of women to school boards was sometimes a separate issue from school suffrage. As early as 1872, the New Hampshire legislature approved the election of women to the prudential committees of school districts, or to school committees of cities and towns of the state. In 1873, Connecticut and Rhode Island also advocated women as *school visitors* (school board members). Boston, in 1872, elected four women to the school committee; and women were also chosen in several other cities. Massachusetts passed an act in 1874 declaring women eligible for membership on school committees. In Philadelphia in 1882, Mary E. Mumford, who was serving as chairman of the Education Committee of the Century Club, a suffragist organization, was asked by the "Committee of One Hundred" to stand as a candidate for the Sectional School Board in the 29th ward. She was elected, served 6 years, and in 1889 was appointed on the Central Board of Education (Woody, 1929/1980, pp. 515–516).

Although school suffrage introduced some women to the vote and some towns to the concept of women as political beings, its overall effect was diminished by legislative efforts to repeal it and by local qualifying mandates, which confused or inhibited would-be female voters. More important, school suffrage demonstrated the continuing historical connection between women's political advancement and public education institutions. Women used the moral edge of motherhood to craft a larger presence in the public world. As mothers, they argued, they had the right and obligation to ensure a proper education for their children.

Further, as voters and school board members they could utilize their particular maternal insights to protect children and communities from the evils of corrupt politicians, tax-evading corporations, and insincere or manipulative school board members. Continuing this domestic feminist rationale, women argued that teachers, as substitute mothers, were peculiarly positioned by virtue of their gender and occupation to demand suffrage as a necessary part of their continuing education. What teacher could teach what she did not really know? Teachers could also argue that they were best informed about the schools and as voters would protect and increase the value of that institution in the community.

TEACHER ORGANIZATIONS AND SUFFRAGE

Teachers worked for suffrage individually and through their representative organizations. For instance, the first president of the Pittsburgh Teachers' Association also served, for 3 years, as secretary of the Pennsylvania Woman Suffrage Association ("Pennsylvania Women," 1910). Teacher-organizer Minnie J. Reynolds organized the state chapters of the Women's Political Union in New Jersey and Washington, and served as editor of the *Woman Voter* (New York City). Emily Pierson, a high school teacher in Bristol, Connecticut, was state organizer for the Connecticut Woman Suffrage Association from 1909 to 1915, and worked on state referendums in Massachusetts in 1910, New Jersey in 1912, and Ohio in 1913, and with the National Women's Party in Washington, D.C., from 1915 to 1919. Kate Hunter, a teacher, was president of the Palestine (Texas) Suffrage League in the same period. In Maryland, Sarah Richmond, a pioneer suffragist, was elected president of that State Teachers' Association in 1915 (Stanton et al., 1922).

The Chicago Federation of Teachers (CTF) pushed for women's suffrage as a facet in their larger campaign to untangle corrupt tax policies that deprived that city's schools of adequate income. The CTF began in 1897 with a group of female elementary teachers, the same year that Carter Henry Harrison became mayor of Chicago. During his campaign, Harrison pledged his backing for a $50-a-year raise for teachers. Many teachers assisted his campaign on the basis of that promise. Yet as one of his first acts, Harrison appointed William Rainey Harper, president of the University of Chicago, to the Chicago Board of Education. Harper wasted no time in announcing that the teachers could forget their raises. When the CTF protested that the money was essential to feeding their families, Harper blithely responded that the teachers were already paid more than his wife's maid. He further inflamed them by suggesting a compromise be reached by granting raises to male teachers only. Margaret Haley, the leader of the CTF, later reflected on the incident, stating, "I think the cause of women's suffrage advanced further on that day than it had gone in fifty years in Illinois. Sometimes the enemies of a cause do more good for it than do its friends. Voting women today owe more than they know to William Rainey Harper" (Haley, 1982, pp. 35–36; "State Correspondence," 1906, p. 20).

Indeed, the episode was a major factor in the 2,500-member federation's unanimous vote to advocate suffrage in 1902. Susan B. Anthony wrote Haley, claiming that the CTF's vote would result in better working conditions for women teachers ("Letter from Miss Susan B. Anthony," 1903; "National American," 1903). Haley became even more closely affiliated with the cause when she served as state auditor for the Illinois State Suffrage Party in 1906, and later as she traveled around the United States speaking on behalf of the vote for women.

In New York City the issue of suffrage became a dividing point in the New York Class Teachers Association (see Chapter 2). In 1915, more than 2,700 women teachers in the Boston Teachers' Club officially endorsed suffrage. The Boston Teachers' Newsletter editorialized on the event, stating, "If teachers want justice on all occasions, if they want better salaries, tenure of office, a safe pension system, proper working conditions, they must secure them by the only certain method to modern civilization—the ballot" ("Boston Teachers Out in Favor," 1915, p. 134).

The *Woman's Journal* Chronicles Teachers' Progress

The *Woman's Journal*, a national suffrage weekly newspaper, chronicled the alliances between teachers and the women's movement. Because no national periodical represented the interests of women teachers, the *Journal* essentially served as a conduit between feminist teachers in cities and towns across the country. Large city presses, often unsympathetic or even hostile to the improvements sought by women, largely overlooked their activities. Lucy Stone, editor of the *Woman's Journal*, had been a teacher for a short time, and her experience confirmed for her the necessity of upgrading the status of school women (Filler, 1974). Though Stone died in 1893, the editorial policy of support for women teachers continued and even escalated as her daughter, Alice Stone Blackwell, became coeditor with her father Henry Blackwell. The *Journal* published special issues for teachers during the Boston meetings of the National Federation of Teachers in 1903 and the National Educational Association in 1910. In 1902, the *Woman's Journal* called for the extension of suffrage to all female teachers, reasoning that they could not satisfactorily teach government and good citizenship if they were not themselves full citizens ("Disenfranchised Teachers," 1902; Porritt, 1911). Such arguments proved powerful in aligning teachers to the cause.

The *Woman's Journal* followed the increasing commitment of women educators to the suffrage movement. The titles told the story: "Why Wisconsin Should Enfranchise Teachers" (1911), "Kansas State Teachers Association Unanimous for Woman's Ballot" (1911), "Teachers Favor Equal Suffrage, Minnesota Educational Association Goes on Record" (1912), "Atlanta Teachers Want Better Pay, Georgia Men Tell Them They Need the Ballot" (1911), "Mississippi Teachers Want Suffrage" (1918), "Women Teachers Can Participate, Birmingham Board of Education Will Not Prohibit Them From Suffrage Work" (1912), "Teachers Ask for Votes in Missouri" (1913), "Rally Teachers to Suffrage in Town" (1917), and "New Jersey Teachers Association Endorses Full Suffrage for Women" (1915).

Suffrage and the School Superintendent

The earliest states to win universal suffrage were also those in which women first moved into county and state school superintendencies. Illinois, the first state east of the Mississippi to grant women the right to vote, also became the first to appoint a woman school superintendent of a large city school district in 1909. Chicago's Ella Flagg Young, an ardent feminist, quickly pointed out the challenges faced by Illinois women teachers previous to the vote:

The teachers of Chicago found that in order to get anything done they had to have the voting power behind them. . . . Before they federated the teachers went in Committees before the Board of Education and asked to have their salaries increased . . . nothing happened. . . . Again, they met the same result. Then they realized they must have the power of the vote behind them. ("Teachers Found Vote Essential," 1916, pp. 225–226; see also Scott, 1993; J. K. Smith, 1979)

While eastern cities were still working on getting women elected to school boards, western states elected them as county and state superintendents of education and to other powerful positions ("Women on Philadelphia," 1906). Cleveland, Ohio, teacher Helen Ring Robinson moved to Colorado where she became a state senator and established a minimum wage guarantee for women teachers ("Teachers' Bill Won," 1913). By 1917, women held at least one half of all the county school superintendencies in nine western states. The majority of these were in woman suffrage states. Furthermore, the same five states to adopt pay equity legislation had also approved woman suffrage. Those with a woman heading their state department of education—Colorado, Idaho, Washington, Wyoming, and Montana—were also suffrage states. In comparison, only one male suffrage state, North Dakota, elected a woman (1891–1895) to serve in this capacity (Boyd, 1917). By 1925, only 5 years after women won the vote, the increase nationwide in women holding leadership positions was phenomenal: 18 state or deputy superintendents of education, 856 county superintendents, and 40 city superintendents of schools (Sullivan, 1925).

Many women voters relished the idea of ushering women into office, and the position of school superintendent seemed most natural for them to fill. And for some this office proved to be only a stepping-stone to more powerful legislative positions. Mary Godat Bellamy of Laramie, Wyoming, a teacher and founding member of that state's Federation of Women's Clubs, was elected county superintendent in 1902, and in 1910 became the first woman elected to the Wyoming legislature ("Mary G. Bellamy," 1965). Nettie Truax followed the same path only a year later (Stanton et al., vol. 6).

The prevailing domestic feminist rhetoric argued that women, especially mothers, had greater insight into matters relating to children's education. Therefore women had a right and obligation to vote for and serve in such capacities ("The Mother and the Schools," 1906). This argument was simply an extension of the one used to justify school suffrage years before.

Other Roads to Suffrage

Teacher institutes served as another vehicle through which teachers and suffrage intersected. Institutes met on a semi-regular basis to provide in-service training for teachers. Many meetings included noted speakers on current issues related to education. At one such institute held in Allen County, Ohio, Dr. Charles B. Taylor presented a talk on suffrage. Later that same group of teachers voted to become an auxiliary unit to the Ohio State Suffrage Association. The *Lexington Herald* found similar results after suffrage lectures were presented at teacher institutes in Kentucky. It noted: "At almost every institute where an address is given on suffrage a County League for Women's Suffrage is formed and a number of members, both teachers and citizens, men and women, are enrolled" ("Teacher Institute," 1913, p. 5). In Nebraska, teacher institutes in Douglas, Clay, and Adams counties all unanimously endorsed women's suffrage ("Teachers Form," 1913).

Some conservative teacher organizations were persuaded to the cause when the NEA passed a resolution supporting women's suffrage. Though women represented over 90% of the membership, the NEA had long held a reputation for being dominated and directed solely by male school super-intendents and university professors and presidents. One effort to end this male monopoly was the election of Ella Flagg Young as the associa-tion's first female president in 1910 ("Suffragists Prominent," 1910). Dur-ing her term, the NEA officially endorsed women's suffrage, a startling departure from business as usual ("National Education," 1912). After the NEA went on record in support of suffrage in 1912, state and local teacher organizations followed suit ("Nevada Teachers to Help Cause," 1913; "Dakota Teachers Go on Record," 1913; "Teachers Want," 1911; "Why Wisconsin," 1911).

Despite its importance to female members, the NEA's decision to support suffrage eluded some, particularly those living in the South. During a 1914 meeting, a resolution recapitulating the association's posi-tion "in favor of the political equality of the sexes," Florida State Superin-tendent W. N. Sheats jumped to his feet demanding clarification of the "vague phrase political equality of the sexes." S. H. Thompson, a state superintendent from Tennessee, asserted that anyone who didn't under-stand it "is in the kindergarten of the school of American politics." Sheats protested, claiming, in the South, "two-thirds of the good women, moth-ers, and intelligent women do not want to vote." Thompson objected to this characterization of southern women, claiming that Sheats was talking about the "Old South" not the "New South." More discussion ensued as to whether the resolution had any binding effect on states, and just why suffrage was an educational issue. An amused Margaret Haley finally brought the matter to a close by reminding everyone that the resolution was already a fait accompli ("Whereas," 1914).

In 1914, the NEA's African American equivalent, the NATNS, founded in 1904 and composed largely of southern teachers, officially endorsed women's suffrage (Salem, 1990, p. 85). In 1910, 6,991 male and 22,441 female African Americans constituted 1.71% and 3.76%, respectively, of the U.S. teaching force. The largest numbers of African American teachers resided in the southern states of Georgia (2,837), Mississippi (1,872), Virginia (1,861), Texas (1,846), North Carolina (1,735), South Carolina (1,560), Tennessee (1,369), and Kentucky (1,006) (*Negro Population*, 1968). The NATCS, renamed the American Teachers Association in 1939 in an effort to attract Black educators from beyond the South, represented teachers who by virtue of their race were closed out of the NEA. Women in this organization struggled against the dual forces of racism and sexism to attain parity with their White counterparts while simultaneously educating African American children to have pride in their race and its achievements (Lewis & Wolcott, 1993). Thus an endorsement of suffrage signified not only a belief in women's rights but also an act against the racism that permeated every region and aspect of American society including the schools and the suffrage movement.

TEACHERS, SCHOOLS, AND ANTI-SUFFRAGISTS

Differences of opinion on suffrage tended to assert themselves forcefully in all areas of the country, but none so much as in the South (Green, 1994; "Teachers on School Suffrage," 1901; Thomas, 1992). There sexism, classism, and racism combined to concoct a powerful brew of anti-suffrage sentiment. The suffrage movement emerged from within the abolition movement, setting the stage for the eventual partition of opinion on women's franchise.

Racism and the Southern Bloc

Southern legislators most often condemned the vote for women on the grounds that a solid bloc of African American voters could affect the precarious balance that maintained segregation and White political dominance. The state's rights strategy supported by most suffrage groups meant that each state could place whatever limitations it wished on women's suffrage as long as it passed into law. African American women feared that many states, especially those in the South, would reject them as potential voters or require them to participate in qualifying tests that would effectively eliminate them. Because the southern states were crucial in ratification of the 19th Amendment, some suffragists endorsed the concept of "expediency" to gain the vote, meaning that they were willing to do almost anything—including sacrificing African American women's political rights—in order to gain the vote (Terborg-Penn, 1978).

Given this situation, African American women generally invested in one of two strategies in their pursuit of the vote: identifying with the mainstream, White women's suffrage associations or creating their own separate organizations and agendas (Gordon, 1997; "Our Women's Number," 1904; Terborg-Penn, 1993). The Alpha Suffrage Club provided an example of the latter strategy. Founded in 1913, the Chicago group counted among its members many women teachers or former educators. Organized as a counterforce to the racism present in many of the states' suffrage organizations led by Anglo-American women, the Alpha Suffrage Club educated members and increased community awareness about the peculiar dilemmas faced by African American women in demanding the vote (Hendricks, 1993a). Ida Wells-Barnett, first president and one of the founders of the ASC, began her career as a teacher at age 16 in Holly Springs, Mississippi, in 1878 (Duster, 1970; Hendricks, 1993b). Later, while a teacher in the Memphis, Tennessee, schools, she took over the editorship of the city's weekly newspaper, the *Evening Star*, one of the few sources of information for and about the Black community. In 1889, she also bought one-third interest in the Memphis *Free Speech and Headlight*, where she wrote many editorials about the poor conditions experienced by African American children in the local schools, including inadequate buildings and improperly trained teachers. As a result, her teaching contract was not renewed the following year. Although her outspokenness threatened her livelihood, and even her life on occasion, Wells-Barnett never wavered in speaking the truth as she saw it.

Another example of her courage occurred when the Alpha Suffrage Club sent Wells-Barnett as an Illinois delegate to the National American Woman Suffrage Association's (NAWSA) parade on March 3, 1913, in Washington, D.C. However, when she arrived and made it known that she anticipated marching with the Illinois suffrage delegation, the group argued that southern women might find it objectionable to allow her to march with their delegation. Instead they asked her to march at the rear of the parade with the other African American women's groups. Wells-Barnett wouldn't acquiesce to such racism and simply slipped into the ranks of the Illinois delegation as it marched down the parade route. Yet it seems that teachers had no similar objections, because Caddie Park marched in a contingent with White women teachers from many states without incident ("Suffrage Paraders," 1913).

Adella Hunt Logan, an American Missionary School teacher for several years before going to Alabama's Tuskegee Institute in 1883, experienced both sides of the racial divide in suffragist work. As an African American with a light complexion, she was able to pass into the segregated National American Suffrage Association conventions held in the South and bring back information to her African American colleagues. For a decade, she was the NAWSA's only Life Member from the state of Alabama and even contributed articles about the NACW to the NAWSA's newspaper (Alexander, 1993).

Another African American teacher-suffragist who used her writing skills on behalf of suffrage and women's rights was Lucie Wilmot Smith, who began teaching in 1877 in Louisville, Kentucky, at age 16. In her second career as a journalist, she edited the column "Women and Women's Work" for the *American Baptist*, where she frequently expressed her strong support for women's suffrage and racial equality. She later contributed to the *Baptist Journal* (Saint Louis, Missouri), *The Journalist* (an African American newspaper in New York City), the *Indianapolis Freeman* (the country's first illustrated newspaper for an African American audience), and was widely reprinted in many papers including the *Boston Advocate* and the *Freeman*.

For Mary B. Martin, suffragist work provided an avenue into political office. After years of suffrage activity, Martin, a teacher, became the first African American and the second woman elected to the Cleveland Board of Education, and she was reelected in 1933 and 1939 (Lewis & Wolcott, 1993). Sarah Smith Tompkins Garnet began her 56-year teaching career at the age of 14 in 1854 at the African Free School in the Williamsburg neighborhood of Brooklyn, New York. In 1863, she became the first African American woman appointed to the principalship of a public (though still segregated) school in Manhattan. While an educator, she helped to organize the Equal Suffrage League, one of the earliest suffrage groups in Brooklyn, and as a member of the NACW, she became the superintendent of its suffrage department (Cash, 1993).

Other Obstacles to the Vote

Racism was only one confounding force in the suffrage question. Lobbyists in large eastern cities like Boston and New York were quick to point to the Catholic Church as another obstacle to franchise (Jablonsky, 1994). Suffragist antipathy toward the Catholic Church stemmed in part from an anti-immigrant bias that suggested that men from "the old countries" were more likely to vote against women's rights and that these new immigrants were less deserving of franchise than were women whose families had been Americans for many generations. The antagonism could also be attributed to the concern that Catholic voters would elect school board members who would realign the schools more in keeping with Catholic religious convictions (Merk, 1956).

The *Woman's Voice and Public School Champion,* a weekly newspaper begun in 1889, became the voice of Boston's Protestant Independent Women Voters group. Advocating full suffrage for women, the paper offered information about women's rights, legislative activities, and suffrage meetings as well as a goodly portion of anti-Catholic propaganda. The newspaper seized on every opportunity to expose the Catholic Church's efforts to extinguish any hope that female parishioners had of obtaining the vote. A revealing example of this occurred in 1912, when teacher Aimee Hutchinson's Catholic school dismissed her for participating in a suffrage parade. According to Hutchinson, the parish priest, Father Taylor, called her into his office several days after the parade and expressed his distress: "You know how much I like you and your work, but since you have marched in the parade of suffragists I cannot have you any longer in the school. The suffragist movement is the next thing to socialism, and I cannot countenance it" ("Suffrage Parader," 1912, p. 24). Harriot Stanton Blatch of the Women's Political Union (WPU), later to become the National Women's Party, immediately came to the young woman's aid, promising to find her a job within the WPU until a teaching opportunity became available in another school ("Black Hand," 1912). Hutchinson became an active participant in the local suffrage movement, writing articles and presenting lectures to encourage the Catholic vote for suffrage (Stanton et al., vol. 4).

Many Catholic teachers deeply resented the church's interference in this political matter. In her travels on behalf of suffrage, Margaret Haley (1912), a Catholic, wrote Chicago friends for immediate funds to counteract a Catholic blitz of anti-suffrage propaganda. She claimed:

Hell is let loose against us here. I enclose you a copy of 6 columns of "stuff" that appeared in most of the Catholic papers throughout Ohio last week and leaflets of this damnable stuff to be distributed at all Churches Sunday. We are trying to offset it but it takes money and the women are exhausted. . . . The local labor council has gone back on us owing to the saloon interests . . . tried to get Gompers but he would not come. . . . I am giving my time free and paying my own expenses up to the limit of my ability.

SUFFRAGISTS SUPPORT TEACHERS

As teachers swelled the ranks of suffrage groups, these groups began taking increasingly aggressive positions on teachers' rights. For instance, the Equal Suffrage Association of Covington, Kentucky, passed a resolution condemning the local school board after teachers there were twice passed over for salary increases. The resolution stated in part:

> Whereas our Covington School Board has seen fit to raise the salaries of all males from superintendent to janitor, ignoring entirely the promise made a year ago and repeated this spring that the salaries of women teachers would be increased. . . . Resolved that we, the Equal Suffrage Association of Covington publicly express our condemnation of this unjust discrimination against women teachers. Resolved. That we assure these women of our sincere and hearty moral support and that we pledge ourselves to greater effort, and to call on all broad minded, liberty-loving men to help us women secure the ballot, so that our women teachers may be fairly represented on School Boards, and that women in all walks of life may be equipped with that which will secure for them both justice and protection. ("Teacher's Pay," 1911, p. 20)

Other examples abound: In Birmingham, Alabama, the Equal Suffrage Association investigated complaints that the school board attempted to keep teachers from getting involved in suffrage work ("Women Teachers Can," 1912).

The election of the first woman president of the Nebraska State Teachers Association resulted with the help of local suffragists who lobbied for her candidacy ("Teachers Choose," 1913). The clubwoman's movement in Waukeska, Wisconsin, originated around the issue of pay equity for female teachers. The Maryland Woman Suffrage Association aided teachers in their campaign for equal pay for equal service (Stanton et al., vol. 6, p. 255). Suffragists participated in a number of activities to advance the causes of teachers, including the right to equal pay for equal work, the right to marry, and the right to become administrators. Sensitive to women teachers' limited financial situation, organizations such as the National Suffrage Party instituted a sliding scale for membership dues. Lawyers, ministers, journalists, doctors, actresses, and college professors were encouraged to contribute a dollar, whereas nurses, teachers, stenographers, and college students contributed 50 cents (Advertisement, 1902).

The growing solidarity between women teachers and the suffrage movement did not go unnoticed by anti-suffrage groups. When the "antis" began courting women teachers with promises of support for better wages, the *Woman's Journal* responded in vehement protest, noting that the "antis" had a history of opposing female teachers on pay equity issues and access to administrative promotions ("The Antis," 1902). In Washington, fellow teachers were quick to expose an anti-suffragist teacher who was seen voting in a local municipal election ("Even the Anti-Suffragists," 1911). Though there is no evidence the "antis" successfully wooed away teachers from suffrage, the power and community prestige held by many of those opposed to suffrage must have given some teachers concern about their jobs.

Frances Smith Whiteside, an Atlanta school principal, was a founding member of that state's suffrage organization and first president of the Atlanta Woman's Suffrage League, of which a large number of members were teachers and businesswomen. Yet Whiteside claimed to be the only teacher "who dared avow herself a member" in 1912, because others feared retaliation by their employers (Stanton et al., vol. 4, p. 133). In Buffalo, New York, a domestic science teacher who joined other suffragists picketing the White House was arrested and sentenced to 60 days in jail, losing her job as a result. Her superintendent, unsympathetic to suffrage, charged her with being absent without leave and with conduct unbecoming a teacher, and dismissed her without appeal (Thomas & Moran, 1991). No wonder the president of the New York Western Federation of Women's Clubs noted that women teachers were at first afraid of dismissal for participating in local campaigns, "but they quietly organized and began work." Quiet organization did have its results, for after 1 year they succeeded in both obtaining salary increases and drawing attention to the need for women's franchise ("How Suffrage," 1911, p. 111).

Similarly, Grace Strachan, leader of the IAWT, felt she had to hide her pro-suffrage stance from the public. Although she privately supported women's franchise, publicly she claimed disinterest because she didn't want to offend the unions and business interests from whom she derived substantial support. It was a compromise with which many disagreed.

In March 1912, the *Woman Voter* wrote a scathing attack on local teachers after that magazine's hawkers felt snubbed at a rally celebrating the passage of the new equal pay bill for teachers. Apparently the celebrants believed the sellers had rudely interrupted the festivities. The *Voter* harshly criticized the teachers for their conservatism. After praising teachers in other cities, the *Voter* editorialized: "In New York, however, teachers are so far behind the more intelligent leaders that suffrage is to them still a thing beyond their ken or utility . . . the rank and file . . . remain indifferent to their own well-being" ("School Teachers and Suffrage," 1912, p. 9). The outburst resulted from a long-simmering feud between some local suffragists and IAWT leader Grace Strachan. In her efforts to secure equal pay for the city's teachers, Strachan had pulled together a forceful coalition of just about every woman's group in the region. During the 4-year campaign, suffragists found Strachan's equivocation on the vote disheartening. Only after winning pay equity for teachers did Strachan become involved in suffrage, at which point she encouraged the 15,000 members of her organization to follow her lead.

By 1915, the editors of *Woman Voter* had forgotten their grudge and reported on New York City teachers' campaign activities for the 19th Amendment, noting that some 8,000 teachers had formed a Teachers' Branch of the Empire State Suffrage Campaign Committee (Blake, 1915; "Teacher Suffragists Organize," 1915). Three thousand signed up to spend their summer working for the vote, touring up-state New York, New Jersey, Pennsylvania, and Massachusetts in their "Franchise Fords" to discuss suffrage with farmers and summer vacationers. One teacher-suffragist noted: "We find the farmers with us to a man. We . . . are much encouraged . . . men at ploughs, the axe, and the fence are 'suffrage fans' throwing up their hats and cheering as we pass along" ("Teachers Help," 1915, p. 224; see also "Teachers to the Front," 1915).

Suffrage Schools

Some of the teachers attended suffrage schools to learn the finer points of working the campaign trail. The New York City school, founded by Carrie Chapman Catt, provided students with instructions on how to study a town, a summer resort, or a hotel to determine who were the most influential people and how to convince these people to hold suffrage meetings. Strachan became one of the school's regular teachers, and many teachers followed in her wake. Teachers had natural assets for this duty. As Katherine Devereux Blake, chair of the Teachers Branch of the Empire State Suffrage Campaign Committee, asserted: "No school teacher need tell me that she can't make speeches, she makes them all day in the schoolroom, and she is well fitted for the work" ("School for Suffrage," 1911; see also "Mail-Order Suffragist," 1916; "Suffrage Evening School," 1915; "Suffrage School," 1913).

Suffrage schools formed in other states, and teachers participated in these as well. In *A History of Women's Suffrage*, Stanton and her colleagues (1922) note their existence in Alabama, Florida, Georgia, Indiana, Iowa, Kansas, Maine, Maryland, Michigan, Nebraska, New Jersey, Rhode Island, South Carolina, Virginia, West Virginia, and Wisconsin. Occasionally, some discriminatory action became the catalyst for teachers' support of suffrage. New Orleans teachers joined the suffrage movement after a salary schedule change that set salaries of the most efficient women on a par with those of the least efficient men ("Teachers Learn," 1913). On another occasion, women teachers in Stark County, Ohio, angered at being excluded from the annual teachers' banquet, used their majority to replace the all-male board with all women ("Teachers Turn," 1907). In Buffalo, New York, teachers organized suffrage clubs in every ward of the city after learning that their failure to receive raises resulted from new tax breaks given to local corporations ("How Suffrage Will Help Teachers," 1911).

Bringing the Students Along

Teachers also influenced students to work for suffrage. In New York, many students engaged in the campaign, largely participating in school suffrage leagues such as the Wadleigh P.E. League of Manhattan, the Julia Ward Howe League of Girls' High of Brooklyn, and the Abigail Adams League of Erasmus Hall High School ("Miss Lenda Hanks," 1910; "Notes," 1910). In Chicago, women teachers organized high school students to march in the 1914 suffrage day parade (Stewart, 1914). In Maryland, pictures of suffrage leaders were installed in public schools, and boys and girls trained to participate in suffrage debates. A Baltimore Women's Club provided prizes for the most convincing arguments for and against suffrage, as did the Atlanta Women's Suffrage League, which awarded business scholarships for the best essay on women's suffrage. Numerous activities of a similar nature took place in cities and towns across the country (Stanton et al., vol. 6; "Name Schools for Women," 1915).

These were not easy accomplishments, because school boards often resisted any attempt to thrust "politics" into the schools. A case in point was the New York City Board of Education's denial of Mrs. H. P. Belmont's offer, in 1910, to fund a prize for the best high school essay on suffrage. The board acted in a characteristically bureaucratic fashion by refusing public discussion of the question. Instead, it simply offered a prepared statement, which said, in part, "No competition, competitive exhibition, or prize contest (other than athletic exhibitions) shall be authorized in any high school except under regulations prescribed by the Board of Education." Few were surprised by this strategy and fewer still by the tone. The *New York Times*, reporting on the incident, claimed: "Knowing [onlookers] said it was the board's means of halting the progress of the spread of woman suffrage propaganda in the schools" ("Bar Mrs. Belmont's Prizes," 1910, p. 13). Nevertheless, suffragists continued to pursue this strategy of reaching students in their classrooms, and the school board eventually relented, or at least tried to ignore most suffrage activities in their schools. Teachers even renovated the curriculum to include the history of the suffrage movement in lessons on government, American history, or social studies (Session, 1913).

Working the Conventions

Suffragists also attempted to win over converts at teacher conventions: In the West, they distributed issues of the *Western Woman Voter*, in the East, the *Woman's Journal*. Adella Parker, a high school teacher of civics and economics in Seattle, served as editor and publisher of the *Western Woman Voter* as well as on the state executive board of the Washington Equal Suffrage Association. In South Dakota, two teachers attended the annual state teachers' convention, passing out pencils embossed "Votes for Women" and sample copies of the *Woman's Journal* (Reed, 1958, p. 71). Teachers also performed "To Vote or Not to Vote," a parody on Shakespeare's *Hamlet*, at both teachers' and suffrage conventions. Originally written as an anti-suffragist piece by Marie Jenny Howe, it was redeveloped into a satirical number that brought audiences to their feet. It began:

> To have the ballot or not to have the ballot that is the question: Whether 'tis nobler in the mind to suffer the slings and arrows of our brother man, or to battle for the franchise and, winning, as win we must some time, for cause is just, end all our trouble. ("Alice Rower," 1913; "Soliloquy on Man," 1903, p. 5)

An even more direct connection was seen in the election of "suffrage" candidate Annie Webb Blanton as superintendent of public instruction of Texas. She became the first woman elected to office by women only 1 day after women got the vote in that state. Some 386,000 women registered in 17 days in order to take part in the vote (Stanton et al., vol. 6, pp. 638–639). The ballot box, many agreed, was a crucial step up in achieving real equity for women.

SUMMARY

The relationship between female educators and the suffrage movement proved to be a potent and symbiotic one. Women teachers composed the most prevalent career group within the campaign for the vote. Well-educated and organized, with access to community and professional colleagues, they had training as speakers and maintained the appearance of refined, middle-class gentlewomen. All these factors persuasively influenced public sentiment about the women's vote. In return, suffrage activists, many of them former or current educators, engaged in the campaigns that teachers waged to improve their professional status.

Feminist teachers' participation in such visibly political roles inside and outside the educational system helped to banish negative and superficial stereotypes of passive and disinterested teachers. They became involved despite their fears about public and administrative disapproval. And some went even further by bringing issues of women's rights into classroom discussions, sponsoring student debates, or encouraging student participation in extracurricular activities such as parades and volunteer work at local suffrage headquarters. They urged their professional organizations to take a position on behalf of women's franchise, a major step forward for the conservative NEA.

Many teachers and other suffragists argued that the woman's vote would result in the improvement of the schools by drawing in more tax dollars and halting scandals such as corrupt textbook contracts, misdirected funds, and hiring and firing based on political patronage. That progressive educators and administrators began to agree with this point of view benefited some teachers and protected their participation in suffrage activities. In fact, some anti-suffragists worried that teacher-voters would end up running the schools. Maria L. Baldwin (1915), principal of the Agassiz Public School in Cambridge, Massachusetts, explored this concern in the *Crisis*:

> Candidates for election to school boards reckon early with the "teacher vote" and hasten to announce their "rightness" on this or that issue supposedly dear to teachers. It is wholly reasonable to infer that the extension of suffrage will enable teachers to secure more consideration for themselves, and to have important influence on the quality of the persons chosen to direct the schools.
>
> At the onset teachers will be confronted by the temptation of power—the temptation to use it for personal or selfish ends. What, as a class, will they do with this temptation! What motives will lie behind their advocacy of men and measures? What tests of fitness will they apply to the candidates for their votes? Will they decline to recognize fine qualities for school service in one who may hold heretical views about increase of salaries, or length of vacation? (p. 1)

Baldwin's questions are only somewhat prescient, because teachers had already been involved in politics far beyond those related to school board positions. In New York City, Grace Strachan and her teachers had helped to bring down a governor and a mayor in their efforts to gain equal pay for equal work in 1911 (see Chapter 2). In Chicago, Maggie

Haley, Catherine Goggin, and the Chicago Teachers Federation enlightened that city about the depth of political corruption that existed and the
corporate tax fraud that deprived schools of much needed budgetary
dollars (see Chapter 1). They also worked hard for the election of city
officials they deemed less corruptible and more sensitive to teachers'
workplace demands.

Over the next decades, female teachers would continue to utilize
the power of franchise and collective activity to improve their schools,
communities, the status of women, and their own occupational situations.
This is illustrated in Chapter 5, which describes the efforts of married
women teachers to maintain their jobs in the face of layoffs during the
1930s Depression. Teachers and their supporters clarified their intention
to use their votes to ensure that fairness and equity were guaranteed to
all school employees regardless of gender or marital status. The election
of school board members, school superintendents, and city officials who
influenced school policies has remained a critical strategy in the reform
efforts of teachers and their benefactors to this day.

Chapter 5

YOUR JOB OR YOUR MARRIAGE: RESTRICTIONS ON TEACHERS DURING THE DEPRESSION

The national optimism of the 1920s quickly faded after the stock market crash of 1929. The proportion of women teachers that had begun to decline in the 1920s plummeted faster and further in the following decade as legislation against employing married women exiled even more (Cott, 1987). During the widespread economic and emotional frustrations and frictions of the early 1930s, working women became branded as culprits whenever men stood on breadlines. Historian Winifred Wandersee (1981, p. 84) notes that society directed the greatest antagonism toward white-collar women, particularly the married women of this group. Teachers constituted the largest percentage and most visible faction of white-collar working women, and as a result they became both the target of anti-married-women legislation and the leaders for married women's right to work. Lois Sharf (1980) notes the Depression fostered a "sex war" (p. 98) in which men attempted to use public fears about the economy to their own benefit. This chapter demonstrates that this was the case in the teaching profession, as some male teachers and administrators used the Depression as an opportunity to improve their own conditions at the expense of women teachers.

THE RIGHT TO WORK: MARRIED WOMEN TEACHERS AND THE LAW

By 1931, 77% of all U.S. school districts had instituted bans on married women teachers. Smaller cities invoked a greater percentage of prohibitions than did larger cities. The differences in whether school districts created discriminatory rulings or not depended on a number of factors: the existence of vigorous women teachers' groups, a lengthy history of dynamic coalitions between teachers and local women's groups, and the receptivity of school superintendents to feminist concerns.

Historians debate whether feminism constituted a significant force in women's lives during the Depression. Some argue that after attainment of suffrage, women's groups returned to the multiple issues in development previous to the vote (Lemons, 1973; Perry, 1993). Others say these groups were factionalized by the social feminist pursuit of protective labor legislation and the radical feminist agenda of the Equal Rights Amendment (ERA) (Banner, 1974; O'Neill, 1969). It is a version of the latter argument that guides this chapter. Though both social feminists and radical feminists supported teachers in their workplace efforts, after the mid-1920s radical feminism, as represented by the National Woman's Party (NWP), offered a position more in keeping with the needs of white-collar women. The NWP split with social feminists over the ERA, introduced in 1921.

The ERA would guarantee complete equality for women under the law by dismantling, in one stroke, a nationwide patchwork of discriminatory rules and restrictions legally imposed on women. However, it would also jeopardize the special protections that limited the hours and types of work that women could perform. The Women's Trade Union League (WTUL) became one of the first and most vociferous opponents of the ERA because the factory women they represented were the major beneficiaries of protective legislation. White-collar women, in physically less-demanding jobs, did not have concerns identical to those of their blue- or pink-collar sisters. Rather, their goals focused on achieving treatment and opportunity equal to those offered men, a position advocated by the NWP and, after 1927, the BPWC.

Workplace discrimination played an important part in the repression of women's advancement to full rights. Even after achieving the vote, women continued to be treated as a temporary labor force. And the myth that women worked for "pin money" persisted, as did men's resentment of women's competition in the labor market. These factors seem to justify BPWC's defense of women in the professions. The teachers' previous advocate, the GFWC, did not make the shift to supporting the ERA until 1944. But many white-collar women made the jump from membership in the GFWC to the BPWC during the 1930s, increasing its membership from 56,000 to 65,000 in only 6 years, a significant accomplishment given that club memberships generally declined in the decade (Lemons, 1973; McGlen, 1995; Sklar, 1988; Swanson & Magiafico, 1992).

White-collar, married women workers received the most public scrutiny and opposition during the 1930s. For it was assumed that they didn't *need* to work for a living but did so out of an uncurbed consumeristic desire. The BPWC kept the question in debate during the Depression with its crusade to annul marriage bans against female public employees, of whom teachers constituted a significant proportion.

Between 1890 and 1920, the percentage of married women in the labor force increased steadily. Yet teachers constituted the smallest percentage of married women in all female occupations, representing only 17% nationwide in 1930 (Punke, 1940, pp. 506–507). This indicates the degree to which entrance to and continuance in the profession were suppressed by decades-long prohibitions against married women teachers, whether or not these prohibitions were always enforced.

Cities of all sizes imposed rules against married women teachers during the Depression. The greatest loss of rights occurred in the smaller cities where, between 1928 and 1931, over 22% of schools established rules against hiring married women as teachers. Another 12.1% also instituted a rule requiring currently employed female teachers who married to resign ("Employment of Married Teachers," 1932, p. 20).

It should come as no surprise that larger cities protected women's rights more assiduously than did smaller towns. As noted in Chapter 1, large cities were more likely to have female teacher associations. These organizations were more likely to work with other local women's groups and take more radical feminist positions than those in smaller communities. Female teachers in large cities were under less individual public scrutiny than those in smaller towns. City dwellers tended to be more diverse in terms of religious, ethnic, class, race, and educational backgrounds and, as a result, more tolerant of liberal thinking. City teachers were more likely to hold higher degrees and to be trained in a college or university, whereas rural teachers often acquired only minimal training from teacher institutes or normal schools. This meant that rural teachers had fewer employment options and were probably less likely to rock the boat. Furthermore, larger cities with their central office staffs were more likely to have investigated court decisions related to married women teachers (Richardson, 1930).

Feminists strongly supported strategies that utilized the courts, but barring that, they suggested women not change their names upon marriage, thereby forestalling the eventuality that they would be revealed as married ("Discrimination Against Married Women," 1902). One of the first court cases involved a New York City teacher who filed a writ of mandamus to force the school board to recognize her as an employee after her dismissal for marrying. The court upheld the teacher, noting that the dismissal conflicted with Section 1117 of the Greater New York state charter that limited the removal of teachers to "gross misconduct, insubordination, neglect of duty, or general inefficiency." During the following decade, other state courts reached similar conclusions (*Blair v. U.S. ex rel. Hellman*, 1916; *Jameson v. Board of Education Union District*, 1914; *Richards v. District School Board*, 1915; *State v. Board of School Directors of City of Milwaukee*, 1923).

A key case heard in the 1930s was *Hutton v. Gill* (1937), in which a New Jersey tenured teacher, Mrs. Gill, was asked to sign a contract that reduced her salary to a level shared only by married women teachers. Gill protested and the state supreme court ruled that the classification of married women teachers for compensation purposes in a different and lower class than unmarried women teachers was "unreasonable and hence invalid" (Davis, 1940). *School Board of the City Elwood v. State* (1932) reached a similar conclusion. In those cases finding for the school—*Baker v. School District* (1931), *Sheldon v. Committee of Hopedale* (1931), and *Backie v. Cromwell Consolidated School District* (1932)—the courts justified the teachers' dismissal on the basis of a clause in their contracts that stated they served at the "discretion of the school committee." This was the rationale in *Sheldon* (1931) in which a Hopewell schoolteacher was terminated even though she had taught as a married woman for 5 years, rendering "constant and competent service and being of good moral character." States with tenure laws, such as California, New York, Wisconsin, and New Jersey, allowed dismissal only for specific causes such as immorality or inefficiency, but not marriage. However, in the absence of limitations imposed by state law, school boards were usually free to set their own policies about married teachers (Edwards, 1925).

Society at large generally believed women to be superior teachers, especially for the lower grades, reasoning that a biological predestination gave them a natural affinity for children. Yet, ironically, teaching *and* motherhood were often regarded as incompatible. Married teachers predominated only in the rural schools where districts had greater difficulty in hiring employees at the wages and conditions offered. When cities had an oversupply of teachers, they could expel experienced married women in favor of less expensive incoming single women. Though the issue was essentially economic, schools more often justified dismissing these teachers on the socially acceptable belief that the married woman's true place was in the home. And as the supply of teachers increased, smaller districts also adopted similarly restrictive policies toward women teachers. However, the enforcement of these policies, in both rural and urban schools, appears to have been haphazardly based on political favoritism, supply, public opinion, and even the personal preferences of school administrators.

A good example of the struggle faced by married women in protecting their right to teach is offered by Cincinnati, Ohio. By following teachers through the decades from 1900 to 1940, we can see the agendas and strategies utilized by school boards, the public, supervisors, and both female and male teachers in dealing with the issue. Moreover, the Cincinnati example clarifies the role that feminist ideology played on the local front in defense of married women's right to work.

CINCINNATI SCHOOLS

In 1829, Cincinnati developed one of the earliest public school systems in the country. From its inception, the Cincinnati system included women on its staff as both teachers and principals. Their proportion grew quickly, constituting 40% of all the public school staff by 1849, though they drew only half the wages of their male counterparts. Cincinnati maintained a separate public school system for African Americans from the 1850s to the 1870s, staffed by African American teachers and principals. During the years of its existence, the African American school system employed from four to ten female teachers and four to seven male teachers and principals. After 1873, Cincinnati's Independent Colored School System was gradually dismantled, undermining an important African American power base in the community as the state legislature granted Black children the right to attend White schools in 1887 (Miller, 1968). Although many in the African American community supported integrating the schools, little desegregation actually occurred. Residential polarity in the city ensured de facto segregation; thus Black schools remained Black. Because African Americans were not permitted to supervise White children, teachers lost their positions when schools actually integrated. By 1912, only seven African American teachers remained in nonintegrated city schools along with 300 African American students (Hurley, 1982).

Early Bars Against Women

In 1850, Cincinnati became the first major city to bar women from serving as principals in its schools. Economist Nancy Bertaux (1994) notes that the prohibition of female principals occurred largely as the result of male bureaucrats' response to the feminization (or critical mass of women) of the schools. She points out that female principals were eliminated on the argument that women were too young and inexperienced for the job, when in actuality female principals averaged 7 years experience to men's 5.

In March 1889, one of the city's newspapers, the *Cincinnati Enquirer* ("Women May Marry," 1889), reported that an investigation by the Cincinnati school board had found that "many of the teachers in the schools were married ladies" (p. 8). School Superintendent E. E. White argued against their removal despite the fact that a rule had existed since 1880 that stated, in part, "Any female teacher shall forfeit her position by marrying during the term of her appointment" (*Cincinnati Board of Education Annual Reports*, 1880, p. 258). It is not clear whether White opposed the dismissal of married women teachers simply because it seemed unjust or because a predominantly female staff was more economical. But his decision would later prove pivotal in married women teachers' ability to retain their position in the hard times of the 1930s.

In 1900, the majority of American cities had wage differentials for male and female teachers. Men, on the average, earned one third to one half more annually than did women teaching at the same grade level. Furthermore, a woman teacher could be retained in her position for several years and still earn less than an incoming male. School Superintendent White agreed that most married women teachers had demonstrated records of superior teaching abilities as well as stability in the work force. For many men, a teaching position was a stepping-stone to more prestigious and higher paying positions in the schools as they moved from teacher to assistant principal to principal. If promotions did not come as quickly as expected, they moved into more lucrative positions with private business firms (Coffman, 1911).

Women had different expectations. Their decision to enter teaching was often based on a lack of career options. In 1900, the majority of Cincinnati women were employed as private household workers (28.7%), dressmakers and seamstresses (7.8%), and teachers (6.1%) (Oppenheimer, 1970). These occupations, and most jobs in which women were employed, were segregated by sex, suppressing wages, and decreasing women's mobility. Though teaching was one of the few female occupations that required a formal education, the reward was more in social status than in wages. A lack of market competition, an oversupply of trained women teachers, and an ingrained societal belief that women's true occupation was motherhood contributed to women's continuing marginality within the labor force.

The Condon Superintendency

It appears that most Cincinnati women teachers voluntarily retired when they married (Jacobs, 1928). To what degree pressures from school or society influenced this *choice* is difficult to access, but some women did not go willingly. This latter group found an ally in Randall J. Condon. Condon was superintendent of the Cincinnati public schools between 1913 and 1927. Hiring Condon in a period of rapid expansion, the district school board hoped that he would increase the efficiency of the large city school system that had become bogged down in politics and "small-town thinking." He appeared eminently qualified for the task. Educated at Colby College and Harvard University, he served a term in the Maine House of Representatives and held positions as school superintendent in Massachusetts, Montana, and Rhode Island ("Superintendent Randall J. Condon," 1919). Within months of his arrival, he astonished many when he responded affirmatively to a women teachers' petition for equal pay and equal opportunity for married and single women teachers ("Small Board Changes," 1914; "Women Teachers Desire," 1919).

He further solidified his feminist inclinations with his nomination of the city's first woman assistant superintendent of schools. The appointment of Anna Logan proved to be so controversial that the school board argued for 6 months before reluctantly agreeing to it. Though they had sought progressive leadership from their new superintendent, board members clearly differed in their definition of the term. The board promptly divided into pro– and anti–working-women factions, with William H. Gibson stating, "In my judgment women are not competent to hold executive positions, and I say this as a business man" ("Refusal to Confirm," 1913, p. 7). James G. Fisk concurred, claiming, "[Logan's] appointment was a bit of an extravagance" ("Sentiment in Logan Case," 1913, p. 8). However, Edith Campbell, the first and then only female board member, countered: "If we refuse endorsement of Mr. Condon's nomination of Miss Logan we are virtually acknowledging that we have one half of our teachers who are incapable of receiving promotion" ("Accused of Bad Faith," 1913, p. 7; "Board Refuses," 1913; Miss Edith Campbell," 1912).

Several community organizations also offered support for the Logan appointment, many of them women's groups, such as the Congress of Mothers Clubs, the Susan B. Anthony Club, and the Cincinnati Business and Professional Women's Clubs (*Cincinnati Board of Education Annual Reports*, 1910; France, 1937). However, one organization, the Hamilton County Association Opposed to Woman Suffrage, vehemently rejected the idea of a female assistant superintendent. To their objections, Condon simply replied:

> If I had known of a man better qualified for the position than Miss Logan, he would have been appointed but not because he was a man. . . . She [Miss Logan] was selected not because she was a woman, but upon the basis of individual merit and fitness. . . . So long as I remain Superintendent of Schools in this city, all appointments will be made on that basis. ("If I Had Known," 1913, p. 2)

In his first annual report to the school board, he also advocated equal pay for equal work, equal opportunity for promotions, and the right of women to retain their teaching positions regardless of marriage or motherhood ("Supt. Condon's Report," 1913). He wrote:

> I cannot reconcile . . . the differences in pay for men and women performing the same kind of work. . . . Merit and justice demand that pay should be equal and that service, not sex, should determine the amount. I cannot bring myself to believe in the value of a rule, however well intended, which by its very terms creates a privileged class upon the basis of sex; it violates the fundamental principles of recognizing merit in service by promoting to positions of larger service and greater reward. Nor do I believe that the marriage of a woman teacher should be considered equivalent to a resignation . . . some of the best teachers I have known have been mothers. (pp. 34–35)

Condon drew national attention for such a radical feminist stance on women teachers. For instance, in 1914 the *Journal of Education* derided the New York City school system for its protracted campaign (begun in 1902) to rid the system of married women teachers while congratulating Cincinnati's progressive support of women's rights ("Progressive Cincinnati," 1914).

Condon's Supporters and Detractors

The climate created by Condon strengthened women's position within the Cincinnati teaching force, and the Cincinnati Women Teachers' Association (CWTA) responded by taking an increasingly prominent role in advocating other developments ("Condon Urged," 1916). The CWTA, a member organization of both the national and the state Federation of Women's Clubs, organized in 1896 under the name of Mathesis "to further the interests of all women teachers of Hamilton County, to meet for educational growth and social intercourse, and to promote education, science and art" ("Cincinnati Women Teachers' Association," 1915, p. 212). The group brought issues before Condon that were met with his respect and attentiveness. One illustration of this relationship occurred in March 1917 when the CWTA's Teacher Welfare Committee sent Condon a list of inequities that they felt still existed in the system. They called for an immediate cost-of-living raise, more promotions for women, the extension of equal pay to high school teachers and to those special teachers not currently receiving it, a spring vacation, higher temperatures in the classrooms, more attention to child welfare issues, a sabbatical year, and sick leave ("Equalized Pay," 1917). By the end of the school year, Condon had negotiated with both the board of education and its secondary school counterpart, the Union of High Schools, to acquire everything on the list except the $100 raise, which he promised to pursue in the following year ("Equal Pay for Men," 1917; "Women in High Schools," 1917).

Not everyone was sanguine about Condon's support of his female work force ("German–American Alliance," 1914). During the 1920s, the Cincinnati Schoolmasters' Club became increasingly vociferous in its opposition to both the increasing number and status of women teachers. The club organized in 1904 for the purpose of promoting "educational interests of Cincinnati and the vicinity" and "the cultivation of good fellowship among men interested in education" ("Cincinnati Schoolmasters Club," 1915, p. 212).

One of the key leaders of this organization was E. D. Roberts. In January 1920, the Schoolmasters held a special conference on the topic, "What Should Be the Proportion of Men Teachers and How Can It Be Maintained?" During the conference they developed a resolution declaring the need for men in schools and deploring their diminishing number. They requested the board of directors of the NEA to "urge upon the American public and boards of education, the necessity of immediately correcting this serious situation by proper means and measures" ("Men," 1920, p. 141). At first the Schoolmasters said that they thought the problem could be rectified by raising all teacher salaries and by making special efforts to appeal to male high school graduates to enter into teaching preparation in college ("Committee Sends Letter to NEA," 1920; "Double Bill," 1920).

However, within a month their meetings had become largely opportunities to castigate female teachers as "inappropriate" instructors of adolescent boys and girls. By drawing selectively on research, the male teachers argued that a feminized profession was a weak and dangerous one (Heer, 1920; Koch, 1920). Revising their initial position, they concluded that not only should men receive higher salaries but women should be restricted from most administrative positions (Condit, 1920; Lorenz, 1920). Several local organizations supported the Schoolmasters' position, including the Chamber of Commerce, the Central Labor Council, the Kennedy Heights Business Men's Club, and the Cincinnati and Norwood Optimist's Clubs ("Study of Public Opinion," 1927; "Why Men and Women Should Receive Equal Pay," 1927).

As the issue droned on over the next year, Superintendent Condon responded only once by giving figures that showed the number of men in the Cincinnati schools had actually increased. Attempting to smooth ruffled feathers, he noted, "There will always be places for men in the Cincinnati schools, and these places will be of increasing importance" ("Men on Increase," 1923, p. 152).

Cincinnati in the 1920s

The equitable environment pursued by Condon's leadership proved to be only part of the explanation for the strengthening agency of the city's female teachers. In the 1920s, women finally achieved the vote after generations of effort, emboldening them to a New World vision in which they played key roles. World War I also had its impact. During the war, men left the profession in large numbers to enter the military or to pursue more lucrative positions in war-related industries, creating teacher shortages in many American cities. As a result, cities that had previously barred married women teachers from teaching suddenly had to plead for their return, going so far as to deem it their patriotic duty to do so. Condon pointed out, none too subtly, that if it were not for his decision to retain married women, Cincinnati too would have faced a "teacher famine" ("Their Bit," 1917; see also "Married Teachers," 1918; "Married Women Teachers," 1918; "Now the Married," 1918).

In the 1920s, child labor legislation pushed many working children into the classroom, leading to the development of vocational education and high schools and creating a further demand for teachers (Lakes, 1995). At the same time, teachers faced escalating certification requirements, which intensified the time and money spent in their own education. Fewer men were willing to make such a large investment for such a little wage compensation, having options in other fields closed to women. In an effort to attract and retain more male teachers to the new high schools, which opened in the 1920s, school boards paid them larger salaries, reasoning that men would be better disciplinarians of older students and better administrators.

By the beginning of the 1920s, women represented just over 80% of the 2,547-member Cincinnati public school teaching staff. About 3% of the women were of African American descent. A majority of female staff was of mature age: 30% between the ages of 45 and 64, and 44% between 25 and 40. Only 14% were 24 years or younger (*Occupations*, 1923, p. 1082). Married women constituted only 6% of female teachers and 4.8% of the entire teaching staff. The proportion of married women in the larger Cincinnati work force proved much greater: 14% for Whites and almost 50% for African Americans (pp. 784, 818).

Cincinnati Schools in the Depression

In the 1930s, Cincinnati public schooling ranged from nursery schools to a municipal university. The system included 67 elementary schools, 6 junior high schools, 4 junior–senior high schools, 2 four-year high schools,

9 vocational high schools, 10 special schools, and 3 night schools. In addition, several elementary and 16 parochial high schools and academies dotted the landscape, along with two Catholic colleges and three theological schools—Catholic, Protestant, and Jewish (*Survey Report of the Cincinnati Public Schools*, 1935).

In 1933, at the depth of the Depression, 30.4% of the Cincinnati labor force stood in the unemployment lines, 28.4% of all Whites and 54.3% of all African Americans ("Employment in Cincinnati, 1936," 1936, p. 873). The Depression increased the student population as unemployment forced young people out of the labor market and into the schools, where many received their only square meal of the day. In Cincinnati the population of 10th graders increased by 20% in this period, whereas the number of students in the 9th, 11th, and 12th grades increased by 50%. The school board tried several avenues to limit expenses: The school year was shortened by 4 days, teachers' salaries were cut, and class size increased. Although the salary cutbacks were not enthusiastically embraced, they were tolerated with some equanimity because Cincinnati teachers were at the top of the salary range for public schools in the nation.

Condon had retired in 1927, turning over the superintendency to Edward Roberts, former assistant superintendent and head of the Schoolmasters' Club. In 1932, the school system faced a $400,000 deficit, and the discussion of layoffs seemed inevitable. Given the earlier stance of the Schoolmasters against equal pay for women, the question of who would be dismissed became an understandably volatile issue. On February 9, 1932, the Cincinnati school board president, William J. Schroeder, declared an "unemployment emergency." Under this edict new teachers could be hired only if there were no other wage earners in the family. Several board members asked Schroeder whether he meant to remove a teacher if someone in "her" family got a job. Though he ventured that this seemed an appropriate response, the rest of the board generally disagreed. They reached a compromise that no current teachers would be dismissed until the end of the school year, at which time each teacher's "family's financial need" would be evaluated ("Door Slams," 1932, p. 1). At that time, Roberts suggested the board take the stronger position that "marriage not be accepted as a basis of a leave of absence, but involve resignation" ("Rules," 1933, pp. 9–10).

Again, though the rule did not specify gender, the presumption was that it would apply to women only. The board, however, was unsure of how to determine the financial status of each woman's family and decided not to pass either bill. In favoring the dismissal of married women teachers, Roberts stood in a minority of school superintendents across the nation.

National Marriage Prohibitions

According to one survey, only 39% of school superintendents approved of marriage prohibitions for teachers, whereas 52% disapproved. Sixty-two percent of superintendents felt that such policies arose from school boards, and 29% thought it was the result of local political pressure. Although 26 states had introduced bills into their legislatures, in 1931 no states yet had laws allowing for the dismissal of married women teachers (Wandersee, 1981, p. 99). Rather, the decision was left to the districts. Although the majority of superintendents may have opposed discrimination against married women, many simply took the path of least resistance when confronted with the issue (Terpenning, 1932, p. 231). If the tax-paying populace opposed married teachers, it would be risky for superintendents to confront them, particularly in this period when emotions ran high.

A 1937 survey of local clubs within the BPWC found that of 460 respondents, 170 thought women teachers suffered greater discrimination than women in any other field. The majority cited marriage bans but also noted inequitable salaries and lack of opportunities for advancement as problematic. The vast majority felt that "women should not be restricted in their choice of careers in spite of possible adverse economic, social, and other situations in their home towns" (Committee on Equal Opportunity, 1939, p. 14). More than 88% indicated that their local clubs advocated legislation for the prevention of discrimination against female employees. Most frequently this was accomplished through conferences with business firms to encourage the adoption of a policy of nondiscrimination. Clubs frequently mentioned "political influence" as responsible for decisions as to whether bans on married women would be levied against all public employees evenly. Clearly clubwomen constituted a factor in holding back the tide of public pressure on school boards to invoke bans on married teachers. This agenda item may have been directly affected by the fact that so many club members were current or former teachers.

Teachers constituted 19.3% of BPWC's national membership, the largest occupational group within the organization. Sixty-seven percent were single, 18% married, 8.5% widowed, and 5.9% separated or divorced. Almost two thirds claimed at least one dependent for whom they were wholly responsible. In replying to questions about workplace discrimination, nearly one fifth of all married women reported that they had been discriminated against by their employers because of their marital status (Byrnes, 1934; see also *Why Women Work*, 1938).

The question as to whether marriage would make women more inefficient or neglectful teachers spawned a proliferation of studies about the competence of married women teachers, scrutinizing everything from the number of sick days they used, what they did on Saturday, their number of dependents, their in-service preparation, to whether eighth graders liked them more than they did single women teachers (Carrothers, 1924; Cooke & Sulzbacher, 1926; Goodler, 1928; Huffaker, 1931; Lewis, 1925; Reeves, 1928; Snyder, 1925). One study, focused specifically on Ohio, found "no distinct differences in the social, recreational, and professional life of married and single women as teachers," leading the researcher to surmise: "Thus it would appear that marital status is not a [valid] criterion for either discrimination or vice versa in the employment of married women as teachers in the public schools" (Waits, 1932b, p. 141).

Married Teachers in Cincinnati

In Cincinnati, as in most cities, the majority of men teachers were married, whereas the majority of women were not; men felt no compulsion to retire upon marriage. Despite societal prejudice and expectations, the percentage of women retaining their teaching positions after marriage increased from 5.8% in 1920 to 12.5% only a decade later (U.S. Census Bureau, 1933, pp. 83, 1,305). The vast majority of married women taught in elementary school, whereas married men were more likely to teach in the high schools. A similar trend existed at the state level, where 10.3% of the approximately 43,500-member teaching staff in 1932 identified as married women, 65% as single women, and 24.5% as men (Waits, 1932b, p. 141; see also Waits, 1932a).

Still the percentage of married women in teaching lagged far behind the percentage of married women in the Cincinnati workforce at large, which was almost triple that in teaching in 1920 and double in 1930. Because teachers were more likely than blue-collar women to be married to white-collar men, they had more choice as to resigning their jobs upon marriage. Some middle-class husbands simply would not allow their wives to work. And other women resigned rather than face adverse public opinion.

Although feminist organizations exposed the innate sexism of bans on married women public employees, taxpayers railed at the selfishness of wage-earning wives who would not retire in favor of some unemployed family man. A 1936 *Fortune* poll asked the American public the question "Do you believe that a married woman should have a full-time job outside the home?" to which 48% responded "no." A year later, an AIPO poll phrased the question differently: "Do you approve of married women earning money in business or industry if she has a husband capable of supporting her?" This time a resounding 82% answered "no" (Oppenheimer, 1970, p. 52). Clearly the public viewed work for women as a privilege justified only under proper conditions—chiefly dire economic necessity (Kessler-Harris, 1989, p. 38). The theories of female economic independence such as those propounded by Charlotte Perkins Gilman in the 1890s remained radical rhetoric to all but the most open-minded citizens of the 1930s.

It is unclear whether Superintendent Roberts was reacting to public pressure when he announced to the board that he had, in a seemingly unilateral move, determined the appropriate criteria for layoffs and already served "informal notice" to 24 women of their impending dismissal ("School Jobs Go One to a Family," 1932). All 24 had husbands also employed in the Cincinnati schools. Whether the couples had a choice as to which spouse would be dismissed was not mentioned. It was simply understood that women would be the ones to go, despite that men stood a better chance of finding employment elsewhere. The couples protested and hired legal counsel for assistance in appealing the ruling ("Legal Fight Planned," 1932). Their lawyers argued that such an edict discriminated against married people and did not take into account employees with brothers, sisters, and other family members within the school system ("Legal Advice," 1932). Though their lawyers felt they had a good case, the couples decided not to pursue the issue out of concern for adverse public sentiment. Instead the women asked that they not be dismissed but suspended until economic conditions improved ("Teachers Ask Suspensions," 1932). This way they could keep their status in the retirement system. Counsel for the couples also requested that the women be given preference in future job openings ("Teachers Ask Preference," 1932). When the board refused even these seemingly minor requests, their decision created such public backlash that the board dropped the matter of layoffs altogether. Instead, salaries of all employees were reduced by another 10% ("Few Changes," 1932).

S. D. Shankland, executive secretary of the Department of Superintendents of the NEA, while speaking in Cincinnati, noted that the question of married teacher layoffs had been one of the most bitterly contested issues since the beginning of the Depression ("School Heads," 1932). The *National Education Association Journal* ran many articles citing arguments, pro and con, about married women teachers (e.g., "Shall Married," 1932). Historian Winifred Wandersee (1981) claims the question of why women worked was a major social issue of the decade. Restrictions against married women's employment also occurred in business and industry. A 1939 survey by the National Industrial Conference indicated that 84% of insurance companies, 65% of banks, and 63% of public utilities had invoked rules against married women workers (Ware, 1981, 1982). In Cincinnati,

Procter and Gamble, Cincinnati Bell Telephone, and Gibson Greeting Card—all large employers of white-collar women—erected similar barriers (Sutherland, 1985).

The teaching profession came under greater scrutiny than did most occupations. The high public visibility of women teachers, their white-collar status, and opposition from their male colleagues made them especially vulnerable to whatever community antipathy existed. Additionally, economic anxiety encouraged conservatism. By 1938, three out of every four cities refused to hire married women teachers, and nearly 50% required resignation upon marriage ("Marriage and Teaching," 1938; Peters, 1934).

Throughout the 1930s, businesses and governments debated the use of prohibitions against married women as a quick fix to budget problems. Some states, such as California, instituted regulations against the hiring of married women for any civil service position (Johnson, 1931). Federal regulations such as Section 231 of the Economy Act mandated that personnel reductions begin with those who had husbands or wives in government service. Representative John J. Cochran, a Missouri Democrat who sponsored this part of the act, repeatedly stated that he wanted this legislation to serve as a model for state and local governments to discourage the employment of married women. The BPWC opposed Section 231 and endorsed its repeal in their monthly publication, *Independent Woman*, by running stories that illustrated the hardships that such regulations brought about. One such article featured the story of a married woman teacher's dismissal in 1932 despite her husband's unemployment and her mother's dependence on her income. After months without a wage, she received a letter offering her a new position "if she was no longer married," which she read as "divorce your husband if you want to work" (Anonymous, 1937; see also Anonymous, 1938; Black, 1936; Ellison, 1946).

Continued Calls for Dismissal

Superintendent Roberts once again broached the issue of married women teachers at the board meeting in August 1933 by suggesting that future openings be limited to single women. He justified his position by noting that he had modeled it on the National Recovery Act (NRA), which declared no more than one member of a household could be employed by the federal government. Thus, in a patriotic gesture, the Cincinnati Board of Education put all married women at the bottom of the preferred list for new jobs ("Wedded Women," 1933). Still Roberts seemed dissatisfied. He ordered a personnel survey and in September 1933 announced its results ("Married Women Teachers Number 344," 1933). The report noted 344 married women teachers, 26 of whom had husbands also employed in the schools. Roberts calculated the average joint salaries of the couples at about $5,500 annually ("Legal Fight," 1933). If one considers that 90.9% of U.S. families earned less than $1,999, this figure doubtlessly raised the hackles of the anti-married-woman crowd (Wandersee, p. 181). Still, despite Roberts's considerable efforts, the board could not agree to take action and the teachers remained employed.

The issue came before the board again when Judge Elmer S. Hunsicker became a new member. He immediately proposed a resolution to dismiss all married teachers to make room for single women teachers ("Women Oppose," 1934). The Cincinnati Business Women's Club vigorously protested. Miss Caroline Hein, president of the organization, stated in a letter to the board that it was the policy of the BPWC (their mother organization) to oppose any action that would use the Depression "as the basis for discontinuing the service of married women teachers" ("Women's Club for Married Women Teachers," 1934, p. 24). Sensitive to negative publicity that might be raised by the larger organization, the board defeated the Hunsicker amendment by a vote of four to two ("Resolutions," 1935). Hunsicker then proposed yet another solution that stated simply that the board could refuse new appointments to married women. This motion passed. Hunsicker unsuccessfully offered several other resolutions, including another attempt to dismiss all married women teachers, to exclude women from principalships, and to remove women whose husbands were employed in the schools ("Wedding Rings," 1934).

Changes and Counter Changes

Despite improvements in Cincinnati's unemployment rate, the Cincinnati Men Teachers' Association (CMTA) continued lobbying the board to improve the status of men in the profession ("Employment Census," 1934). In May 1934, they obtained a bill which placed all men at the top of the eligibility list for teaching positions for the next year ("Men Teachers," 1934). That November, the Cincinnati Teachers' Association (CTA), an organization representing both male and female teachers, responded by sending the board a resolution of its own. In it the CTA insisted that the board retain a single salary schedule for all teachers, male or female, elementary or secondary ("Letter from Cincinnati," 1935). The dispute escalated and eventually became public when the CMTA wrote an article for the *Cincinnati Post* in which it stated its case against the woman teacher. The CWTA immediately asked for equal time, and throughout the month of January 1935 Cincinnatians read the almost daily charges and counter charges of both groups.

Among other things, the men's group cited claims by psychologist G. Stanley Hall that "undue retardation and misgrouping of boys" was caused by biased female elementary school teachers and that taxpayers were unfairly saddled with the burdens of resultant retarded students ("Girls with No More Ability," 1935, p. 2; see also Diehl, 1986). The CMTA also asserted that both boys and girls preferred heroes to heroines and thus would naturally prefer male to female teachers ("Boys Worship Hero Not Heroine," 1935). Female teachers responded that women had educated many outstanding American men and that, on the whole, the psychological literature showed "no striking dissimilarities exist between the sexes as teachers" ("Pupils Want Kind, Patient Teachers," 1935, p. 11). They further noted, "If the boys in our schools see our men paid more than women for doing the same work they will grow up convinced of the inferiority of women, and ready to put this conviction into social and economic practice" ("Ability Unrelated to Sex," 1935, p. 9). They charged the men with using the system as a refuge during hard times and fleeing it during prosperity ("Men Forced Out?" 1935). They further opined that schools should not be welfare systems, giving out jobs to those who could prove they were the neediest ("Women Teachers Uphold Single Schedule," 1935).

Despite the assertion by its competitor, the *Cincinnati Enquirer*, that the public was not interested in the issue, the *Post* articles created a community furor ("Tempest," 1935). It especially resonated among Cincinnati's women's groups. The school board received letters from the Cincinnati branch of the American Association of University Women, the Cincinnati Business Women's Club, the Central Women's Christian Temperance Union, and the Cincinnati League of Women Voters, all insisting on a married woman's right to work. In May 1935, the Cincinnati Business Women's Club increased the pressure when it warned that the BPWC, their parent group, would pull its national convention from Cincinnati if the school board did not immediately cease its harassment of married women ("Wage Fight," 1935).

The combination of pressure from women's groups and the community's disapproval of the board's inability to settle the issue as well as admonishments from the U.S. Commission of Education finally curtailed the continuing debate about married women teachers. The commission, at the request of the board, had undertaken a year-long survey of the district, visiting the schools and administrative offices and collecting data on the general status of the system. As to the married teacher question, the commission's report recommended that marital status be disregarded in teacher employment or retention in service (Survey Report of Cincinnati Public Schools, 1935). The debate cooled until sparked again during the late 1940s as returning military men flooded the employment market, but it quickly cooled once more as the baby boom created teacher shortages. As shown in the next chapter, even motherhood no longer stood as a critical obstruction to women who would become teachers in the overcrowded classrooms of 1950s and 1960s.

SUMMARY

Teachers proved fairly successful in achieving public support for the right to marry in the economic prosperity of the 1920s. However, sentiments shifted toward conservatism in the Depression. Though the public supported women's need to work when their husbands could not, only a small percentage advocated women's right to work regardless of financial need. Given public antipathy to the issue, it would have been natural if female teachers had switched their approach to the more politically expedient argument that women worked primarily out of financial need. However, this argument had the unfortunate effect of confirming the traditional stereotype of women's employment as related to a temporary economic emergency. Thus the real issue—a woman's right to work—was obscured. The split between progressive reformers and feminists only aggravated this tension. Reformers saw working women as dangerous to the ideals of family, whereas feminists considered employment a prerequisite for female independence.

This chapter has illustrated that organizations like the NWP, the BPWC, and a growing number of others supported teachers' and other white-collar women's right to work regardless of economic need. Given that their membership was drawn from the same population that they tended to help, they understood, firsthand, the degree to which the conditions of the Depression became rationales for placing limits on women's economic independence. The support of such outside organizations proved essential to the protection of teachers and pivotal in keeping the issue before the public.

The higher the visibility of a job, the more likely it was to encounter discrimination. Teachers and other white-collar workers faced greater public pressure than did factory and domestic workers. That teachers' salaries were drawn from the public trough only increased the antagonism. The rationalization for firing married women in order to hire single women was little more than a thinly veiled attempt to factionalize women. To their credit, single women usually did not take advantage of the situation, perhaps because they could see a time when they too might want to marry.

The degree to which women wanted and needed to work is evident in the increasing national marriage rate for female teachers during the Depression, from 17.9% in 1930 to 24.6% in 1940 (Punke, 1940). The substantial increase in working women in general during the Depression is further confirmation of a shift in public opinion due, in part, to the concerted efforts of women's groups to heighten awareness of women's right to work (Wandersee, 1981, p. 83; see also Murphy, 1981, pp. 145–156; Pederson, 1987).

It is tempting to wonder what might have happened during the 1930s had Cincinnati retained Condon as superintendent. Would he have kept the question of married women teachers out of debate? Or, conversely, how might the situation have differed had Condon not supported women's rights previous to the Depression, and allowed women to form the bond of solidarity, which sustained them through the hostilities of the 1930s? More than likely their situation would have followed in the pattern of other similar-sized cities that eliminated teachers from the rolls only to plead for their return later when shortages arose.

Chapter 6

PREGNANT BUT EQUAL:
THE FIGHT FOR MATERNITY RIGHTS

In the earliest decades of the 20th century, U.S. feminists were divided on issues relating to work and motherhood. Reformers, including many social feminists, considered much of the paid work performed by women, like that in sweatshops and factories, potentially harmful to women's health, especially during pregnancy. Their concerns led them to lobby local and state governments to create laws, called protective labor legislation, that limited women's hours, night work, and access to dangerous jobs. Key in the development of protective labor legislation was the 1908 case *Muller v. Oregon* in which the U.S. Supreme Court tried to settle conflicting findings by lower courts that variously struck down and upheld the validity of female-specific industrial labor legislation (Stetson, 1991). The Court found the state's interference in a woman's contractual powers was justified by its prevailing interest in the future health and well-being of her children. Though the Court claimed "that in the matter of personal and contractual rights [women] stand on the same plane as the other sex," it determined that woman's maternal role and its meaning for the greater good of the state justified the state's interference in the contractual freedoms of women. It noted in part:

> Her physical structure and proper discharge of her maternal functions—having in view not merely her own health, but the well-being of the race—justify legislation to protect her from [the] greed as well as the passion of man. The limitations which this statute places upon her contractual powers . . . are not imposed solely for her benefit, but also largely for the benefit of all. (Goldstein, 1988, p. 22)

Reformers welcomed the decision, finding it an important first step in a greater nationwide plan for the protection of both male and female industrial workers. With the help of these reformers, most notably representatives of the National Consumer League, *Muller v. Oregon* resulted in a wave of new or revitalized state labor legislation. By 1924, 43 states had laws restricting hours and/or night work for women. Eventually laws expanded to include mandatory meals and rest periods, restricted types of jobs, and even regulated lighting, ventilation, weight lifting, seating, washrooms, and toilet facilities. Several states also enacted legislation prohibiting women from working in the months before or after childbirth (Kessler-Harris, 1982, p. 181).

Though professional women sympathized with the unhealthful conditions faced by factory workers, they rejected such proscriptions being placed on their own occupations. Aligned with radical feminist sentiments, most preferred equal treatment under the law and contested the limits imposed on them as a special class of workers simply because of their reproductive potential. They argued that not all women would be mothers, that many were past their child-bearing years, and that not all workers suffered under the same kind of horrendous conditions found in the worst shops and factories. However, because professional women constituted only a small proportion of female workers, their protests were largely ignored in the halcyon days of reform in the 1920s. Thus professional women, in groups such as the BPWC, coalesced with radical feminists, such as the NWP, to demand their need be recognized by the state.

Some historians have attributed the resultant factionalization of working women in the 1920s and 1930s to class division or antifeminist sentiments. However, another position is that women simply divided, reasonably enough, along employment lines. That is, they viewed protective labor legislation from the perspective of their own careers. From this perspective they could see how well the legislation would help or hinder their admission to or advancement within that field. Although the majority of the NWP and BPWC members admittedly had middle-class careers or were "professionals," this did not necessarily imply a class antagonism with those who benefited from protective labor legislation. In fact, many female teachers were from working-class backgrounds, whereas some of the strongest advocates of protective labor laws were from the upper class and were not employed outside the home. Rather, the NWP and BPWC opposed protective labor legislation because of its short-sightedness in treating all female workers as having a similar need to be "protected."

This is also not to say that middle-class women disagreed with the long-term goals of protective labor legislation. As Goldstein (1988, p. 24) explains, protective labor reformers pursued a three-step strategy that would first gain protection for women, then establish minimum wage statutes, before finally extending all these advantages to men. Unfortunately, the strategy collapsed at phase two, leaving the country with a legacy of labor policies that, however inadvertent, led to false assumptions about the physical inability of women to work during pregnancy and only further inscribed Victorian notions about the impropriety of pregnant women appearing in public (Cott, 1987; Kessler-Harris, 1982, 1990).

These social attitudes, which existed well into the second half of the 20th century, not only proscribed working women's contractual rights but also unfairly stigmatized pregnant workers and mothers as careless, neglectful, or greedy. From the beginning of the century, teachers worked at the cutting edge of efforts to diminish such attitudes and to achieve the right to maternity leave.

EFFORTS FOR MATERNITY LEAVE IN NEW YORK CITY

The New York City public school teachers' fight for maternity leave provides a good illustration of the differences in feminist perspectives about the appropriate place of work in women's lives. Though teachers might have supported protections for pregnant factory workers, they steadfastly argued against the extension of such rules to their own work lives. Teachers claimed the right to maternity leave, the length of which was to be determined by themselves and their physicians, as well as the right to return to their positions without loss of status or pay. Though they were not able to achieve all these rights, their campaign preceded the more successful efforts of 1970s feminists by many decades.

The local New York City fight for teacher-mothers' rights brought together a broad coalition of women's groups representing both local social and radical feminist perspectives, including the League for the Civic Service of Women, the City Mothers' Club, the Women's Political Union, the Woman Suffrage Party (and by extension the National American Suffrage Association), the Women Lawyers' Club, and the Feminist Alliance. The coalition's most noted spokesperson was Henrietta Rodman, a high school English teacher at Wadleigh High School. Rodman, secretary of the League for the Civic Service of Women and a founding member of the New York City Feminist Alliance, dabbled in many radical feminist and socialist—if not utopian—schemes and dreams, including a feminist apartment house. This structure, based on the economic theories of Charlotte Perkins Gilman, would have freed the professional woman from the drudgery of housekeeping and child-rearing while allowing her time to pursue her career and family on the same basis that her husband enjoyed. Such a plan, though not embraced by a wide segment of the population, denotes the stimulating intellectual, cultural, social, and political fusion in the feminist community of New York City during this period. And it was largely owing to the willingness of diverse women's groups to co-alesce on single issues that made the teacher-mother victory possible.

The Great Mother–Teacher Debate

On November 29, 1911, Abraham Stern, chair of the New York City Board of Education, announced the board's intention to begin barring women with small children from teaching in the local public schools. He noted: "A married woman's sphere is the home, if she has a family. A woman who has infant children to rear has no business trying to take care of these and at the same time teach school" ("Bar Out Teachers," 1911, p. 13).

Just hours before this announcement, the board's Elementary School Committee had formally suspended four young mothers on the charge of chronic absenteeism. Stern acted immediately in his recommendation of a by-law that he felt would prevent any future abuses. When asked by a *New York Times* reporter if a teacher could return to her job after the child had grown, Stern replied, "Yes, if she resigned and later came up to the regular requirements imposed on former teachers who returned to work. However, if she were discharged for cause it is improbable that she could ever be reinstated" ("Bar Out Teachers," 1911, p. 13). Stern left no doubt that deciding whether a woman should teach or stay at home with her child belonged to the board, not to the woman or even to her doctor. The message was clear: If she did not leave on her own volition, she would lose not only her job but any future possibility of working in the local public schools.

The New York City school board was not alone in creating regulations that prevented mothers of young children from teaching (a rule that did not extend to fathers). In May 1910, the Chicago Board of Education formally adopted Section 94 of Article 5, which stated: "No mother with a child under two years of age shall be appointed to a position as teacher." A similar rule applied to teachers in Indianapolis, where mothers could not return to teaching until their youngest reached his or her second birthday. Even then her return required her to begin again at the bottom of the pay scale. A 1914 survey of 48 U.S. cities with populations over 100,000 found 37 prevented the employment of women after marriage. Of the other 11, only 3—Cincinnati, Los Angeles, and Milwaukee—instituted policies granting leaves of absence for childbirth. Both Los Angeles and Milwaukee limited the leave to 1 year, whereas Cincinnati stipulated no time limit ("Duties of Teachers," 1908).

Within only a few months of the New York City board's decision to suspend mothers, the case of Lily R. Weeks hit the news. Weeks, a teacher for P.S. 84 in Long Island City, received notice of her suspension and charges against her for neglect of duty. Weeks had applied to her principal for a leave of absence, citing reasons of restoration of health, travel, and study. Her application was approved and forwarded to the district superintendent, Seth Stewart. However, just a few days before giving birth, Weeks received a notice of suspension that declared that she had attempted to obscure the real reason for her leave. A hearing was set on the day after the child's birth. Although she requested an extension so that she could attend the hearing, her request was denied. Yet a final vote on the case was not taken until almost 10 months later. The delay was, reportedly, due to the illness of one of the committee members ("Lost Job," 1913). In the interim, another woman, Catherine Campbell Edgell, who taught physical culture at Erasmus High School in Brooklyn, applied for a year's leave without pay so that she could give birth and then nurse her child. Perhaps because her request was unprecedented or because several of the members of the Committee on High Schools were friends of Edgell and her husband, the committee approved the petition. Dr. Ira S. Wile headed the committee and became the only board of education member who steadfastly supported the rights of the teacher-mothers. When the committee forwarded its approval to the board of education chair, Abraham Stern, he made a motion that the board refuse to even discuss the concept of providing leaves to pregnant teachers. By ignoring Edgell's plea for leave, the board forced her to take a leave without permission, thus creating grounds for her dismissal.

Henrietta Rodman

The news of the board's treatment of the teacher-mothers aroused the feminist sentiments of many in the local community. Henrietta Rodman, a vocal advocate of what became known as the "silent agreement" among married women in the public schools, felt that a woman's marital status should be of no consequence to her professional life as a teacher. Those who agreed protected each other's secret marriages. In spite of the state commissioner's previous ruling that a woman teacher could not be removed from her position for getting married, the board still insisted on immediate notification of any change in the marital status of women in their employ. Rodman protested against this position publicly, fervently, and much to the chagrin of the board of education.

She further encouraged the board's wrath on March 18, 1913, when she announced that she had married without giving the board notice. She broke the news to the press at a league meeting that was held to discuss its advocacy of the teacher-mothers. She explained her action:

The moment a woman teacher announces her marriage she puts herself, no matter what her abilities may be, in a class that is not in line for promotion. The only way a teacher can protect her interests is to keep silent as long as she can whether or not she is married. ("Aided Mrs. Edgell," 1913, p. 8)

With this admission she firmly aligned the already natural allies of married teachers and teacher-mothers. Immediately, members of the league expressed concern that Rodman had given the board ample cause for her dismissal. But, uncharacteristically, the board did not take advantage. The day after Rodman's admission, Stern responded contemptuously to queries from reporters about Rodman's future: "Whenever a woman marries she cannot keep the fact from her associates. . . . It has been our experience that no woman can keep a secret from a woman friend" ("Won't Act," 1913, p. 22).

The board's apparent leniency did not encourage reciprocity from Rodman who, with the league, announced plans to wage a campaign intended "to make the Board of Education and every one else in the city and the state realize that bearing a child is a civic service and that discrimination by the Board of Education or any employer is wrong" ("Motherhood Held as Civic Service," 1913, p. 25). Among the league's strategies was to obtain endorsements for their cause from various organizations throughout the state. When the City Mothers Club announced it would join the coalition, the league knew that they would have little trouble attracting a diversity of women from various political and social perspectives ("Motherhood and Teaching," 1913; "Penalizing Motherhood," 1913).

By this time the league had found another case that would draw attention and sympathy to the cause when teacher Bridgett Peixotto received notice of her suspension (Young, 1914). In February, she sent a letter from her physician to her principal notifying him of her absence due to a nose and ear infection. However, "an anonymous writer" revealed the real reason for her absence was childbirth. Her dismissal presented the board with an opportunity to issue a report containing opinions on several issues related to teacher-mothers, including their deleterious effect on older girls in the schools:

It is within our knowledge that in the congested districts, and in the crowded tenements, whence come many of our pupils, conditions which exist preclude all possibility of privacy and reserve. Natural reserve is a girl's greatest charm. . . . Can this teaching be given by those whose very presence in the school is in violation of the very laws of reserve? ("Minutes of the Board for June 25, 1913," 1913, p. 1169)

The rest of the report contained similar personal opinions and anecdotal evidence. Apparently the board felt the opinions of the five men and one woman committee mirrored those of society at large. Throughout the report the board placed emphasis on the welfare of others—the schoolchildren, the teacher's child, the unemployed—without ever admitting that the regulation might also restrain women's salaries through the dismissal of more senior faculty, as women generally waited longer to marry and have children than did their male colleagues. Nor did they ever seek substantial outside expert opinion on maternal health or solicit comments from the teachers themselves.

Many teachers were incensed by the board's actions. They pointed out that as an 18-year veteran, Peixotto was only 2 years away from a full pension. But the board's only response was to undertake an investigation of other possible cases. They followed closely the lives of women who had recently reported marriages, considering each a likely suspect for similar transgressions ("Dr. Elliot," 1913; "Minutes of the Board of June 25, 1913," 1913). This, of course, further suppressed the desire of teachers to share information about their nuptials.

A VICTORY FOR THE TEACHER-MOTHERS

In November of 1913, the feminist community celebrated the news that Bridgett Peixotto had won a peremptory writ of mandamus that compelled the board to return her to her job. Justice Seabury of the state appeals court wrote in part:

> Married women becoming lawfully employed as teachers and excusable for absence caused by personal illness, the idea that because the illness resulting in absence is caused by maternity it therefore becomes "neglect of duty" is repugnant to the law and good morals. (*People ex rel Peixotto v. Board of Education of the City of New York*, 1913)

Upon hearing the decision, the conservative *New York Times* characteristically editorialized:

> Obviously our public school system is a victim of that comparatively new and distressing malady called feminism. . . . This woman is representative of a new order. She claims the right to hold her place in the public service when she is obviously unfit to perform the duties attached to it. ("Teacher's Right to Motherhood," 1913, p. 1051)

Days later, 800 people attended a meeting sponsored by the League for the Civic Service of Women at the Cooper Union to celebrate Peixotto's victory and to protest the board's continued prosecution of cases against other teachers. Harriet Burton Laidlaw, a former English teacher and Manhattan Borough chair of the Woman Suffrage Party, cautioned the audience that the fight was far from over and that Seabury's decision might be reversed in a higher court. Beatrice Forbes Robertson Hale, president of the league, applauded its efforts, claiming that their stand on behalf of the teacher-mothers made them "the most radical organization in the feminist movement" ("Find Mothers," 1913, p. 20). The cause of woman suffrage, she said, was almost conservative in comparison. Norman Hapgood, editor of *Collier's Weekly*, claimed that the feminist movement was "a revolt against the medieval estimate of womanhood which regarded woman as an inferior being and condemned her to household labor and menial tasks" (p. 20). Dr. James P. Warbasse, a well-respected New York City surgeon, condemned what he called "the social hypocrisy which regarded child-bearing as something to be ashamed and avoided" (p. 20). Edwin Slosson, editor of the *Independent*, explained that the New York City teachers fought not "for a strange principle" (p. 20) but one already possessed by teachers in Russia, France, and Great Britain. Other prominent voices came to the defense of the teacher-mothers, including educator-philosopher John Dewey, Reverend Howard Mellish, Reverend Anna Howard Shaw, actor Fola La Follette, and Columbia University Professor James T. Shotwell.

In October 1914, the teacher-mothers' coalition received news of a case that they hoped would settle the issue once and for all. Henrietta Rodman announced that she had been in contact with a pregnant teacher who intended to postpone her dismissal by remaining in the classroom for as long as she could. In doing so, Rodman explained, the teacher would embarrass the board, who contended that pregnant women were physically incapable of teaching properly. The press soon revealed that the woman, Lora Wagner, a teacher at Curtis High School, gave birth only 13 hours after leaving her last class. While in the hospital, she mailed a request for a leave to her school and an appeal to the mayor, asking him to use his influence in the matter. Somewhat unexpectedly, the board granted the leave, whereas the mayor responded that he didn't want to become involved ("Leave for Mother," 1914; "A Married Teacher's Ruse," 1914; "Teacher Becomes Mother," 1914; "Teacher Mother Appeals," 1914; "Teacher-Mother to Mayor," 1914).

The teachers pursued a ruling at the state level in an effort to remove the issue from the board's case-by-case approach. They wanted a guaranteed maternity leave that would allow them to return to their former positions when their doctors advised. In December, the question went before New York State Assistant Commissioner of Education Thomas E. Finnegan, who heard the cases of six teachers, reinstated one, and denied three. He refused to hear the cases of Lora Wagner and another teacher because he felt that they had not exhausted all other remedies before appealing to him ("Miss Rodman's Pen Again Jabs Board," 1914; "Teacher Mothers Case," 1914). In the meantime, the board had arrived at a compromise measure allowing for maternity leaves for a mandatory period of 2 years. Although many, including Rodman, protested that the time was excessive, they celebrated their Pyrrhic victory. Over the next few years, they fought to have the mandatory maternity leave decreased, and to have it determined by only the woman and her physician. But their pleas were ignored.

It was not until labor shortages during World War I began to shrink the teacher work force that the New York City public schools began to ignore pregnancy and motherhood in their hiring and leave practices. And this was only for the duration. The irony of U.S. Commissioner of Education Dr. P. P. Claxton's appeals to married women to return to teaching, out of sense of patriotism, did not go unnoticed by feminists, including those at the *Woman's Citizen* (formerly the *Woman's Journal*). The editor summarized the situation:

> Fashions in teachers change, if one waits long enough, like fashions in hats. Only three years ago the idea of marriage in connection with a woman school teacher so revolted the taste of the masculine school boards of New York state that the married woman teacher was either driven into hiding the guilt of matrimony or was hounded out of her position. The distaste against her ran so high that the public consciousness had some difficulty in determining whether it was the married state, maternity itself, or their mere conjunction in the person of a woman teacher, which was so scandalous. The situation was more anomalous in a state, which chanted the duty of maternity and the beauty of wifehood as reasons for not giving woman the vote. ("Now the Married Teacher," 1918, p. 367)

The *Woman Citizen* presented an accurate assessment not only of the period but also of several decades to come. Changing economic and social forces saw mothers being pushed out of the classroom only to be enticed back almost every other decade. In the Depression of the 1930s, mothers belonged at home with their children, but in the post–World War II labor shortages, mothers again became ideal teachers of a burgeoning student population.

FEDERAL LEGISLATION AND THE PREGNANT WORKER

After World War I, social feminists lobbied intently for the Sheppard-Towner Act of 1921, which provided the first major piece of federal social legislation in the United States as well as the first successful federal lobbying effort by now enfranchised women. The act gave funds to states to provide for the health and welfare of mothers and their children, regardless of the mother's work or economic status. Though funding for the act stopped after the start of the Depression in 1929, it had already done much to insinuate its protectionist theories into the public consciousness and the policies of the federal Women's Bureau. The Women's Bureau joined with the Children's Bureau in 1942 to pressure public and private employers to institute a maternal health standard that limited work hours of pregnant and nursing mothers, required on-the-job rest periods, and set 6 weeks of prenatal and 2 months of postnatal leave ("Maternity Legislation," 1930). Though never enacted into law, the standard was incorporated by some of the more "progressive" U.S. companies and institutions.

Radical feminists, as represented by the BPWC and the NWP, opposed the Sheppard-Towner Act and similar protectionist bills. Concerned that the act treated all women as potential mothers who required and desired its protection and assistance, the BPWC and the NWP believed that women would not be truly free until society allowed absolute equality in the treatment of both genders (Stetson, 1991). As a result, the BPWC and the NWP advocated a different approach to women's rights as embodied in a new bill, the ERA, that would amend federal and state constitutions to provide a basis for the *equal* treatment of women under the law.

First introduced into the 68th Congress in 1923, the ERA would have eliminated thousands of laws at the state and federal levels that allowed for differential treatment of women in matters relating to work, family, and government. Organizations such as the League of Women Voters (LWV) (the successor of the NAWSA), though in favor of some changes in sex-biased legislation, feared that the whole-scale abolition of protective labor legislation would harm far more women than it helped (Chafe, 1991; Lindgren & Taub, 1988). These differing points of view examined the question of whether women were fundamentally different from men. The reformers, as historian Susan Hartmann (1989) points out, believed there was a critical difference: "Women's maternal roles, along with their weaker physical constitutions, necessitated laws which regulated the conditions of their employment" (p. 129). Those in favor of the ERA felt that a special status for women almost always resulted in inferior treatment.

Historians have noted that social welfare reformers portrayed NWP and BPWC members as upper-class professionals with little regard for the working conditions of the masses of women. Reformer Molly Dewson sneered: "Some of these hard-boiled females seem to forget the virtues of generosity and sympathy for the underprivileged." And U.S. Secretary of Labor Frances Perkins agreed: "There is one whole group of women who is always greatly excited about the word 'equality.' You make them equal and that suits them splendidly" (Ware, 1982, p. 109). Embedded in such criticisms was the belief that class antagonism was responsible for the rift between pro- and anti-protective labor legislation activists. And though teaching (the largest occupation among this latter group) was considered a middle-class occupation, few, if any, teachers felt antagonism toward their factory sisters. In fact, a large proportion of teachers were born to working-class families and knew well the conditions under which the "underprivileged" were employed (Hartmann, 1982; Ware, 1982). Rather, the differences in political perspectives derived from their educational and employment experiences in working and competing on the same level as their male colleagues. Too, as a critical mass within the female professional class, they felt that they deserved a right to have their employment needs considered.

The ERA did not pass, nor was there significant progress in abolishing sex-biased laws through the piecemeal strategy advocated by the LWV. Thus between the two world wars teachers continued to struggle, mostly on a district-to-district basis, to expand their rights as married women and working mothers. Courts often provided the only relief women found in the ever-shifting social and economic attitudes about married teachers and teacher-mothers. J. S. Brubacher (1927), in researching the attitude of the courts on work, marriage, and maternity in the late 1920s, found that the most important cases involved teacher-plaintiffs. He pointed out the inherent conflict between the concept of "modern education [as an avenue to] the liberation of [the] personality" and the limits continually placed on their adult roles. "There is thus, an inconsistency between the way girls are educated and the extent to which they may profit by it" (pp. 428–429). Although educational and work opportunities were expanding for women, social attitudes confined their employment to far shorter periods than those experienced by men.

Compared with other countries in Europe, South America, and Africa, the United States lagged in developing rational policies involving pregnant women's work rights. The 1929 International Labor Conference drafted an agreement that signing countries would provide women in commerce and industry (teachers were not specifically covered) the right to a 6-week maternity leave before and after the birth, and protection of her position during her leave ("Maternity Legislation," 1930, pp. 53–56). The United States was not a signatory.

A new federal conceptualization of work and maternity emerged in the 1960s as the Women's Bureau broke from its protectionist past and began to work for the Equal Pay Act, a first step in eliminating sex discrimination in the workplace. Working closely with President Kennedy's new Commission on the Status of Women and its descendent, the Citizen's Advisory Council on the Status of Women, the Women's Bureau eventually adopted the earlier radical feminist concept of pregnancy (as seen in the New York City campaign) as a temporary disability that should not impinge on a woman's workplace rights. But employers objected to this definition on several grounds. Some claimed that pregnancy was not a disability due to accident or disease but rather a normal and usually voluntary disposition. They also pleaded that coverage of pregnancy would prove too costly, especially if covered by disability and health insurance benefits. Also, some argued that many pregnant women did not return to work after childbirth, unlike those workers with "true" temporary disabilities (Rupp & Taylor, 1987; Stetson, 1991). But the days in which employers could view women as a temporary and insignificant work force were numbered.

THE BABY BOOM AND TEACHER-MOTHERS

Serious teacher shortages began during World War II and continued afterward, increasing to crisis proportions in the 1950s. The profession suffered during the war as male and female teachers left the schools for more lucrative positions in war-related industries. The expanded job opportunities of the 1940s alerted the college-educated women of the 1950s to options outside of teaching. Assistant Professor of Education Isabel Stephens (1947, pp. 78–81) of Wellesley College examined why teaching was no longer the appealing career it once was. Calling the American school system a "huge new machine," she cited five forms of resistance expressed by undergraduate women to teaching careers. They believed that (1) good teachers are born, not made; (2) teaching is a safe, stodgy thing to do; (3) teachers have to be old maids; (4) teaching is dull and monotonous; and (5) getting a teaching certificate involved too many requirements.

In talking to women who left the teaching profession, she found five primary reasons for their departure: (1) lack of community support, (2) lack of intellectual interchange, (3) petty gossip in the schools, (4) objection to a system where scientific efficiency was valued over ideas, and (5) objection to the practice of firing women if they married. Women's increasing lack of interest in teaching combined with expanding options in other fields coincided with the baby boom to create a distinct opportunity for teacher workplace reform in the 1950s and 1960s.

With a new classroom of children reaching school age every 10 minutes, the elementary schools of the mid-1950s were swamped. By 1960, the high schools too would see the deluge. At least 100,000 more teachers would be needed to staff new classrooms to reduce overcrowding and replace the approximately 57,600 untrained persons teaching on emergency certificates (Wilson, 1957).

The teacher crisis reached proportions that some felt jeopardized U.S. national security during the cold war with the U.S.S.R. One writer (Fischer, 1956) in a letter to *Harper's* editors claimed that "already we are falling behind the Russians in the production of scientists, linguists, and mathematicians—a failure which could easily prove just as dangerous as a lag in turning out jet bombers or guided missiles" (p. 12). His suggestion? Draft college "girls" into a 2-year commitment to teach in grade schools. Letters soon appeared in subsequent issues responding to the idea. Most were against the draft, and several voiced confidence that the problem would be solved through less compulsory measures ("Teacher Shortage," 1956).

Alice K. Leopold, head of the U.S. Women's Bureau, offered an alternative. She pushed for hiring mothers to fill the gap. Leopold, a 44-year-old, middle-class suburbanite from Weston, Connecticut, and mother of two grown sons, commented that many of her friends had expressed envy of her working life. They had tired of their volunteer activities, committee meetings, and teas, and yearned for careers where they could use their college education. "Why," she asked, "not hire such women as teachers?" (Lake, 1956, p. 38).

In 1954, approximately 50,000 women were college graduates, 55 years or younger, and were neither employed nor caring for preschool children. That year Leopold and Dr. Samuel M. Brownell, U.S. Commissioner of Education, began promoting these women to fill the teacher shortage in talks to women's and teacher-educator groups. Although women's groups were enthusiastic, teacher-educators proved more skeptical, many doubting "the emotional stability" of women who would leave their homes for paid labor. "We're not running a mental-hygiene program for a bunch of restless middle-aged women," one professor commented (p. 38).

Despite such concerns, the Women's Bureau and the U.S. Office of Education established the Committee on New Teachers for the Nation's

Schools in August 1954 to promote "special intensive college courses to equip older women for teaching careers." Several model programs were set up, including one in Ohio that turned out some 250 new teachers in the first year, and others at the University of Southern California at Claremont, San Diego State University, and Wayne State University in Detroit.

Many of these programs screened potential teachers to determine their emotional stability. Temple University in Philadelphia put its applicants through a full-day battery of personality tests, and Wayne State turned down 40% of all applicants, feeling their motivation for teaching was not "psychologically sufficient." What were acceptable motives for teaching? Among successful applicants were idealistic mothers who felt a social responsibility to their communities, women who demonstrated a love of children, and those who wanted a career that allowed them to keep the same hours and vacations as their own children.

Somewhat surprisingly, salaries were thought to be another socially acceptable motivation. However, salaries probably presented as many difficulties as remedies for the new career women. Clare Louise Jameson of Katonah, New York (whose husband was a New York University professor), complained that the $300-a-year sitter bill took "an unpleasant bite" out of her annual salary of $3,900. Furthermore, her "double day" took its toll as each afternoon she had to decide whether to "make the beds, do the marketing, wash the laundry, prepare the dinner, or iron last week's wash." She admitted to seldom being in bed before 11 p.m. (Black & Miles, 1959, pp. 24–25). Additionally, many teachers had to contend with husbands' resentment about their wives' absence and new economic independence. Some men saw their wives' earning power as a subtle affront to their own.

Yet money remained a strong factor in attracting new teachers, according to a study discussed in a 1959 issue of the *National Parent-Teacher* (Black & Miles, 1959). But among other reasons, mothers included personal satisfaction, contribution to the community, a wish to use their college education, and opportunity to fill the "empty nest" years. Graduates of the Bank Street College of Education in New York City noted that they found their home and work lives mutually enhancing and that their husbands (for the most part) cooperated in and approved of their new jobs. Their greatest anxieties revolved around how they would care for a sick child, and how to get children and husbands to take on more responsibility in household chores.

By the end of the 1950s, husbands and children increasingly played a key role in the lives of young women. Seventy percent of all women married by the age of 24, compared with just 42% in 1940 and 50% in the later 1980s. The average marital age fell to a record low—men at 22 and women at 20—altering a 20th-century pattern in which men tended to marry in their mid- to late 20s, whereas women married in their early- to mid-20s. The 1950s also reversed the trend in fertility, as women gave birth earlier, more frequently, and to children closer in age than had their mothers. The fertility rate rose by 50% from 1940 to 1957. Nearly one third of all American women had their first child before the age of 20 (Mintz & Kellogg, 1989).

Married women in their 30s and 40s, specifically those with a college diploma and school-age children, became the natural targets of the nationwide drive for new teachers. In the 2 years between 1954 and 1956, some 5,000 to 10,000 were recruited. After decades wherein teacher-mothers were pushed out of the schools, now they were being touted as "superior" instructors. Schools particularly sought out the woman whose "liberal arts education had given her a rich scholastic background," whose instincts were "sharpened by raising children of her own," and whose "maturity ripened her wisdom and humor" (Lake, 1956, pp. 38–39; "Married Women Teachers," 1961). In 1953, married women teachers outnumbered unmarried for the first time in the nation's history (Attridge, 1953). Moreover, just over 40% of women teaching in this period were in their childbearing years (U.S. Census Bureau, 1964).

THE PSYCHOLOGICAL MOTIVATIONS OF FEMALE TEACHERS

As the number of teaching applications mounted, the psychological motivations of women teachers entertained researchers throughout the Freudian 1950s and 1960s. One example of such research asked the questions, "Why do women become teachers?" and "Why do they teach in high school or grade school?" This intensive study of childhood experiences of prospective female teachers tried to determine how childhood identification with adult role models informed their decisions to become teachers. The researchers believed that women chose a teaching career as a means of resolving childhood conflicts or reenacting unresolved conflicts through identification with their pupils. In essence, they suggested that those who chose elementary school teaching did so because of a desire to recreate a "romance" they had had with their fathers as children and/or to compensate for a disappointment in their relationships with their mothers. Those who became high school teachers did so to recreate a "romance" with a former teacher and/or to reenact an unhappy or unfulfilled relationship with her own parents. Somewhat ironically, the study found only nonteachers had positive, fulfilling relationships with their mothers.

And these women eschewed teaching for motherhood (Wright & Tuska, 1968).

Underlying such psychological inquiry was the belief that women worked not because they wanted to but because they had to, and that only dysfunctional women willingly gave up full-time homemaking for full-time careers. Psychologists, for the most part, were far more comfortable with programs that utilized young mothers as "volunteer" teachers' aides, playground monitors, tutors, and clerical assistants because these roles fit within the expected framework of women as altruists (Levenson, 1967). Society's continued unease with economically independent married women paralleled the growing restlessness and repression of women cited by Betty Friedan and others in this period.

Psychologists generally encouraged the belief that marriage was a necessary part of a fulfilled adult role. Those who avoided this commitment were accused of "homosexuality," "emotional immaturity and infantile fixations," "unwillingness to assume responsibility," and/or "narcissistic pursuit of career ambitions." Of these possibilities it was the latter, the narcissistic pursuit of career ambitions, that was most often attributed to women who sought outside employment opportunities during marriage and motherhood. One bestseller, the *Modern Woman: The Lost Sex*, admonished that careers would lead to the "masculinization of women with enormously dangerous consequences to the home, the children dependent on it, and the ability of the woman, as well as her husband, to obtain sexual gratification" (Mintz & Kellogg, 1989, pp. 181–182).

During this time, a postwar economic boom facilitated a move to suburbia and promoted greater consumerist urges. By 1960, 31 million out of 44 million families owned their own homes, and 75% had a car in the garage. The suburbs accounted for 64% of the nation's population growth. Because of the demands of commuting, fathers spent little time with their families. Mothers isolated in their bungalows tended to focus on children to the exclusion of their own personal and intellectual development. This dovetailed with psychological theories that stressed the essential importance of early childhood development, to magnify the apprehensions and restlessness experienced by mothers (Meyerowitz, 1994; Mintz & Kellogg, 1989). Thus the solution proposing young mothers as saviors of the schools generated complex reactions.

TEACHER-MOTHERS IN THE 1970S AND BEYOND

The decades between 1950 and 1980 experienced a virtual revolution regarding social attitudes about women, motherhood, and employment.

Although only about 10% of women with preschool-age children were employed in 1950, almost half of this entire cohort were engaged in the labor force by the early 1970s (Lindgren & Taub, 1988, p. 109). The significance of the introduction of large percentages of women into the work force can be seen in accompanying federal legislation including the Equal Pay Act of 1963; the Executive Order of 1968 (which required federal contractors to adopt affirmative action employment policies); Title VII of the Civil Rights Act and Title IX of the Education Amendments of 1972 (which covered sex discrimination in employment and federally funded educational institutions, respectively); and the formation of the Equal Employment Opportunity Commission (EEOC). This legislation sought to remedy the government's decades-long inability to set a realistic approach to women's employment rights. This legislation, although not instantly and vigorously enforced, did eventually prove useful in several milestone cases involving teacher-mothers, the most significant being *Cleveland Board of Education v. LaFleur* (1973) and *Cohen v. Chesterfield County Board* (1971).

By 1970, the women's movement had penetrated society's consciousness with a force unseen in the previous five decades. The meaning that this held for teacher-mothers, and schools in general, was palpable in that national women's groups such as the Women's Education Equity League (WEAL) and NOW dedicated themselves to seeing the enforcement of the new federal legislation that guaranteed women fair treatment in employment and education. Schools bore the greatest scrutiny because they were the most accessible and ubiquitous institutions that received federal funding. In 1970, one third of all women leaving the teaching profession did so for reasons related to maternity (*Status of American Public School Teachers*, 1972), despite the fact that Title IX specified: "Leaves of absence and fringe benefits must be offered to pregnant employees as they are offered to temporarily disabled."

If teachers looked to their two national teacher organizations, the American Federation of Teachers (AFT) and the NEA, for assistance, they were certainly disappointed. Researchers Fishel and Pottker (1973) found that neither the national nor the local unions "actually fought hard for the reform of maternity policies in their contract negotiations" (p. 41). They also accurately predicted: "If forced maternity leave is overthrown it will be due to the efforts of individual teachers and not to the efforts of teacher organizations" (p. 41). It was the individual teachers who jeopardized their jobs and reputations to test unjust maternity policies and spent years of their lives seeing the cases through the various levels of the judiciary along with the assistance of women's organizations such as WEAL and NOW.

A case in point was *Cleveland Board of Education v. La Fleur*. During the 1970–71 school year, Cleveland public school teachers Jo Carol LaFleur and Ann Elizabeth Nelson each reported her pregnancy to her local school board as required by a rule first adopted in 1952. The rule required a pregnant woman to begin a nonpaid maternity leave 5 months prior to the expected birth of her child. Application for leave had to be filed no later than 2 weeks before her date of departure. The teacher was also prevented from returning to work before her child was 3 months old, and then only at the beginning of the next regular school semester following that date. A doctor's certification testifying to her good health was an additional prerequisite to her return. The school did not guarantee that the teacher could return to her former position or even reemployment after the birth of her child, but merely that she would be given priority consideration should a position for which she was qualified open up. Failure to comply with the mandatory leave provisions provided grounds for dismissal.

Neither LaFleur nor Nelson wanted to take an unpaid maternity leave. Both were early enough in their pregnancies that they could finish the semester before leaving to give birth. They requested that they be allowed to stay on until the end of the school year, but each was required to leave in March 1971. The two women then filed separate suits in the U.S. District Court in Ohio challenging the constitutionality of the maternity-leave rule. The district court tried the cases together and rejected the plaintiffs' pleas. However, this finding was reversed on appeal, when the Sixth Circuit Court held that the Cleveland school board had violated the Equal Protection Clause of the Fourteenth Amendment.

About this same time, a similar plea was being heard in the U.S. District Court in Virginia. In this case, Susan Cohen, a teacher employed by the school board of Chesterfield County, Virginia, informed her board in November 1970 that she was pregnant. County policy regarding maternity provisions for women teachers required Cohen notify the school board at least 6 months in advance of the expected birth and resign 4 months prior to delivery. Job termination could be delayed only under special conditions and with written recommendations from the pregnant teacher's physician, her principal, and the superintendent. She could then be reemployed on the first day of the next school year with written certification from her physician and only if she previously had a record of satisfactory performance. She would not be returned to her former position but had to accept an offer for the first vacancy available.

Similar rules covered most U.S. teachers. Those fortunate enough to be allowed a maternity leave were not guaranteed that they could return to their former position or to any position at all. Yet male teachers were almost always guaranteed a position on their return from military service or a disabling illness. Furthermore, because maternity was not considered a medical problem, teachers could not use their paid sick-leave days for childbirth. As a result, one third of all women who left the profession permanently did so because of such requirements (Fishel & Pottker, 1973, p. 20). Ironically, this led to the most consistent complaint about women teachers: They weren't dedicated to the profession.

In fact, it was the educational institution's lack of dedication to its workers that created this condition. As was the case in most of society's other occupations, education continued to be guided by men who were insensitive to the needs of their female employees. In 1970, only one state superintendent in 50 was a woman, only 18% of the members of the 50 state boards were female, and only just over 0.5% of the 14,379 local superintendents of schools were women. Women held only 1 in 10 school board positions, and 56% of all local school boards had no female members at all. To compound the problem, until 1970, no woman ever served in any major policy-making position in the U.S. Office of Education. Although two thirds of all teachers were women, 85% of all principals were men.

While women might have entered teaching with aspirations to become administrators, the reality soon set in and few bothered to obtain the necessary academic credentials to do so. Although women received three quarters of all the bachelor's degrees in education, they obtained only half of all the master's degrees and one fifth of all the doctorates in education. Single women teachers sought the greater number of advanced degrees and moved more readily into administrative positions than did married women (Fishel & Pottker, 1973; Simpson & Simpson, 1969). Clearly, maternity and stellar careers in education were not viewed as companionate. Moreover, maternity was seen as something best not seen. Administrators voiced the concern that students would ask inappropriate questions and get "ideas" if they were to see their teachers in advanced stages of pregnancy. It is surprising that few questioned the rationality of this position, especially in light of the fact that many children had pregnant mothers at home.

It was this environment that Cohen faced when she requested permission to continue teaching to within a month before giving birth. The school board rejected this request, as it did her subsequent petition that she be allowed to teach until the end of the first semester, which ended on January 21, 1971. Instead she was forced to leave her position on December 18, 1970, only a month before the end of the semester. In the trials that followed, the U.S. District Court held that the Virginia school board had violated the Equal Protection Clause of the Fourteenth Amendment, but the appeals court reversed this decision. In order to resolve the apparent conflict in the findings by the two U.S. Courts of Appeals (the LaFleur/Nelson cases and the Cohen case), the U.S. Supreme Court granted a hearing on the constitutionality of such mandatory leaves for public school teachers.

In this case, cited as *Cleveland Board of Education v. LaFleur*, the Court heard all three cases together. The Court noted that the school boards offered "two essentially overlapping explanations" (p. 53) for the mandatory maternity leaves. First, they claimed that the leaves were necessary to maintain continuity of classroom instruction, because advanced warning of the teacher's impending leave helped facilitate the finding and hiring of her replacement. Second, the schools argued that some teachers were physically inadequate to the job of teaching during the final months of pregnancy, and thus the leave helped protect that teacher and her unborn child while assuring the schoolchildren of a capable teacher ("Cleveland Board of Education," 1973). In scrutinizing these explanations the Court, although agreeing that the continuity of instruction was a significant and legitimate educational goal, nevertheless asked the litigants to look at the case of *Green v. Waterford Board of Education* (1973). That case exposed the real intent of mandated maternity leave as in part "to insulate schoolchildren from the sight of conspicuously pregnant women." The Court in this case noted, "Whatever may have been the reaction in Queen Victoria's time, pregnancy is no longer a dirty word" (p. 53). The Court also found that the arbitrary cut-off dates laid out in the mandatory leave policies had "no rational relationship to the valid state interest of preserving continuity of instruction" (p. 53). In the cases of both LaFleur and Nelson, each was required to leave with only a few months left in the school year, even though both were willing and apparently able to continue to teach until the end of their contract year. This scenario, the Court stated, would have been far more in keeping with the school board's desire to keep continuity of instruction than was the situation resulting from the forced leave.

The majority opinion of the Court also held that the school board's mandatory maternity policy had contained "an irrebuttable presumption of physical incompetency, and that presumption applies even when the medical evidence as to an individual woman's physical status might be wholly to the contrary" (p. 56). Further, Justice Stewart noted in a footnote to the majority opinion that the factual hypothesis of such a presumption—that no mother is physically fit to return to work until her child reaches the age of 3 months—"is neither necessarily nor universally true" (p. 56). In summary, the U.S. Supreme Court found:

The mandatory termination provisions of Cleveland and Chesterfield County maternity regulations violate the Due Process Clause of the Fourteenth Amendment because of their use of unwarranted conclusive presumptions that seriously burden the exercise of protected constitutional liberty. For similar reasons, we hold the three months' provision of the Cleveland return rule unconstitutional. (p. 61)

Although in agreement with the result, Justice Powell, in writing the minority opinion, argued against the use of "irrebuttable presumption" (p. 61), suggesting instead that the case should have been based on the Equal Protection Clause of the Fourteenth Amendment of the Civil Rights Act (which specifically looks at sexual discrimination). But he concurred with the majority opinion, finding:

It appears that by forcing all pregnant teachers undergoing a normal pregnancy from the classroom so far in advance of term, the regulations compel large numbers of able-bodied teachers to quit work . . . such policies, inhibit, rather than further, the goal of continuity of teaching. (p. 63)

The Legal Legacy of LaFleur

A number of other important cases following the *LaFleur* decision attempted to clarify the judicial integrity of this view. These included *Phillips v. Martin Marietta* (1971) that held the refusal of private employers to hire women with preschool-age children to be in violation of Title VII of the 1964 Civil Rights Act. In *Turner v. Department of Employment Security of Utah* (1975), the U.S. Supreme Court followed the reasoning of *Cleveland v. LaFleur*, noting: "Freedom of personal choice in matters of marriage and family life is one of the liberties protected by the due process clause." In this case, the state denied women unemployment insurance during the last 3 months of pregnancy and the first 6 weeks following childbirth under the presumption that during this time women were unfit for gainful employment. The Court declared such a presumption an unconstitutional infringement on the right to privacy (Goldstein, 1988, p. 464).

Richmond Unified School District v. Berg (1977) considered the question of whether a school district was guilty of sex discrimination if it denied a female employee the use of accrued sick leave for pregnancy and childbirth. The case involved Sonja Berg, a Richmond, California, teacher, who on becoming pregnant filed suit and secured a temporary injunction to keep her district from enforcing two separate policies regarding pregnancy leave. The first required a pregnant teacher to cease working at a time determined by the school board rather than the woman or her doctor, and the second denied her use of any accrued sick leave for the pregnancy or childbirth. The case invoked Title VII of the Civil Rights Act of 1964, and the court agreed to issue a permanent injunction against the school's enforcement of these policies. On appeal, the court held that the school's policies violated a U.S. Equal Employment Opportunity Commission (EEOC) guideline that required employers to treat pregnancy the same as all other temporary disabilities.

The Richmond school board then appealed to the U.S. Supreme Court, but before the case could be heard the Court issued a decision in *General Electric Co. v. Gilbert* (1976). Here the Supreme Court held that disability programs that refused to cover pregnancy did not violate the Equal Protection Clause of the Fourteen Amendment. Justice Rehnquist, in the majority opinion, reasoned that pregnancy is a special condition of women only, and to provide disability coverage for this condition would, in fact, require discriminating against men. A similar rationale was used a year later, in 1977, when the Court examined another case, *Nashville Gas Company v. Satty* (1977), in which pregnant employees, but not those disabled for other reasons, were required to take unpaid leaves of absence and to lose job seniority upon their return. The Court permitted the mandatory unpaid maternity leave policy, but found the loss of seniority in violation of Title VII, reasoning that although pregnant women could be treated differently while pregnant, on return to their jobs they were again like men and required the same treatment (Williams, 1984). The Court considered *Berg* along with *Satty*, leaving open the possibility that sex discrimination could be proved if "it was shown that distinctions involving pregnancy are mere pretexts designed to effect an invidious discrimination against the members of one sex or the other." These cases were then sent back to the lower courts to determine if this condition existed (Flygare, 1978, pp. 558–559).

In another teacher-mother case, *Gedulig v. Aiello* (1974), the Supreme Court upheld the constitutionality of a state's right to exclude disabilities relating to normal pregnancy from the state disability insurance program coverage. Using the same logic applied in *General Electric v. Gilbert* (1976), the Court reasoned that such policies were not necessarily sex-based because they did not divide women from men but the pregnant worker from the nonpregnant worker (French, 1974; Trzinski & Alpert, 1994).

Federally Structuring Pregnancy Leave

Another approach to solving this dilemma came through the U.S. Department of Health, Education, and Welfare (HEW), which had tried to enforce a regulation regarding pregnancy leave issued under Title IX of the Education Amendments of 1972. The HEW regulation stated: "A recipient (i.e.

school district) shall treat pregnancy, childbirth, false pregnancy, termination of pregnancy, and recovery therefrom and any temporary disability resulting therefrom as any other temporary disability for job-related purposes." However, in *Romeo Community Schools (MI) v. HEW* (1979), a federal district court found that the HEW had no authority under Title IX to regulate the employment practices of school districts. The court argued that Congress intended Title VII of the Civil Rights Act of 1964 to cover school employment issues and not Title IX.

Title IX of the Education Amendments of 1972 specified that "no person in the United States shall, on the basis of sex, be excluded from participation in, be denied the benefits of, or subjected to discrimination under any educational program or activity receiving federal financial assistance." Worded exactly like Title VII of the Civil Rights Act except for the substitution of the word *sex* for *race*, this legislation opened the door through which feminists proposed to confront a variety of curricular and other educational grievances. Moreover, it provided teachers with specific protections by requiring "nondiscrimination in employment, criteria, recruitment, compensation, job classification and structure, fringe benefits, marital or parental status, advertising of jobs and handling of pre-employment inquiries" (Epstein & Hursh, 1985, pp. 27–28).

Title IX came about largely through the efforts of WEAL and its advisory board member Representative Edith Green, chair of the House Special Committee on Education. WEAL had its origins in NOW, which formed in 1968, when some delegates to the NOW annual convention, disturbed by NOW's pro-abortion rights stand, decided to start their own organization with a focus on educational equity. Their early strategies included advocating the implementation of Title IX as well as litigating against those institutions that abused it. Both WEAL and NOW had their work cut out for them. Title IX covered not only curriculum reform but educational access, equitable funding for curricular and extracurricular activities, employment, counseling, and a plethora of other issues probably not even considered when the bill first passed into law (O'Connor, 1977; Smith & Pingree, 1980).

Within a year of its passage, NOW learned that HEW officials had not been responsive to numerous complaints about Title IX violations by school systems across the country. After lengthy and circumvented efforts to obtain information from HEW about these complaints, NOW decided to do its own investigation. Using HEW's own records obtained through the Freedom of Information Act, NOW's Project for Equal Educational Rights (PEER) followed up on each complaint filed from the time of the law's enactment through October 1, 1976. They conducted interviews with HEW staffers, parent, student, and teacher complainants, and school administrators whose districts had been charged with the violation(s). PEER determined that HEW had failed its duty to implement, enforce, and respond to complaints in regard to Title IX.

Most common among the complaints were grievances filed by women about employment discrimination (564 out of 1,585). According to PEER, HEW managed to resolve only one out of five violations. Delays of 2 and 3 years were not uncommon and most investigations proved cursory at best. During this time HEW did independent checks on only 12 of the country's 16,000 school districts and did no follow-up on several nation-wide surveys that indicated the existence of many more Title IX violations. PEER concluded that indecision proved the major obstacle to action in that HEW failed to "issue clear and consistent rulings on important issues it considers controversial" (p. 4). For 10 months the department almost entirely stopped making any determination on cases, failing even to answer its mail, fearing any decision might prove controversial (Project on Equal Rights, 1977).

Given the courts' uncertainty about Title IX's relevancy to teacher employment issues, women's organizations looked to Congress to aid them in developing an explicit rule governing the treatment of pregnant workers. They did so in 1978 in an amendment to Section 701(k) of Title VII. Called the Pregnancy Discrimination Act (1978), the law tried to clarify the appropriate treatment of pregnancy in the workplace by explaining in part:

> The terms of "because of sex" or "on the basis of sex" include, but are not limited to, because of, or on the basis of pregnancy, childbirth, and related medical conditions. [Such conditions] shall be treated the same for all employment-related purposes, including [the] receipt of benefits under fringe benefit programs, as other persons not so affected but similar in their ability or inability to work. (Flygare, 1978, pp. 418–420)

The Pregnancy Discrimination Act provided the ground on which many new controversies were tested; for instance, the issue of whether separate-treatment statutes and disability policies that provided benefits for pregnancy and childbirth-related disabilities, but not for other disabilities, violated the law. In 1987, *California Federal Savings and Loan Association v. Guerra* (1987) tested this question. California Federal argued that the California statute mandated preferential treatment and was in violation of Federal law. However, the U.S. Supreme Court found that Title VII (as amended by the Pregnancy Discrimination Act) did not preempt the state statute. Rather, the Court noted that Congress had intended that the federal provision of the Pregnancy Discrimination Act "be a floor beneath which pregnancy disability benefits may not drop, not a ceiling above which they may rise." In 1990, the EEOC issued new guidelines that intended to allay confusion about the differences between pregnancy-related disability leave and parental leave. Three years later, President Clinton signed into law the Family and Medical Leave Act (FMLA) (U.S. Public Law 103–3), which extended the conditions and the period for employee leave to companies with at least 50 employees.

FMLA provided from 1 hour to 12 weeks unpaid leave to employees who had worked at least 1,250 hours in the last year with their current employer. It allowed leave for the birth or placement of a child for adoption or in foster care, the care of an immediate family member with a serious health condition, or the serious health condition of the employee. School systems, as public agencies, were covered by FMLA and all full-time elementary and secondary teachers met the 1,250-hour eligibility requirement. However, special conditions have been set by the law in reference to teacher's leave in order to minimize the "disruption factor" in classroom continuity. For example, an employer may transfer the employee temporarily to an alternative position with equivalent pay and benefits if the request is for an intermittent leave that would prove disruptive. A "disruptive leave" is defined as more than 20% of the total number of working days over the leave period. If a teacher normally works 5 days a week and requests 2-days-a-week leave for 6 weeks, this would be considered "disruptive leave." Special conditions also govern teachers taking leave in larger blocks of time. For instance, the law allows the employer of a teacher who takes a leave that begins less than 3 weeks before the end of the term to require that teacher to continue the leave until the end of the term (Wyld, 1995, pp. 301–307; see also Buell, 1996; Marczely, 1994; Scanlon, 1988; Simpson, 1993; Weidlich, 1995). Though a coherent federal understanding of many facets of pregnancy leave for teachers is still incomplete, most teachers still work under more specific regulations spelled out in state civil rights acts or in collective bargaining contracts.

The 1970s began with a reevaluation of women, work, and motherhood that continues today. Though both judicial opinion and federal and state laws now in place substantiate the pregnant teacher's right to work, public notions about the appropriateness of this still hold sway in actual day-to-day academic practices, forcing some teachers to leave the classroom sooner than they would like. Although women now compose almost half the nation's labor force, the system is far from accommodating. Women are still forced to make decisions that may ultimately impede their careers. In the 1980s, the concept of the "mommy track" emerged. The idea offered mothers the "opportunity" to move to a subordinate status in the workplace, where expectations and responsibilities—as well as advancement opportunities—would be less. Most women understandably rejected such proposals, feeling that agreement would brand them as less committed employees (Hopkins, 1990; Rose, 1992).

SUMMARY

During the 20th century, women's organizations as diverse as the Feminist Alliance, the City Mothers Clubs, the NWP, the BPWC, NOW, and WEAL supported a multitude of strategies to expand the rights of pregnant women teachers. These included public information campaigns; pressure groups to force local and state boards of education to eliminate gender-biased rules; appeals for the involvement of city and state government officials; test cases at the local, state, and federal judiciary levels; and federal legislation involving agencies such as the Women's Bureau, the Equal Employment Opportunity Commission, the Department of Education, and professional teachers' organizations such as the National Education Association and the American Federation of Teachers. Each approach tried to diminish the price paid by female employees for taking on the double burdens of family and workplace responsibilities. The success of these efforts has been informed by public opinion that was in turn influenced by the growing percentage of women in the work force at large as well as the efforts of women's rights organizations.

As more women became employees, the public tended to support issues such as paid maternity leaves. And as a rapidly growing percentage of mothers of preschool children entered the workplace in the 1970s and 1980s, public resistance to the concept of working mothers tended to subside. A secondary factor influencing public opinion has been the ebb and flow of the American economy and the national birthrate. Correspondingly, women were seen as either a burden to the labor force or a priceless commodity. In eras of teacher shortages, such as World War I, World War II, and the baby boom of the 1950s, the public and the school boards were willing to overlook pregnancy and motherhood as invalidating factors in the employment of women.

The case for maternity rights built slowly, incrementally, and substantially through the efforts of national women's organizations that kept their constituent groups apprised of tactics that could be utilized at both the national and local levels. Local groups were often able to personalize the issue by providing examples of individuals within the community who had experienced personal hardships because of such unjust regulations. Individuals bore the brunt of the stress, risk, and public antipathy involved in the struggle, but coalitions proved successful in swaying public opinion, raising funds for lawyers, and providing an esprit de corps necessary to revive weary colleagues over the long road to change.

Appendix

ORGANIZATIONS AND THEIR ACRONYMS

Below is a list of frequently noted organizations and their acronyms.

American Federation of Teachers (AFT)
American Teachers Association (ATA)
Association of Men Teachers and Principals (AMTP)
Chicago Federation of Teachers (CFT)
Cincinnati Men Teachers' Association (CMTA)
Cincinnati Teachers' Association (CTA)
Cincinnati Women Teachers' Association (CWTA)
Equal Employment Opportunity Commission (EEOC)
General Federation of Women's Clubs (GFWC)
Interborough Association of Women Teachers (IAWT)
Interborough Teacher's Association (ITA)
National Association for the Advancement of Colored People (NAACP)
National Association of Teachers in Colored Schools (NATCS)
National American Woman Suffrage Association (NAWSA)
National Association of Colored Women (NACW)
National Education Association (NEA)
National Federation of Business and Professional Women's Clubs (BPWC)
National Organization for Women (NOW)
National Woman's Party (NWP)
National Union of Women Teachers (NUWT)
New York Class Teachers' Association (NYCTA)
NOW's Project for Equal Educational Rights (PEER)
U.S. Department of Health, Education, and Welfare (HEW)
Women Teachers' Organization (WTO)
Women's Christian Temperance Union (WCTU)
Women's Educational Action League (WEAL)
Women's Political Union (WPU)
Women's Trade Union League (WTUL)
Young Women's Christian Association (YWCA)

REFERENCES

Ability unrelated to sex, women teachers say. (1935, January 17). *Cincinnati Post,* p. 9.

Accused of bad faith, refusal to confirm Miss Logan starts controversy. (1913, July 22). *Cincinnati Times Star,* p. 7.

Acker, S. (1992). Creating careers: Women teachers at work. *Curriculum Inquiry, 22,* 141–163.

Advertisement. (1902, May 17). *Woman's Journal, 33,* 156.

Aided Mrs. Edgell, married herself. (1913, March 19). *New York Times,* p. 8.

Alcoff, L. (1988). Cultural feminism versus post-structuralism: The identity crisis in feminist theory. *Signs, 13,* 405–436.

Alexander, A. L. (1993). Adella Hunt Logan. In D. C. Hine (Ed.) *Black women in America: An historical encyclopedia* (pp. 729–731). Bloomington: Indiana University Press.

Alexander, C. (1910). *Some present aspects of the work of teacher voluntary associations in the United States.* New York: Teachers College, Columbia University.

Alice Rower and Emily Wheeler at the Ohio teachers' association in a misleading headline. (1913, July 10). *Everywoman, 1,* 8.

Allen, S. L. (1988). Progressive spirit: The Oklahoma and Indian Territory Federation of Women's Clubs. *Chronicles of Oklahoma, 66,* 4–21.

Allen, W. H. (1911). *Woman's part in government: Whether she votes or not.* New York: Dodd, Mead.

Alliance of teachers rent by dissension. (1906, December 9). *New York Times,* p. 1.

A long way to reach the maximum. (1915, November). *School Index, 2,* 5.

Anonymous. (1937, September). I am the victim of a school board. *Independent Woman, 16,* 281, 300.

Anonymous. (1938, December). Are married women people? *Independent Woman, 17,* 376–378, 396.

The antis and the teachers. (1902, May 17). *Woman's Journal, 33,* 6.

Apple, M. W. (1985). Teaching and "women's work": A comparative historical and ideological analysis. *Teachers College Record, 86,* 457–471.

Apple, M. W. (1993). In K. Casey, *I answer with my life: Life histories of women teachers working for social change* [foreword]. New York: Routledge.

Association of Men Teachers and Principals of New York City. (1907). Argument against the White Bill, some resolutions: The economic talley of equalization theory [a political curricular distributed in the New York City area in 1907]. Held by the New York City Public Library, special collections.

Atlanta teachers want better pay, Georgia men tell them they need the ballot. (1911, March 4). *Woman's Journal, 42,* 165.

Attridge, R. (1953, July 25). Old maid schoolma'ams had their pleasant side. *Saturday Evening Post, 226,* 10–11.

Backie v. Cromwell Consolidated School District (Minnesota), No. 13, 242 N. W. 389 (April 1932).

Baker v. School District (Nebraska), 233 N. W. 897 (1931).

Baldwin, M. L. (1915). Votes for teachers. *Crisis, 10,* 1.

Banner, L. W. (1974). *Women in modern America: A brief history.* New York: Harcourt, Brace & Jovanovich.

Bar Mrs. Belmont's prizes: Board of education won't permit high school essay contest. (1910, January 16). *New York Times,* p. 7.

Bar out teachers with small babies. (1911, November 30). *New York Times,* p. 13.

Bayard, V. (1947, April). Sidelight on the teacher shortage. *Independent Woman, 26,* 107–108.

Beecher, C. (1858). *Treatise on domestic economy.* New York: Harper & Brothers.

Beecher, C., & Stowe, H. B. (1869). *The American woman's home.* New York: J. B. Ford.

Berkeley, K. C. (1984). The ladies want to bring about reform in the public schools: Public education and women's rights in the post–civil war south. *History of Education, 24,* 45–58.

Berkeley, K. C. (1985). Colored ladies also contributed: Black women's activities from benevolence to social welfare, 1866–1896. In W. Fraser, Jr. (Ed.), *The web of south social relations: Women, family & education* (pp.181–203). Athens: University of Georgia Press.

Bertaux, N. E. (1994). Exploring the connections among gender, race, and ethnicity in the public schools of the 19th century Cincinnati, Ohio. *Humanity & Society, 18,* 37–48.

Biklen, S. K. (1978). The progressive education movement and the question of women. *Teachers' College Record, 80.*

Biklen, S. K. (1995). *Schoolwork: Gender and the cultural construction of teaching.* New York: Teachers College Press.

Black hand to suffragists. (1912, May 24). *New York Times,* p. 2.

Black, I. S., & Miles, B. (1959, March). Look who's teaching—Mother! *National Parent-Teacher, 53,* 24–26.

Black, R. A. (1936, January). Repeal section 213. *Independent Woman, 15,* 19, 28–29.

Blackwell, A. S. (1905, October 31). Do teachers need the ballot? *Woman's Journal, 36,* 174.

Blackwell, A. S. (1909, July 1). Do women teachers need the vote? *Journal of Education, 75,* 8.

Blair, K. J. (1980). *Clubwoman as feminist: True womanhood redefined, 1868–1914.* New York: Holmes & Meier.

Blair, K. J. (1989). *The history of American women's voluntary organizations, 1810–1960: A guide to sources.* Boston: G. K. Hall.

Blair v. United States ex rel. Hellman, 45 District of Columbia Appeals 353 (1916).

Blake, K. D. (1915, August). Signs of victory. *Woman Voter, 6,* 12.

Block, L. (1972). *The history of the public school teachers of Baltimore city: A study of the internal politics of education*. Unpublished doctoral dissertation, Johns Hopkins University, Baltimore, MD.

Board refuses Miss Anna E. Logan. (1913, July 22). *Cincinnati Enquirer*, p. 8.

Board retracts threat. (1908, November 12). *New York Times*, p. 6.

Board rules against women teachers. (1906, May 10). *New York Times*, p. 9.

Boring, P. (1977). *Some thoughts on the equal pay act and coaching salaries*. Washington, DC: Women's Educational Equity League.

Boston teachers out in favor. (1915, April 24). *Woman's Journal 46*, 134.

Boyd, M. S. (1917, January). The woman educator and the vote. *Headquarters Newsletter National Women Suffrage Association*, 10–11.

Boys worship hero not heroine. (1935, January 23). *Cincinnati Post*, p. 11.

Brokaw, M. K. (1946, January). Shall I reconvert? *Independent Woman, 25*, 15, 28.

Brown, C. A. (1987). The new patriarchy. In C. Bose (Ed.), *Hidden aspects of women's work* (pp. 137–159). New York: Praeger.

Brown, H. Q. (Comp.). (1926). *Homespun heroines and other women of distinction*. Xenia, OH: Aldine.

Brown, V. B. (1990). The fear of feminization: Los Angeles high schools in the progressive era. *Feminist Studies, 16*, 493–515.

Brown v. Board of Education of Topeka, Kansas, 347 U.S. 483 (1954).

Brubacher, J. S. (1927, October 1). Reports: The judicial status of marriage and maternity in teaching. *School and Society, 25*, 428–429.

Buechler, S. M. (1990). *Women's movements in the United States: Woman suffrage, equal rights, and beyond*. New Brunswick, NJ: Rutgers University Press.

Buell, J. (1996). The politics of family leave. *Humanist, 56*, 41–43.

Bullock, W. B. (1916, September). The era of the teacher's cottage. *National Magazine, 44*, 997.

Bunch, C. (1987). *Passionate politics: Feminist theory in action*. New York: St. Martin's Press.

Bush, C. G. (1987). He isn't half so cranky as he used to be: Agricultural mechanization, comparable worth, and the changing farm family. In C. Groneman & M. B. Norton (Eds.), *To toil the livelong day: America's women at work, 1780–1980* (pp. 213–232). Ithaca, NY: Cornell University Press.

Byrnes, H. A. (1934). *Age as a factor as it relates to women in business and the professions: Bulletin of the Women's Bureau, no. 117*. Washington, DC: U.S. Government Printing Office.

California Federal Savings and Loan Association v. Guerra, 107 S. Ct. 683 (1987).

Calloway-Thomas, C., & Garner, T. (1996). Daisy Bates and the Little Rock school crisis: Forging the way. *Journal of Black Studies, 26*, 616–629.

Carney, M. (1912). *Country life and the country school*. Chicago: Row, Peterson.

Carrothers, G. E. (1924). *The physical efficiency of teachers: Contributions to education no. 155*. New York: Teachers College, Columbia University.

Carter, P. A. (1992a). Becoming the new women: The equal rights campaigns of New York City schoolteachers, 1900–1920. In R. J. Altenbaugh (Ed.), *The teacher's voice: A social history of teaching in twentieth-century America* (pp. 40–58). London: Falmer Press.

Carter, P. A. (1992b). The social status of women teachers in the early twentieth century. In R. J. Altenbaugh (Ed.), *The teacher's voice: A social history of teaching in twentieth-century America* (pp. 127–138). London: Falmer Press.

Carter, S. B. & Savoca, E. (1992). The teaching procession? Another look at teaching tenure 1845–1925. *Explorations in Economic History, 29,* 401–416.

Cash, F. L. B. (1993). Sarah S. T. Garnet. In D. C. Hine (Ed.), *Black women in America: An historical encyclopedia* (p. 479). Bloomington: Indiana University Press.

Cattell, J. M. (Ed.). (1932). Dr. Josephine Corliss Preston. *Leaders in education: A biographical dictionary.* New York: Science Press.

Census statistics of teachers, bulletin 23. (1905). Washington, DC: U.S. Government Printing Office.

Chafe, W. H. (1972). *The American woman: Her changing social, economic, and political roles, 1920–1970.* New York: Oxford University.

Chafe, W. H. (1991). *The paradox of change: American women in the 20th century.* New York: Oxford University.

Chicago teachers join labor union. (1902, November 22). *Woman's Journal, 21,* 370.

Chicago women's club. (1900, March 31). *Woman's Journal, 21,* 104.

Cincinnati Board of Education Annual Reports. Annual unpublished documents, 1880–1937.

The Cincinnati Schoolmasters Club. (1915). *School Index, 2,* 212.

Cincinnati Women Teachers' Association. (1915). *School Index, 2,* 212.

City comforts for country teachers: A Minnesota neighborhood sets an example to the nation. (1917, April). *American Review of Reviews, 55,* 403–408.

Clark, S. (1962). *Echo in my soul.* New York: Dutton.

Class teachers wage war over equality plan. (1905, May 10). *New York Times,* p. 9.

Cleveland board of education v. Jo Carol LaFleur. (1973). *Nolpe School Law Journal, 3,* 53.

Cleveland Board of Education v. La Fleur, 414 U.S. 632 (1973).

Clifford, G. J. (1978). Home and school in the 19th century America: Some personal history reports from the United States. *History of Education Quarterly, 18,* 3–34.

Clifford, G. J. (1982). Marry, stitch, die, or do worse. In H. Kantor & D. Tyack (Eds.), *Work, youth and schooling* (pp. 161–183). Stanford, CA: Stanford University Press.

Clifford, G. J. (1987). Lady teachers and politics in the United States, 1850–1930. In M. Lawn & G. Grace (Eds.), *Teachers: The culture and politics of work* (pp. 3–30). London: Falmer Press.

Coffman, L. D. (1911). *The social composition of the teaching population.* New York: Teachers College, Columbia University.

Coffman, L. D. (1913, April). Mobility of teaching population in relation to economy of time. *School & Home Education, 32,* 292–296.

Cohen v. Chesterfield County Board, 42 U.S.C. 1983 (1971).

Collier-Thomas, B. (1982). The impact of Black women in education: An historical overview. *Journal of Negro Education, 51,* 173–180.

Collins, C. W. (1976). *Schoolmen, schoolma'ams and school boards: The struggle for power in urban school systems in the progressive era.* Unpublished doctoral dissertation, Harvard University, Cambridge, MA.

Committee on Equal Opportunity. (1939). *Protecting the employment status of women.* Washington, DC: National Education Association.

Committee sends letter to NEA. (1920). *School Index, 6,* 3.

Compensation of male and female teachers. (1855, May). *New York Teachers, 4,* 94–95.

Condit, A. T. (1920). Men teachers in the public schools. *School Index, 6,* 190.

Condon urged to consider woman teacher for the position of writing supervisor. (1916, October 15). *Cincinnati Enquirer,* p. 30.

Coney, C. (1920, September). The social isolation of the teacher. *School and Home Education, 40,* 14–17.

Conway, J. K. (1987). Politics, pedagogy, and gender. *Daedalus, 116,* 137–152.

Cooke, D. H., & Sulzbacher, D. E. (1926). Married women as teachers. *Pennsylvania School Journal, 75,* 242–243.

Cordier, M. H. (1992). *Schoolwomen of the prairies and plains: Personal narratives from Iowa, Kansas, and Nebraska, 1860–1920s.* Albuquerque: New Mexico University Press.

Cott, N. F. (1987). *The grounding of modern feminism.* New Haven, CT: Yale University Press.

Cott, N. F. (1989). What's in a name? The limits of social feminism; or expanding the vocabulary of women's history. *Journal of American History, 76,* 809–829.

Cottages for country school teachers. (1916). *World's Work, 32,* 226.

Cowan, J. R., & Bird, J. (1925). Reports: Equal pay for equal service. *School and Society, 22,* 596–597.

Cowan, R. S. (1983). *More work for mother: The ironies of household technology from open hearth to the microwave.* New York: Basic Books.

Culley, M., & Portuges, C. (1985). *Gendered subjects.* Boston: Routledge & Kegan Paul.

Dakota teachers go on record. (1913). *Woman's Journal, 44,* 394.

Davis, A. F. (1967). *Spearheads for reform: The social settlements and the progressive movement, 1890–1914.* New York: Oxford.

Davis, H. (1940). Can married women be legally discriminated against in salary scheduling? *School and Society, 52,* 111–112.

Davis, H. (1943, July). Teaching is a war job! *Independent Woman, 22,* 202.

Dickson, L. F. (1987). Toward a broader angle of vision in uncovering women's history: Black women's clubs revisited. *Frontiers, 9,* 62–8.

Diehl, L. A. (1986). The paradox of G. Stanley Hall: Foe of coeducation and educator of women. *American Psychologist, 41,* 868–878.

Discrimination against married women. (1902, November 29). *Women's Tribune, 19,* 1.

Discriminatory dismissals of Negro teachers. (1965). *School and Society, 93,* 338.

Disenfranchised teachers. (1902, January 18). *Woman's Journal, 33,* 22–23.

Do teachers need the ballot? (1908, October 31). *Woman's Journal, 39,* 174.

Dr. Elliot opposes married teachers. (1913, July 26). *New York Times,* p. 6.

Dodge, G. H. (1895). Women and the public schools. *Pennsylvania School Journal, 43*, 439–440.

Doherty, R. E. (1979). Tempest on the Hudson. *History of Education Quarterly, 18*, 413–434.

Door slams on new teachers. Wage earner in family is barrier to job. (1932, February 9). *Cincinnati Enquirer*, p. 1.

Double bill at the schoolmasters club. (1920). *School Index, 6*, 1.

Duster, A. (Ed.). (1970). *Crusade for justice: The autobiography of Ida B. Wells*. Chicago: University of Chicago.

Duties of Teachers. (1908). Rules of the Education Department of the Board of Education of the City of Chicago. Unpublished document located at the Chicago Historical Society, p. 11.

Echols, A. (1989). *Daring to be bad: Radical feminism in America, 1967–1975*. Minneapolis: University of Minnesota Press.

Educating the Negro: Tuskegee convention studies vocational problems. (1938, August 8). *Newsweek*, 19.

Education. (1915). *Crisis, 10*, 1.

Edwards, I. N. (1925). Marriage as legal cause for dismissal of women teachers. *Elementary School Journal, 25*, 692–695.

Ehrenberg, R. G., Goldhaber, D., & Brewer, D. J. (1995). Do teachers' race, gender, and ethnicity matter? Evidence from the national educational longitudinal study of 1988. *Industrial and Labor Relations Review, 48*, 547–561.

Ellis, A. M. (1945, September). What price teaching? *Independent Woman, 24*, 247, 262–264.

Ellison, L. (1946, September). The sentence. *National Educational Association Journal, 35*, 294.

Ellsworth, E. (1989). Why doesn't this feel empowering? Working through the repressive myths of critical pedagogy. *Harvard Educational Review, 59*, 297–324.

Employment census of Cincinnati, 1934. (1934). *Monthly Labor Review, 39*, 647–649.

Employment in Cincinnati, 1936. (1936). *Monthly Labor Review, 41*, 873.

Employment of married teachers: Administrative practices affecting classroom teachers, Part 1. (1932). *Research Bulletin of the National Education Association, 10*, 20.

Englehardt, C. (1987). Compulsory education in Iowa, 1872–1919. *Annals of Iowa, 49*, 58–75.

Epstein, B. L. (1981). *The politics of domesticity: Women, evangelism, and temperance in nineteenth-century America*. Middletown, CT: Wesleyan University Press.

Epstein, T., & Hursh, H. (1985, April). National Organization for Women (NOW) bill of rights for 1969. *OAH Magazine of History, 1*, 27–28.

Equal compensation for New Jersey high school teachers. (1929). *School and Society, 26*, 261.

Equal pay dinner to women teachers. (1908, June 21). *New York Times*, p. 8.

Equal pay for men and women teaching in public schools provided by board. (1917, March 10). *Cincinnati Enquirer*, p. 8.

Equal pay for White and Negro school teachers. (1941). *Monthly Labor Review, 52*, 350.

Equalization of salaries. (1907, March 16). *Outlook*, p. 595.

Equalized pay and a chance of promotion sought. (1917, March 11). *Cincinnati Enquirer*, p. 23.

Ethridge, S. B. (1979). Impact of the 1954 *Brown v. Board of Education of Topeka* decision on Black educators. *Negro Educational Review, 30*, 217–232.

Evans, M. J. (1898). Women's clubs as an educational factor. *National Education Association Proceedings and Addresses of the 37th Annual Meeting.* Chicago: University of Chicago Press.

Even the anti-suffragists voted. (1911, March 11). *Western Woman Voter, 1*, 16.

Extra pay and dependency allowances: Are they fair? (1960, November). *NEA Journal, 49*, 52–54.

Ferguson, K. (1984). *The feminist bureaucracy.* Philadelphia: Temple University Press.

Ferree, M. M., & Hess, B. B. (1985). *Controversy and coalition: The new feminist movement.* Boston: Twayne.

Few changes of teachers made, staffs to be intact. (1932, September 3). *Cincinnati Enquirer*, p. 5.

Filler, L. (1974). Lucy Stone. In E. T. James (Ed.), *Notable American women: A biographical dictionary* (pp. 387–390). Cambridge, MA: Belknap Press of Harvard University.

Find mothers make best teachers. (1913, November 25). *New York Times*, p. 20.

Fink, D. (1988). Sidelines and moral capital: Women on Nebraska farms in the 1930s. In W. G. Haney & J. B. Knowles (Eds.), *Women and farming: Changing roles, changing structures* (pp. 55–72). Boulder, CO: Westview Press.

The first federal injunction against salary differentials for Negro teachers. (1939). *School and Society, 50*, 717.

Fischer. (1956, April). Greetings girls. *Harpers, 212*, 12, 14, 16.

Fishel, A., & Pottker, J. (1973). Women teachers and teacher power. *Urban Review, 6*, 41.

Flygare, T. J. (1978). A legal embarrassment: Paid sick leave for pregnant teachers. *Phi Delta Kappan, 59*, 558–559.

Force, A. L. (1922). Preliminary report of committee on the status of the American woman teacher. *National Education Association Proceedings and Addresses* (pp. 564–570). Washington, DC: National Education Association.

Forderhouse, N. K. (1985). The clear call of thoroughbred women: The Kentucky Federation of Women's Clubs and the crusade for educational reform, 1903–1909. *Register of the Kentucky Historical Society, 83*, 19–35.

Forderhouse, N. K. (1987). Eve returns to the garden: Women reformers in Appalachian Kentucky in the early twentieth century. *Register of the Kentucky Historical Society, 85*, 237–261.

Foster, M. (1991, Spring). Constancy, connectedness, and constraints in the lives of African-American teachers. *NWSA Journal, 3*, 248–252.

France, R. (Ed.). (1937). *Women of achievement: A record of their achievement.* n.p.: S. J. Clarke.

Freedman, E. (1974). The new woman: Changing views of women in the 1920s. *Journal of American History, 61*, 372–393.

Freedman, E. (1979). Separatism as strategy: Female institution building and American feminism, 1870–1930. *Feminist Studies, 5*, 512–529.

Freedman, E. (1995). Separatism revisited: Women's institutions, social reform, and the career of Miriam Van Waters. In L. Kerber (Ed.), *U.S. history as women's history: New feminist essays* (pp. 170–188). Chapel Hill: University of North Carolina Press.

French, L. L. (1974). LaFleur, Cohen and Aiello: An aftermath. *School Law Journal, 4*, 160–165.

Fultz, M. (1995). Teacher training and African-American education in the South, 1900–1940. *Journal of Negro Education, 64*, 196–211.

Gedulig v. Aiello, 417 U.S. 484 (1974).

General Electric Company v. Gilbert, 429 U.S. 125 (1976).

General Federation of Women's Clubs. (1911). *U.S. Bureau of Education Report, 1910.* Washington, DC: U.S. Government Printing Office.

German-American Alliance against employment of married women teachers and female teachers. (1914). *Cincinnati Board of Education Proceedings, 29*, 405.

Gibbons, M. W. (1979). *The American woman in transition: The urban influence, 1870–1920.* Westport, CT: Greenwood Press.

Giddings, P. (1984). *When and where I enter: The impact of Black women on race and sex in America.* New York: Bantam Books.

Gilkes, C. T. (1980). Holding back the ocean with a broom: Black women and community work. In L. F. Rodgers-Rose (Ed.), *The Black woman* (pp. 217–232). Beverly Hills, CA: Sage.

Gill, L. (1901). The scope of the Department of Women's Organizations. *National Education Association Proceedings and Addresses, 39*, 75.

Gilman, C. P. (1898). *Women and economics.* New York: McClure, Phillips.

Girls with no more ability beat boys in school—Why? (1935, January 12). *Cincinnati Post,* p. 2.

Goldstein, L. F. (1988). *The constitutional rights of women: Cases in the law and social change.* Madison: University of Wisconsin Press.

Goodler, F. T. (1928). Another conclusion regarding the married woman teachers. *Nation's Schools, 2*, 51–52.

Gordon, A. D. (with Collier-Thomas, B., Bracey, J. H., Avakian, A. V., & Berkman, J. A.). (1997). *African American women and the vote, 1837–1965.* Amherst: University of Massachusetts Press.

Gordon, J. A. (1995). Why minority students don't teach. *Education Digest, 60*, 49–53.

Graham, A. (1926). *Grace H. Dodge: Merchant of dreams.* New York: Woman's Press.

Gray, A. A. (1916). The teacher's home. *Elementary School Journal, 17*, 201–208.

Green, E. (1994). Ideals of government of home and of women: The ideology of southern white anti-suffragism. In V. Bernhard (Ed.), *Hidden histories of women in the new South* (pp. 96–113). Columbia: University of Missouri Press.

Green v. Waterford Board of Education (Connecticut), 473 F. 2d 629 (1973).

Grenfell, H. L. (1909). The constitution of the ideal school board and the citizen's duty toward it. *NEA Addresses and Proceedings, 47*, 998–999.

Grier, K. C. (1988). *Culture and comfort: People, parlors, and upholstery 1850–1930.*

Rochester, NY: The Strong Museum. [Distributed by The University of Massachusetts Press.]

Grumet, M. (1981). Pedagogy for patriarchy: The feminization of teaching. *Interchange, 12,* 165–184.

Gulliford, A. (1984). *America's country schools.* Washington, DC: Preservation Press.

Haley, M. (1912, August 12). [Letter to Miss Kendall on Cincinnati Woman's Suffrage Party letterhead]. Located in Chicago Teachers' Federation Collection, file box 18, Chicago Historical Society.

Haley, M. (1982). *Battleground: The autobiography of Margaret Haley* (R. Reid, Ed.). Urbana: University of Illinois.

Hansen, K. V. (1986). The women's unions and the search for a political identity. *Socialist Review, 16,* 67–95.

Harley, S. (1982). Beyond the classroom: The organizational lives of Black female educators in the District of Columbia, 1890–1930. *Journal of Education, 51,* 254–265.

Harris, B. (1978). *Beyond her sphere: Women in the professions in American history.* Westport, CT: Greenwood Press.

Harris, J. H. (1906, February 3). Everybody's paid but the teacher. *The Women's Journal, 37,* 20.

Hartmann, S. M. (1982). *The home front and beyond: American women in the 1940s.* Boston: Twayne.

Hartmann, S. M. (1989). *From margin to mainstream: American women and politics since 1960.* Philadelphia: Temple University Press.

Hayden, D. (1981). *The grand domestic revolution: A history of feminist designs for American homes, neighborhoods, and cities.* Cambridge, MA: MIT Press.

Hecker, E. A. (1914). *A short history of women's rights.* Westport, CT: Greenwood Press.

Heer, A. L. (1920). Men teachers needed by adolescent boys and girls. *School Index, 6,* 180.

Hendricks, W. (1993a). The Alpha Suffrage Club. In D. C. Hine (Ed.), *Black women in America: An historical encyclopedia* (pp. 25–26). Bloomington: Indiana University Press.

Hendricks, W. (1993b). Ida Bell Wells-Barnett. In D. C. Hine (Ed.), *Black women in America: An historical encyclopedia* (pp. 1242–1246). Bloomington: Indiana University Press.

Herrick, M. B. (1921, April). Teacherages. *School and Home Education, 40,* 145–147.

Hervey, H. D. (1925). Discussion: The equal pay law in New York State. *School and Society, 21.*

Hewitt, N. A., & Lebsock, S. (Eds.). (1993). *Visible women: New essays on American activism.* Urbana: University of Illinois Press.

Hill, M. A. (1980). Charlotte Perkins Gilman: A feminist's struggle with womanhood. *Massachusetts Review, 21,* 503–526.

Hine, D. C. (1990). We specialize in the wholly impossible: The philanthropic work of Black women. In K. D. McCarthy (Ed.), *Lady bountiful revisited: Women, philanthropy, and power* (pp. 70–93). New Brunswick, NJ: Rutgers University Press.

Hoffert, S. D. (1985). Yankee schoolmarm and the domestication of the South. *Southern Studies, 24,* 188–201.

Hoffman, N. (1981). *Women's true profession: Voices from the history of teaching.* Old Westbury, NY: Feminist Press.

Hopkins, E. (1990, October). Who is Felicia Schwartz and why is she saying those terrible things about us? *Working Woman, 15,* 116–121.

How suffrage will help teachers. (1911, April 8). *Woman's Journal, 42,* 111.

Hudson, M. J. (1994). Missing teachers, impaired communities: The unanticipated consequences of Brown v. Board of Education on the African American teaching force at the precollegiate level. *Journal of Negro Education, 63,* 388–394.

Huffaker, C. L. (1931). *Teacher supply and demand in Oregon education series* (Vol. 2). Eugene: University of Oregon Press.

Hummer, P. M. (1979). *The decade of elusive promise: Professionals in the United States, 1920–1930.* Ann Arbor, MI: UMI Research Press.

Hurley, D. (1982). *Cincinnati: The queen city.* Cincinnati, OH: Cincinnati Historical Society.

Hutchinson, L. D. (1994). Anna Julia Haywood Cooper. In D. C. Hine (Ed.), *Black women in America: An historical encyclopedia* (pp. 275–281). Bloomington: Indiana University Press.

Hutton v. Gill (8 N.E. (2d) 81188), transferred (Appl.) (7 N.E. (2d) 1011) (1937).

If I had known of a man better qualified. (1913, July 26). *Cincinnati Times Star,* p. 2.

Integration and dismissal of southern Negro teachers. (1965). *School and Society, 93,* 468, 470.

Jablonsky, T. J. (1994). *The home, heaven, and mother party: Female anti-suffragists in the United States, 1868–1920.* Brooklyn, NY: Carlson.

Jacobs, F. R. (1928). *Teacher turnover in Cincinnati, 1917–18 to 1926–27.* Unpublished master's thesis, University of Cincinnati, Cincinnati, OH.

Jaggar, A. (1983). *Feminist politics and human nature.* Totowa, NJ: Littlefield & Adams.

Jameson v. Board of Education of Union District,. 81 N.E. 1126 (1914). (W. Va. 389).

Jeffrey, J. R. (1987). Women in the southern farmer's alliance: A reconsideration of the role and status of women in the late nineteenth-century south. In J. E. Friedman, W. G. Shade, & Capozzolli, M. J. (Eds.), *Our American sisters: Women in American life and thought* (pp. 273–296). Lexington, MA: D.C. Heath.

Jensen, J. M. (Ed.). (1991). Butter-making and economic development in mid-Atlantic America, 1750–1850. In *Promise to the land: Essays on rural women* (pp. 153–169). Albuquerque: University of New Mexico.

Johnson, A. F. (1931, March 26). Legislation and women in industry. *Los Angeles City Teachers Club Bulletin,* pp. 14–15.

Johnston, J. (1973). *Lesbian nation: The feminist solution.* New York: Simon & Schuster.

Jones, B. (1994). Mary Eliza Church Terrell. In D. C. Hine (Ed.), *Black women in America: An historical encyclopedia* (pp. 1157–1159). Bloomington: Indiana University Press.

Jones, J. (1985). *Labor of love, labor of sorrow: Black women, work, and the family, from slavery to present.* New York: Basic Books.

Jones, J. (1988). Tore up and a-movin': Perspectives on the work of Black and poor White women in the rural south, 1865–1940. In W. G. Haney & J. B. Knowles (Eds.), *Women and farming: Changing roles, changing structures* (pp. 15–34). Boulder, CO: Westview Press.

Jones, L. G. (1937). *The Jeanes teacher in the United States, 1908–1933.* Chapel Hill: University of North Carolina Press.

Kansas Federation of Colored Women's Clubs, 1900–1930. (1986). *Kansas History, 9,* 19–30.

Kansas State Teachers Association unanimous for woman's ballot. (1911). *Woman's Journal, 42,* 369.

Kaufman, P. W. (1991). Building a constituency for school desegregation: African-American women in Boston, 1962–1972. *Teachers College Record, 92,* 619–631.

Keatley, V. B. (1951, October). They work to give millions away. *Coronet, 30,* 133–136.

Keen, H. (1990). *Deeds not words: The lives of suffragette teachers.* London: Pluto Press.

Kellogg, R. S. (1916). *Teachers' cottages.* Chicago: The National Lumber Manufacturers Association.

Kerber, L. K. (1988). Separate spheres, female worlds, woman's place: The rhetoric of women's history. *Journal of American History, 75,* 9–39.

Kessler-Harris, A. (1982). *Out to work: A history of wage-earning women in the U.S.* New York: Oxford University Press.

Kessler-Harris, A. (1989). Gender ideology in historical reconstruction: A case study from the 1930s. *Gender & History, 1,* 38.

Kessler-Harris, A. (1990). *A woman's wage: Historical meanings and social consequences.* Lexington: University of Kentucky.

King, S. (1987). Feminists in teaching: The National Union of Women Teachers, 1920–1945. In M. Lawn & G. Grace (Eds.), *Teachers: The culture and politics of work* (pp. 31–49). London: Falmer Press.

Kleinfeld, J. (1992). *Teaching in the North: Gender tales.* Fairbanks: University of Alaska-Fairbanks.

Knowles, J. B. (1988). It's our turn now. In W. G. Haney & J. B. Knowles (Eds.), *Women and farming: Changing roles, changing structures* (pp. 303–315). Boulder, CO: Westview Press.

Koch, H. E. (1920). Men in the schools. *School Index, 6,* 234–235, 240.

Koehler, L. (1984). Women's rights, society and the schools: Feminist activities in Cincinnati, Ohio, 1864–1880. In *Women in Cincinnati: Century of achievement, 1870–1970* (pp. 3–17). Cincinnati, OH: Cincinnati Historical Society.

Lafferty, H. H. (1948). It pays to be ignorant. *Elementary School Journal, 49,* 133–136.

Lake, A. Look who's teaching school. (1956). *Saturday Evening Post, 228,* 38.

Lakes, R. D. (1995). Social welfare and vocational education in progressive era Cincinnati. *Journal of Vocational and Technical Education, 11,* 12–21.

Lasch, C. (1979). *Haven in a heartless world: The family besieged.* New York: Basic Books.

Lather, P. (1991). *Getting smart: Feminist research and pedagogy with/in the postmodern.* New York: Routledge.

Leave for mother. (1914, November 5). *New York Times*, p. 11.

Legal advice for teachers likely. (1933, August 20). *Cincinnati Enquirer*, p. 8.

Legal fight planned by married teachers. (1933, August 19). *Cincinnati Post*, p. 15.

Leloudis, II, J. L. (1983). School reform in the new South: The Women's Association for the Betterment of Public School Houses in North Carolina, 1902–1919. *Journal of American History, 69*, 886–909.

Lemann, N. (1991). *The Promised Land: The great Black migration and how it changed America.* New York: Alfred A. Knopf.

Lemons, J. S. (1973). *The woman citizen: Social feminism in the 1920s.* Urbana: University of Illinois Press.

Lerner, Gerda (Ed.). (1977). *The female experience: An American documentary history.* Indianapolis, IN: Bobbs-Merrill.

Lerner, Gerda (Ed.). (1979). *The majority finds its past: Placing women in history.* New York: Oxford University Press.

Lesser, S. T. (1991). Paradigms gained: Further readings in the history of women in the progressive era. In N. Frankel & N. S. Dye (Eds.), *Gender, race, class and reform in the progressive era* (pp. 180–193). Lexington: University of Kentucky Press.

Letter from Cincinnati Teacher's Association, November 12, 1934. (1935). *Cincinnati Board of Education Proceedings* (p. 3). Cincinnati, OH: n.p.

Letter from Miss Susan B. Anthony. (1903, July 7). *Chicago Teachers' Federation Bulletin, 2*, 2.

Levenson, D. (1967). Mothers bring their skills. *Parents Magazine, 42*, 48–49.

Lewis, C. D. (1937). *The rural community and its schools.* New York: American Book Company.

Lewis, E., & Wolcott, V. (1993). American Teachers Association. In D. C. Hine (Ed.), *Black women in America: An historical encyclopedia* (pp. 26–28). Bloomington: Indiana University Press.

Lewis, E. E. (1925). *Personnel problems of the teaching staff.* New York: Century.

Lichter, M. (1946). Social obligations and restrictions placed on women teachers. *School Review, 54*, 15–33.

Lieberman, M. (1957). Civil rights and the NEA. *School and Society, 85*, 167.

Linden-Ward, B., & Green, C. H. (1993). *American women in the 1960s: Changing the future.* New York: Twayne.

Lindgren, J. R., & Taub, N. (1988). *The law of sex discrimination.* St. Paul, MN: West.

Link, W. A. (1986). *A hard country and a lonely place: Schooling, society, and reform in rural Virginia, 1870–1920.* Chapel Hill: University of North Carolina Press.

Littlefield, V. W. (1994). A yearly contract with everybody and his brother: Durham County, North Carolina Black female public school teachers, 1885–1927. *Journal of Negro History, 79*, 37–54.

Lorenz, E. J. (1920). Salary as a factor in determining the proportion of men and women teachers. *School Index, 6*, 182.

Lost job as teacher for bearing a child. (1913, March 16). *New York Times*, sec. II, p. 10.

Louisiana legislature passes suffrage amendment; women allowed to serve on school boards. (1912, July 20). *Woman's Journal, 43,* 1.

Lowth, F. (1926). *Everyday problems of the country teacher.* New York: MacMillan.

Maguire, M. (1993). Women who teach. *Gender and Education, 5,* 269.

The mail-order suffragist. (1916). *Independent, 86,* 143.

Manning, D. (1990). *Hill Country teachers: Oral histories from the one-room school and beyond.* Boston: Twayne.

Manson, G. E. (1931). *Occupational interests and personality requirements of women in business and the professions.* Ann Arbor: University of Michigan Bureau of Business Research.

Marczely, B. (1994). The Family and Medical Leave Act and the public school teacher. *Clearing House, 67,* 339–343.

Marriage and teaching: Revolt spreads against the drive to enforce celibacy. (1938, August 1). *Newsweek,* 28.

Married teachers. (1918). *School and Society, 3,* 226–227.

A married teacher's ruse. (1914, October 13). *New York Times,* p. 18.

Married women teachers. (1918). *Journal of Education, 71,* 156.

Married women teachers number 344, 26 have husbands in schools here. (1933, September 15). *Cincinnati Post,* p. 4.

Married women teachers urged to stem shortage. (1961, November 4). *Science Newsletter, 80,* 304.

Marti, D. B. (1991). *Women of the Grange: Mutuality and the sisterhood in rural America, 1866–1920.* New York: Greenwood Press.

Martin, J. R. (1982). Excluding women from educational realm. *Harvard Educational Review, 52,* 133–148.

Martin, P. Y. (1990). Rethinking feminist organizations. *Gender and Society, 4,* 183.

Mary G. Bellamy. (1965). In *Let your light shine: Pioneer educators of Wyoming* (pp. 15–21). Sheridan, WY: Alpha Xi State Delta Kappa Gamma.

Maternity legislation for working women in foreign countries. (1930). *Monthly Labor Review, 30,* 53–56.

Maxwell, W. H. (1903). Teachers' salaries in New York City. *Journal of Education, 56,* 255–257.

McBride, G. G. (1994). *On Wisconsin women: Working for their rights from settlement to suffrage.* Madison: University of Wisconsin Press.

McClymer, J. F. (1991). Gender and the American way of life: Women in the Americanization movement. *Journal of American Ethnic History, 10,* 3–20.

McGlen, N. E. (1995). National Federation of Business and Professional Women's Clubs of the USA. In S. Slavin (Ed.), *U.S. women's interest groups: Institutional profiles* (p. 374). Westport, CT: Greenwood Press.

McFadden, G. J. (1993). Septima Poinsette Clark. In D. C. Hine (Ed.), *Black women in America: An historical encyclopedia* (pp. 249–252). Bloomington: Indiana University Press.

McIntosh, M. (1978). The state and the oppression of women. In A. Kuhn & A. M. Wolpe (Eds.), *Feminism and materialism* (pp. 254–289). London: Routledge & Kegan Paul.

McMurry, S. (1988). *Families and farmhouses in the nineteenth-century America: Vernacular design and social change*. New York: Oxford University Press.

McNaught, M. S. (1917). The enfranchised woman teacher: Her opportunity. *School and Society, 6*, 155.

Meeting of the Board of Education, October 28, 1908. (1908). *Journal of the Board of Education of the City of New York* (pp. 2126–2127). New York: n.p.

Men. (1920). *School Index, 6*, 141.

Men forced out? (1935, January 19). *Cincinnati Post*, p. 5.

Men on the increase. (1923). *School Index, 9*, 152.

Men teachers assured of positions. (1934, May 24). *Cincinnati Enquirer*, p. 10.

Merk, L. B. (1956). Boston's historic public school crisis. *New England Quarterly, 31*, 172–199.

Meyerowitz, J. (Ed.). (1994). Beyond the feminine mystique: A reassessment of postwar mass culture, 1946–1958. *Not June Cleaver: Women and gender in postwar America, 1945–1960* (pp. 229–262). Philadelphia: Temple University Press.

Miller, Z. L. (1968). *Boss Cox's Cincinnati*. Chicago: University of Chicago Press.

Minkoff, D. C. (1995). *Organizing for equality: The evolution of women's and racial-ethnic organizations in America 1955–1985*. New Brunswick, NJ: Rutgers University Press.

Mintz, S., & Kellogg, S. (1989). *Domestic revolutions: A social history of American family Life*. New York: The Free Press.

Minutes of the board of education for June 25, 1913. (1913). *Journal of the Board of Education of the City of New York*. New York: n.p.

Miss Edith Campbell first woman on board. (1912, January 1). *Cincinnati Enquirer*, p. 14.

Miss Lenda Hanks, Girls' High representative of suffrage party. (1910). *Woman Voter, 1*, 7.

Miss Rodman's pen again jabs board. (1914, November 28). *New York Tribune*, p. 7.

Mississippi Teachers Want Suffrage. (1918). *Woman's Journal, 49*, 225.

Moses, W. J. (1987). Domestic feminism conservatism, sex roles, and Black women's clubs. *Journal of Social and Behavioral Studies, 24*, 166–177.

The mother and the schools. (1906, June 12). *Woman's Journal, 37*, 75.

Motherhood and teaching. (1913). *Outlook, 68*, 462.

Motherhood held as civic service, on the ground league of women will insist on Mrs. Edgell's rights. (1913, June 28). *New York Times*, p. 25.

Motz, M. F., & Browne, P. (1988). *Making the American home: Middle-class women and domestic material culture, 1840–1940*. Bowling Green, OH: Bowling Green State University Press.

Mrs. Chapman's warning. (1897, June 4). *New York Tribune*, p. 5.

Mrs. Ella Flagg Young. (1901). *Western Journal of Education, 26*, 515.

Mueller, F. W., & Bunn, E. M. (1951). Salaries: City public school teachers. *Monthly Labor Review, 72*, 286–288.

Muerman, J. C. (1922). *District owned housing or controlled teacher's home. Bulletin 16*. Washington, DC: U.S. Government Printing Office.

Murphy, K. A. (1981). *Boston Teachers Organize, 1919–65.* Unpublished doctoral dissertation, Harvard University, Cambridge, MA.

Murphy, M. (1990). *Blackboard unions: The AFT and the NEA, 1900–1980.* Ithaca, NY: Cornell University Press.

Name schools for women. (1915, January 10). *New York Times,* sec. III, p. 2.

Nashville Gas Company v. Satty, 34 U.S. 136 (1977).

Nathan, B. S. (1956). *Tales of a teacher.* Chicago: Henry Rignery.

National American Woman Suffrage Association. (1903). *Chicago Teachers' Federation Bulletin, 2,* 12.

National Center for Education Statistics America's teachers: Profile of a profession. (1992). Washington, DC: U.S. Department of Education.

National Education Association in convention at Chicago favors votes for women. (1912, July 20). *Woman's Journal, 43,* 225.

National Federation of Teachers. (1902, September 5). *Chicago Teachers' Federation Bulletin, 1,* 1.

Negro population in the United States, 1790–1915. (1968). New York: Arno Press and the New York Times.

Nevada teachers to help cause. (1913). *Woman's Journal, 44,* 1.

Neverdon-Morton, C. (1989). *Afro-American women of the south and the advancement of the race, 1895–1925.* Knoxville: University of Tennessee.

New Jersey Teachers Association endorses full suffrage for women. (1915, January 9). *Woman's Journal, 46,* 9.

New teacherages should be everywhere. (1916). *Ladies Home Journal, 33,* 4.

New York women teachers. (1906). *Journal of Education, 59,* 479.

Nicholson, L. J. (1980). Women & schooling. *Educational Theory, 30,* 225–234.

Nolan, J. E. (1992). Irish-American teachers and the struggle over American urban public education, 1890–1920: A preliminary look. *Records of the American Catholic Historical Society of Philadelphia, 103,* 13–22.

Notes. (1910). *Woman Voter, 1,* 1.

Now the married teacher. (1918, April 6). *Woman Citizen, 1,* 367.

Occupations, population—1920, 14th census of the US. (1923). Washington, DC: U.S. Government Printing Office.

O'Connor, K. (1977, September 4–6). *The use of the courts by women's groups to obtain rights* (p. 17). Paper presented at annual meeting of the American Political Science Association, Washington, DC.

On the resolution of the Federation relating to salary and examinations. (1902). *Chicago Teachers' Federation Bulletin, 1,* 2.

O'Neill, W. (1968). Feminism as radical ideology. In A. F. Young (Ed.), *Dissent: Explorations in the history of American radicalism* (pp. 273–300). DeKalb: Northern Illinois University Press.

O'Neill, W. (1969). *Everyone was brave: A history of feminism in America.* Chicago: Quadrangle Books.

Oppenheimer, V. K. (1970). *The female labor force in the United States.* Berkeley: University of California.

Our women's number. (1904). *Voice of the Negro, 1,* 1.

Pardee, J. S. (1916, March). The teacherage. *Country Life in America, 29*, 24.

Pederson, S. (1987). Married women and the right to teach in St. Louis, 1941–1948. *Missouri Historical Review, 81*, 141–158.

Peiss, Kathy. (1986). *Cheap amusements: Working women and leisure in turn-of-the-century New York*. Philadelphia: Temple University Press.

Penalizing motherhood. (1913). *Independent, 99*, 605.

Pennsylvania Women. (1910). *Journal of Education, 63*, 100.

Pennybacker, Mrs. Percy V. (1915). The need of teachers' homes. *Ladies Home Journal, 32*, 25.

People ex rel. Peixotto v. Board of Education of the City of New York, 82 Misc. Rep. 684 (1913).

Perkins, Linda (1983). Impact of the cult of true womanhood on the education of Black women. *Journal of Social Issues, 39*, 17–28.

Perry, E. (1993, September). Why suffrage for American women was not enough. *History Today, 43*, 36–42.

Peters, D. W. (1934). *The status of married woman teacher*. New York: Teachers College, Columbia University.

Phillips v. Martin Marietta, 400 U.S. 542 (1971).

Pickens, D. K. (1989). Domestic feminism: The structure of American history. *Contemporary Philosophy, 12*, 17–18.

A Plea for Negro Education. (1944). *School and Society, 59*, 22–23.

Porritt, A. G. (1911). The feminization of our schools and its political consequences. *Educational Review, 41*, 441–448.

Preston, J. A. (1993). Domestic ideology, school reformers and female teachers: Schoolteaching becomes women's work in nineteenth-century New England. *New England Quarterly, 66*, 531–552.

Preston, J. C. (1915). Community center work. *National Education Association Proceedings and Addresses of the 53rd Annual Meeting* (pp. 687–691). Washington, DC: National Education Association.

Preston, J. C. (1916a). Cottages for country school teachers. *World's Work, 32*, 266.

Preston, J. C. (1916b). Teachers' cottages. *National Education Association Addresses and Proceedings of the 55th Annual Meeting* (pp. 142–145). Washington, DC: National Education Association.

Preston, J. C. (1916c). Teachers cottages and rural home economics. *Journal of Home Economics, 3*, 109–112.

Price, E. E. (1898, January). More women on school boards. *Pennsylvania School Journal, 46*, 299–300.

Progressive Cincinnati. (1914). *Journal of Education, 67*, 155.

Project on Equal Education Rights. (1977). *Stalled at the start*. Washington, DC: NOW Legal Defense and Education Fund.

Punke, H. H. (1940). Marriage rate among women teachers. *American Sociological Review, 5*, 505–511.

Pupils want kind, patient teachers only, women say. (1935, January 14). *Cincinnati Post*, p. 11.

Quantz, R. A. (1985). The complex of female teachers and the failure of unionization in the 1930s: An oral history. *History of Education Quarterly, 25*, 197–213.

Rally teachers to suffrage in town. (1917, April 17). *Woman's Journal, 48,* 89.

Rankin, C. E. (1990). Teaching: Opportunity and limitation for Wyoming women. *Western History Quarterly, 21,* 163–164.

Rapeer, L. W. (1920). *The consolidated rural school.* New York: Charles Scribner's Sons.

Recommends equal pay. (1910, October 29). *Woman's Journal, 41,* 184.

Reed, D. R. (1958). *The woman suffrage movement in South Dakota.* Vermillion: Governmental Research Bureau, State University of South Dakota.

Reese, W. J. (1978). Between home and school: Organized parents, clubwomen, and urban education in the progressive era. *School Review, 87.*

Reeves, C. E. (1928, October). Opinion of superintendents. *Nation's Schools, 2,* 103–104.

Refusal to confirm Miss Logan starts controversy. (July 22, 1913). *Cincinnati Post & Times Star.* 7.

Reid, J. (1991). A career to build, a people to serve, a purpose to accomplish: Race, class, gender, and Detroit's first Black teachers, 1865–1916. *Michigan Historical Review, 18,* 3–32.

Report of the commissioner of education for the year ending June 30, 1906 (Vol. 1). (1907). Washington, DC: U.S. Government Printing Office.

Resolutions re: married women teachers February 12, 1934. (1935). *Cincinnati Board of Education Proceedings* (pp. 4–7). Cincinnati, OH: n.p.

Richards v. District School Board (Oregon), 153 Pac. 482 (1915).

Richardson, A. S. (1930, December). When mother goes to business. *Woman's Home Companion, 57,* 22, 108.

Richmond Unified School District v. Berg, 434 U.S. 158, 98 S.Ct. b23 (1977).

Ridley, W. N. (1966). NEA-ATA unification. *NEA Journal, 55,* 49–50.

Riley, G. (1988). *The female frontier: A comparative view of women on the prairie and the plains.* Lawrence: University of Kansas.

Ripley, E. C. (1915, February). What can clubwomen do for rural schools? *GFWC Magazine, 14,* 19–20.

Romeo Community Schools v. HEW, 62 L. Ed. 2d 388 (1979).

Rose, J. (1992, July–August). From career to maternity: A feminist reconsiders the mommy track. *Washington Monthly, 24,* 51–54.

Rules for granting leaves of absence, June 27, 1932. (1933). *Cincinnati Board of Education Proceedings* (pp. 9–10). Cincinnati, OH: n.p.

Rupp, L. J., & Taylor, V. (1987). *Survival in the doldrums: The American women's rights movement, 1945 to the 1960s.* New York: Oxford University Press.

Rural teacher notes complaints. (1907, January). *Woman's Voice & Public School Champion, 16,* 4.

Rural vs. city schools. (1911). *Journal of Education, 64,* 410.

Ryan, M. (1975). *Womanhood in America: From colonial times to the present.* New York: New Viewpoints/Franklin Watts.

Sadker, M., & Sadker, D. (1994). *Failing at fairness: How America's schools cheat girls.* New York: Charles Scribner and Sons.

Salaries of Negro public-school teachers in 15 states. (1936). *Monthly Labor Review, 43,* 1242.

Salem, D. C. (1990). *To better our world: Black women in organized reform, 1890–1920.* Brooklyn, NY: Carlson Publishing.

Salem, D. C. (1993). National Association of Colored Women. In D. C. Hine (Ed.), *Black women in America: An historical encyclopedia* (pp. 842–851). Bloomington: Indiana University Press.

Sauce for the gander. (1929). *School and Society, 29,* 519.

Scanlon, J. P. (1988). What helps the working parent? *National Law Journal, 11,* 13.

Scharf, L. (1980). *To work and to wed: Female employment, feminism, and the Great Depression.* Westport, CT: Greenwood Press.

Scharf, L., & Jensen, J. M. (Eds.). (1983). *Decades of discontent: The women's movement, 1920–1940.* Westport, CT: Greenwood Press.

Schneider, D., & Schneider, C. J. (1993). *American women in the progressive era, 1900–1920.* New York: Facts on File.

School Board of the City of Elwood v. State (Indiana), 180 N.E. 471 (1932).

School Board of the City of Norfolk v. Alston, 61 Sup. Ct. 75 (1939).

School for suffrage. (1911). *Woman's Journal, 42,* 298.

School heads are at odds, differ in questions of married teachers. (1932, September 17). *Cincinnati Post,* p. 10.

School jobs go one to a family. (1932, August 19). *Cincinnati Enquirer,* p. 1.

School teachers and suffrage. (1912, March). *Woman Voter, 3,* 9.

Schoolma'ams want men teachers' pay. (1905, April 30). *New York Times,* p. 8.

Schuler, M. (1922). Making teachers welcome. *American Review of Reviews, 65,* 195–198.

Scott, A. F. (1990). Most invisible of all: Black women's voluntary associations. *Journal of Southern History, 56,* 3–22.

Scott, A. F. (1993). *Natural allies: Women's associations in American history.* Urbana: University of Illinois Press.

Sentiment in Logan case aroused. (July 23, 1913). *Cincinnati Post & Times Star.* 8.

Session, J. (1913, May 8). The place of woman in school histories. *Everywoman, 1,* 11.

The sex of teachers in high and elementary schools. (1905). In *Salaries and pensions of the public school teachers in the United States, 52.* Ann Arbor, MI: National Educational Association.

Sexism. (1972). *Learning, 1,* 77.

Shall married women be barred from teaching? (1932). *National Education Association Journal, 21,* 299.

Sharf, L. (1980). *To work and to wed: Female employment, feminism, and the Great Depression.* Westport, CT: Greenwood Press.

Shaw, S. (1996). *What a woman ought to be and to do: Black professional women workers during the Jim Crow era.* Chicago: University of Chicago Press.

Sheldon v. Committee of Hopedale (Massachusetts), 177 N. E. 94 (1931).

Shelton, B. K. (1976). *Reformers in search of yesterday: Buffalo in the 1890s.* Albany: State University of New York Press.

Should women have equal pay? (1904). *Woman's Journal, 5,* 356.

Simpson, M. (1993). Congratulations! It's a law! *NEA Today, 12,* 17–18.

Simpson, R., & Simpson, I. (1969). Women and bureaucracy in the semi-professions. In A. Etzioni (Ed.), *The semi-professions and their organizations* (pp. 196–265). New York: Free Press.

Sitton, T., & Rowald, M. C. (1987). *Ringing the children in, Texas country schools.* College Station: Texas A & M Press.

Sklar, K. K. (1988). Organized womanhood: Archival sources on women and progressive reform. *Journal of American History, 75,* 176–183.

Small board changes number of rules; lifts ban on married teachers. (1914, January 24). *Cincinnati Times,* p. 1.

Smith, D., & Pingree, S. (1980). *Directory of organizations working for women's educational equity.* San Francisco: Women's Educational Equity Communications Network.

Smith, D. S. (1979). Family limitation, sexual control, and domestic feminism in Victorian America. In N. F. Cott & E. H. Pleck (Eds.), *A heritage of her own: Toward new social history of American women* (pp. 222–245). New York: Touchstone.

Smith, J. K. (1979). *Ella Flagg Young: Portrait of a leader.* Ames, IA: Educational Studies Press.

Smith-Rosenberg, C. (1975, Fall). The new woman and the new history. *Feminist Studies, 3.*

Snyder, G. R. (1925). *The health of teachers.* Unpublished master's thesis, Ohio State University, Columbus, OH.

Soliloquy on man. (1903). *Chicago Teachers' Federation Bulletin, 2,* 5.

Stanton, E. C. (1898). *Eighty years and more: Reminiscences of Elizabeth Cady Stanton.* London: T. Fischer Unwin.

Stanton, E. C., Anthony, S. B., Gage, M. J., & Harper, I. H. (1922). *History of women's suffrage* (Vols. 1–6.) New York: Fowler & Wells.

State correspondence, Illinois. (1906, February 3). *Woman's Journal, 37,* 20.

State v. Board of School Directors of City of Milwaukee, 191 N. W. 746 (1923).

Statistics of women at work. (1907). Washington, DC: Department of Commerce and Labor, U.S. Government Printing Office.

Status of American public school teachers, 1970–71. (1972). Washington, DC: Research Division, National Educational Association.

Status of the American public school teachers 1990–91. (1992). n.p.: National Education Association.

Steinschneider, J C. (1994). *An improved woman: The Wisconsin Federation of Women's Clubs, 1895–1920.* Brooklyn, NY: Carlson.

Stephens, D. M. (1990). *One-room school: Teaching in 1930s western Oklahoma.* Norman: University of Oklahoma Press.

Stephens, I. (1947). What hope for women teachers? *Atlantic, 179,* 78–81.

Stetson, D. M. (1991). *Women's rights in the USA: Policy debates and gender roles.* Pacific Grove, CA: Brook/Cole.

Stewart, H. (1914). Letter to Margaret Haley, April 28, 1914. Unpublished document located at the Chicago Historical Society, Chicago Teachers Federation file, box 43.

Strachan, G. C. (1910). *Equal pay for equal work: The story of the struggle for justice being made by women teachers of the city of New York.* New York: Buck & Company.

Strasser, S. (1982). *Never done: A history of American housework.* New York: Pantheon.

Strom, S. H. (1975). Leadership and tactics in the American woman suffrage movement: A new perspective from Massachusetts. *Journal of American History, 62,* 300.

A study of public opinion favoring more men in our high schools. (1927, March). *Cincinnati Teachers Association Bulletin, 2,* 8–17.

Suffrage evening school. (1915, March 12). *New York Times,* p. 15.

Suffrage parader loses teaching job. (1912, May 22). *New York Times,* p. 24.

Suffrage paraders. (1913, April). *Crisis, 5,* 2.

Suffrage school well attended. (1913, September 25). *Everywoman, 1,* 6.

Suffragists prominent in NEA. (1910). *Woman's Journal, 41,* 111.

Sullivan, J. E. (1925). Report of the committee on women as administratives [sic] in the educational fields. *National Education Association Proceedings and Addresses 63* (pp. 378–380). Washington, DC: National Education Association.

Superintendent Randall J. Condon. (1919). *School Index, 5,* 1.

Supt. Condon's report. (1913). *84th Annual Report of the Cincinnati Schools* (pp. 44–47). Cincinnati, OH: n.p.

Suratt, J. (1974). Ella Flagg Young. In E. T. James (Ed.), *Notable American women: A biographical dictionary* (pp. 697–699). Cambridge, MA: Belknap Press of Harvard University.

Survey on salaries, tenure of office and pension provisions of teachers. (1891). Washington, DC: National Educational Association.

Survey report of the Cincinnati public schools. (1935). Cincinnati, OH: Cincinnati Bureau of Governmental Research.

Sutherland, L. (1985). From baby shoes to bank vaults: Alberta Burke, founder of Burke Marketing [unpublished paper furnished by author].

Swanson, C. N., & Magiafico, L. C. (1992). *Guide to the archives of the General Federation of Women's Clubs.* Washington, DC: GFWC.

Tax, M. (1980). *The rising of the women: Feminist solidarity and class conflict, 1880–1917.* New York: Monthly Review Press.

Teacher becomes mother. (1914, November 1). *New York Times,* sec. II, p. 13.

Teacher institute and suffrage. (1913, September 11). *Everywoman, 1,* 5.

Teacher mother appeals to mayor. (1914, November 5). *New York Tribune,* p. 14.

Teacher-mother to mayor. (1914, November 6). *New York Times,* p. 11.

Teacher-mothers case at Albany. (1914, December 15). *New York Times,* p. 6.

Teacher shortage. (1956, June). *Harpers, 212,* 4, 6.

Teacher suffragists organize. (1915, April 11). *New York Times,* p. 6.

Teacher's pay. (1911, July 11). *Woman's Journal, 42,* 20.

The teacher's right to motherhood. (1913, November 29). *Literary Digest,* 1051.

The teacherage. (1914, September). *Ladies Home Journal, 31,* 5.

Teacherage in Texas. (1930). *School and Society, 3,* 731.

Teachers and their pay. (1906, March 31). *Woman's Journal, 37,* 50.

Teachers ask equal pay. (1907, March 9). *Woman's Journal, 38,* 1.

Teachers ask for votes in Missouri. (1913, November 8). *Woman's Journal, 44,* 360.
Teachers ask preference in future jobs. (1932, August 22). *Cincinnati Post,* p. 1.
Teachers ask suspensions. (1932, August 20). *Cincinnati Post,* p. 8.
Teachers choose woman president. (1913). *Woman's Journal, 44,* 369.
Teachers favor equal suffrage, Minnesota Educational Association goes on record. (1912). *Woman's Journal, 43,* 408.
Teachers form many leagues. (1913, September 27). *Woman's Journal, 44,* 305.
Teachers found vote essential. (1916, July 15). *Woman's Journal, 47,* 225–226.
Teachers help during vacations. (1915, July 17). *Woman's Journal, 46,* 224.
Teachers in the rural districts. (1922). *World's Work, 45,* 355.
Teachers lack diversity. (1996). *American School Board Journal, 183,* 15.
Teachers learn they need to vote. (1913, November 1). *Woman's Journal, 44,* 352.
Teachers on school suffrage. (1901, June 29). *Woman's Journal, 32,* 201.
Teachers to the front. (1915, July). *Woman Voter, 6,* 23.
Teachers turn tables. (1907, December 7). *Woman's Journal, 38,* 194.
Teachers want the vote. (1911, November 25). *Woman's Journal, 42,* 369.
Teachers' bill won, Ohio women envy Colorado. (1913). *Woman's Journal, 44,* 176.
Teachers' cottages. (1916). *School and Society, 3,* 415–416.
Teachers' election fight. (1905, May 7). *New York Times,* p. 12.
Teachers' equal pay bill. (1907, May 25). *Woman's Journal, 38,* 82.
Teachers' pay is below janitors: Recent Detroit survey reveals. (1916). *Woman's Journal, 17,* 409.
Teachers' salaries and the cost of living. (1913). Ann Arbor, MI: National Education Association.
Tell men teachers they shan't meddle. (1909, June 10). *New York Times,* p. 16.
Tempest. (1935, May 3). *Cincinnati Enquirer,* p. 4.
Terborg-Penn, R. (1978). Discrimination against Afro-American women in the women's movement, 1830–1920. In S. Harley & R. Terborg-Penn (Eds.), *The Afro American woman's struggles and images* (pp. 17–27). Port Washington, NY: Kennikat.
Terborg-Penn, R. (1993). Suffrage movement. In D. C. Hine (Ed.), *Black women in America: An historical encyclopedia* (p. 1125). Bloomington: Indiana University Press.
Terpenning, W. A. (1932, October). The educational veil. *Forum and New Century, 88,* 231–233.
Terrell, M. C. (1940). *A colored woman in a White world.* Washington, DC: Ransdell.
Their bit done by those women who continue teaching after marriage says Condon. (1917, December 9). *Cincinnati Enquirer,* p. 25.
$37 a week for teachers. (1947, April 1). *Ladies Home Journal, 64,* 54.
Thomas, M. M. (1992). *The new woman in Alabama: Social reforms and suffrage, 1890–1920.* Tuscaloosa: The University of Alabama Press.
Thomas, W. B., & Moran, K. J. (1991). Women teacher militancy in the workplace, 1910–1922. *Pedagogica Historica* [Belgium], *27,* 35–53.
Thomason, C. W. (1915, March). Washington's new slogan. *Sunset Magazine, 34,* 554–555.
Threlkeld, A. L. (1923). Conclusions based on questionnaire concerning aspects

of the professional and social status of American women teachers. In *National Education Association Proceedings and Addresses of the 61st Annual Meeting* (pp. 484–486). Washington, DC: National Education Association.

Title IX: Parity of coaches' salaries for male and female athletic teams. (1979). Washington, DC: National Education Association.

Trzinski, E., & Alpert, W. T. (1994). Pregnancy and parental leave benefits in the United States and Canada: Judicial decisions and legislation. *Journal of Human Resources, 29,* 535–555.

Turner v. Department of Employment Security of Utah, 423 U.S. 44 (1975).

Tyack, D., & Hansot, E. (1982). *Managers of virtue: Public school leadership in America, 1820–1980.* New York: Basic Books.

U.S. Census Bureau. (1933). *Population, Volume IV, Occupations by States, 15th Census of the United States, 1930.* Washington, DC: Government Printing Office. 8, 1305.

U.S. Census Bureau. (1964). *Characteristics of teachers: U.S. Census of the populations, 1960 final report pc(2)-7d.* Washington, DC: U.S. Government Printing Office.

Van Horn, S. H. (1988). *Women, work, and fertility, 1900–1986.* New York: New York University Press.

Vaughn-Roberson, C. A. (1984). Sometimes independent but never equal— Women teachers, 1900–1950: The Oklahoma example. *Pacific Historical Review, 53,* 39–58.

Vaughn-Roberson, C. A. (1985). Having a purpose in life: Western women teachers in the twentieth century. *Great Plains Quarterly, 5,* 107–124.

Vincent, G. E. (1916). The spread of the school manse idea. *Annals of the American Academy of Political and Social Science, 67,* 167–169.

Vincent, G. E. (1917). City comforts for country teachers: A Minnesota neighborhood sets an example to the nation. *American Review of Reviews, 55,* 403–408.

Wage fight. (1935, May 29). *Cincinnati Enquirer,* p. 1.

Waits, L. A. (1932a). A study of the comparative efficiency of single and married as teachers. *Educational Administration and Supervision, 8,* 630–633.

Waits, L. A. (1932b). *A study of the status of married women teachers in the public schools of Ohio: A comparative study of efficiency in teaching.* Unpublished doctoral dissertation, Ohio State University, Columbus.

Wandersee, W. D. (1981). *Women's work and family values, 1920–1940.* Cambridge, MA: Harvard University Press.

Want five women named: City Federation of Women's Clubs presents candidates for board of education. (1913, November 16). *New York Times,* p. 6.

Ware, S. (1981). *Beyond suffrage, women in the new deal.* Cambridge, MA: Harvard University Press.

Ware, S. (1982). *Holding their own: American women in the 1930's.* Boston: Twayne.

Watkins, M. P. (1993). Political activism and community-building among Alliance and Grange women in western Washington, 1892–1925. *Agricultural History, 67,* 197–213.

Wedded women teachers to be continued. (1933, August 29). *Cincinnati Post,* p. 16.

Wedding Rings No Bar to Teachers. (1934, February 13). *Cincinnati Enquirer*, p. 1.

Weider, Alan. (1992). One who left and one who stayed: Teacher recollections and reflections of school desegregation in New Orleans. In R. J. Altenbaugh (Ed.), *The teacher's voice: A social history of teaching in the twentieth century America* (pp. 107–120). London: Falmer Press.

Weidlich, T. (1995). Leave law still draws ire despite employer wins. *National Law Journal, 18*, B1.

Weiler, K. (1988). *Women teaching for change: Gender, class and power*. New York: Bergin & Garvey.

Weiler, K. (1989). Women's history and the history of women teachers. *Journal of Education, 171*, 11.

Weiler, K. (1994). Women and rural school reform: California, 1900–1940. *History of Education Quarterly, 34*, 25–47.

Weiner, L. Y. (1985). *From working girl to working mother: The female labor force in the United States, 1820–1980*. Chapel Hill: University of North Carolina.

Where shall the country teacher live? (1916). *Survey, 36*, 505.

Whereas. (1914). *Journal of Education, 80*, 90.

White, D. G. (1993). The cost of club work, the price of Black feminism. In N. Hewitt & S. Lebsock (Ed.), *Visible women: New essays on American activism* (pp. 247–269). Urbana: University of Illinois Press.

White, M. E. (1903). Work of the woman's clubs. *Atlantic Monthly, 93*, 614–623.

Who's who and why in after-war education. (1921). New York: Institute for Public Service.

Why men and women teachers should receive equal pay for equal preparation and for equal service. (1927). *Cincinnati Teachers Association Bulletin, 2*, 8–17.

Why Wisconsin should enfranchise teachers. (1911). *Woman's Journal, 42*, 369, 371.

Why women work: Based on a study made by the National Federation of Business and Professional Women's Clubs, Inc. (1938). New York: Public Affairs.

Williams, W. (1984). Equality's riddle: Pregnancy and equal treatment/special treatment debate. *New York University Review of Law & Social Change, 13*, 325, 345–346.

Wilson, J. D. (1990). I am here to help if you need me: British Columbia's rural teachers' welfare officer, 1928–1934. *Journal of Canadian Studies, 25*, 94–118.

Wilson, M. G. (1979). *The American woman in transition, the urban influence 1870–1920*. Westport, CT: Greenwood Press.

Wilson, S. (1957). A new deal for the teachers. *Parents Magazine, 32*, 40–41, 91, 93.

Women and the schoolboards. (1913, September 18). *Everywoman, 1*, 4.

Women in high schools to receive same salary as men. (1917). *School Index, 4*, 1.

Women in the school board. (1901, April). *Chicago Teachers & School Board, 4*, 24.

Women may marry and still teach in schools. (1889, March 12). *Cincinnati Enquirer*, p. 8.

Women on Philadelphia school boards. (1906, March 10). *Woman's Journal, 37*, 37.

Women oppose Hunsicker plan. (1934, January 12). *Cincinnati Post*, p. 8.

Women teachers begin higher salary fight. (1906, November 4). *New York Times*, p. 3.

Women teachers can participate, Birmingham board of education will not prohibit them from suffrage work. (1912). *Woman's Journal, 43*, 408.

Women teachers desire equal salaries. (1919, October 8). *Cincinnati Times Star*, p. 5.

Women teachers envy fish. (1915, December 25). *Woman's Journal, 46*, 414.

Women teachers uphold single schedule. (1935, January 19). *Cincinnati Post*, p. 5.

Women teachers want equal pay with men. (1906, September 30). *New York Times*, p. 9.

Women's Bureau. (1965). *Digest of state equal pay laws*. Washington, DC: U.S. Government Printing Office.

Women's club for married women teachers. (1934, January 12). *Cincinnati Enquirer*, p. 24.

Won't act against teacher, notice of marriage forthwith elastic. (1913, March 20). *New York Times*, p. 22.

Wood, M. I. (1912). *The history of the General Federation of Women's Clubs for the first twenty-two years of its organization*. New York: History Department of the GFWC.

Wood, M. I. (1915). The school manse in reality. *Ladies Home Journal, 32*, 25.

Woody, Thomas. (1929). *A history of women's education in the United States* (Vol. 1). New York: The Science Press. (Reprinted 1980, New York: Octagon Books)

Wright, B. D., & Tuska, S. A. (1968). Career dreams of teachers. *Trans-Action, 6*, 43–47.

Wright, G. (1985). *Building the dream: A social history of housing in America*. Cambridge, MA: MIT Press.

Wyld, D. C. (1995). The FMLA and the changing demand for substitute teachers. *Clearing House, 68*, 301–307.

Young, R. Guilty of motherhood. (1914, January). *Good Housekeeping, 73*, 27–33.

INDEX

169

ABOUT THE AUTHOR

Pat Carter has been an administrator and faculty member in Women's Studies at the University of Cincinnati, the University of Connecticut, and Oglethorpe University. She is the author of several articles on women's history, the executive producer of two documentary films, the special editor for two history anthologies, and an artist whose work is held in public and private collections.